THE WAY OF SPLENDOR

*Jewish Mysticism and
Modern Psychology*

Edward Hoffman

SHAMBHALA
BOULDER & LONDON 1981

Shambhala Publications, Inc.
1920 13th Street
Boulder, Colorado 80302

© 1981 by Edward Hoffman
All rights reserved.

Distributed in the United States by Random House
and in Canada by Random House of Canada Ltd.

Distributed in the United Kingdom by Routledge & Kegan Paul Ltd.,
London and Henley-on-Thames

Printed in the United States of America

Library of Congress Cataloging in Publication Data
Hoffman, Edward, 1951-
   The way of splendor.
   Bibliography: p.
   Includes index.
   1. Cabala—Psychological aspects.   2. Mysticism—Judaism—
Psychological aspects.   I. Title.
BM526.H63   296.1'6   81-50967
ISBN   0-87773-209-4   AACR2
ISBN   0-87773-210-8 (pbk.)
ISBN   0-394-52152-8 (Random House)
ISBN   0-394-74885-9 (Random House : pbk.)

CONTENTS

ACKNOWLEDGMENTS

This book would scarcely have been possible without the valuable cooperation of many persons. The initial impetus for the project came from my colleague and friend, Professor W. Edward Mann of York University. I am greatly indebted to Harvey Gitlin for his masterful research efforts and conceptual contributions. Jack Fei and Aaron Hostyk provided me with many hours of stimulating discussion related to the topics of this book. I wish to offer special thanks to my parents, brother, and above all to my wife Laurel for their unflagging encouragement throughout the progress of the writing; gratitude is extended too to Gertrude Brainin and John White. The enthusiastic support and editorial judgment of Samuel Bercholz and Larry Mermelstein is likewise very much appreciated.

To The Memory of My Grandparents

PREFACE

THE KABBALAH, the esoteric offshoot of Judaism, has entranced many persons from all faiths for centuries. It provides a detailed, massive, and coherent world view of the nature of human existence and our relation to the cosmos. Its powerful, poetic vistas have excited the imagination of Jews and non-Jews alike in nearly every country of the globe. Yet, in modern times, large numbers of people are just beginning to become aware of this fascinating tradition.

My own involvement with this vast and provocative subject has grown steadily over the years. Having attended Orthodox *yeshiva* (Hebrew day school) as a child, from my earliest memories I have been intrigued by the visionary aspects of Judaism. My teachers did not, of course, present formal lessons on the Kabbalah. This would have been forbidden. Nor could we have grasped at our tender ages the subtle complexities of Jewish mysticism. But in their retelling of legends and tales they offered a tantalizing glimpse into another world. On my mother's side, my grandfather was a leading American cantor for many years; though he died when I was only five, he infused me with an awareness of the power of the Jewish spirit to transcend the constraints of verbal language.

Later, my religious and secular education converged in the 1960s, when the ancient Far Eastern traditions came like a tidal wave upon the West—initially affecting the campus generation and within a few years the wider society. While pursuing my undergraduate degree in psychology at Cornell

University, I remember reading with considerable excitement
Martin Buber's evocative works on Jewish mysticism and
Hasidism. In their own way, they seemed to strangely com-
plement the quite different volumes on Yoga, Hinduism, and
Buddhism that I was also absorbing.

But I confess that it was not until several years later, when
completing my doctorate in psychology at the University of
Michigan, that I again turned to the Kabbalistic tradition.
Gershom Scholem's authoritative books on its history were
not designed for psychologists, but nevertheless appeared to
describe definite theories about the human mind. His impec-
cably documented allusions to Kabbalistic interest in dreams,
meditation, and altered states of consciousness piqued my
curiosity. The symbolism was indeed abstruse. Yet, perhaps,
the new breed of humanistic and transpersonal psychologists,
in their rush to embrace the Orient, were overlooking an
extremely relevant, forgotten system of knowledge.

I began to study the major works of the Kabbalah in more
detail and discovered that my hunches were correct. Far from
being a hodgepodge of medieval fears and superstition as it
was often portrayed, the Jewish visionary tradition was clearly
an immense—if at first bewildering—treasure house of psychological insight and speculation. In the summer of 1978, I
summarized my initial findings in a paper, "The Kabbalah
and Humanistic Psychology," at the annual convention of the
American Psychological Association. Greatly encouraged by
the response, I expanded my observations into an article which
was published shortly thereafter in the *Journal of Humanistic
Psychology*. Before long, friends and colleagues had succeeded
in persuading me to develop a still more comprehensive treatment of these ideas. The task has been a most enjoyable one.

My aim here has been to introduce the Kabbalah's psychological insights to the general public, unfamiliar with the
intricacies of either Jewish philosophy or mysticism. This
book is intended to serve as a bridge to the actual body of
Kabbalistic lore; it has not been planned as a substitute or
replacement for the primary sources, but rather, as a guide
across their often complex and difficult terrain. To this end, I

have drawn substantially upon key Kabbalistic texts, using direct quotations whenever appropriate.

In writing from the vantage point of my particular field of training, I hasten to stress that in no way is this work designed to reduce the Kabbalah to the terms of modern psychology. Nor do I believe that such an approach would be very meaningful or even at all desirable. The Kabbalistic thinkers have a great deal to offer us today concerning our inner makeup and higher potentialities. But above all, the Jewish esoteric system encompasses a religious dimension and must ultimately be met in that sphere. If this book manages in some small way to illumine the grandeur of this tradition, it will have fulfilled its purpose.

INTRODUCTION

THOUGH FOR MANY YEARS the Kabbalah lapsed into obscurity, today it seems to be undergoing a true renaissance of interest. Beginning in the 1960s, with the rediscovery of the relevance of many longstanding spiritual traditions, the Kabbalistic allure was felt once more. More and more persons from many diverse creeds have become drawn to this ancient branch of Judaism. Around the world, explorations into this body of hidden wisdom are now occurring at a quickening pace. Several interesting developments appear to be responsible for this encouraging trend.

For one thing, the study of what has been loosely called "Jewish mysticism" has become viewed as a much less dubious or unrespectable field. For much of the nineteenth and even twentieth centuries, Jewish academicians and other professionals would not even touch the subject, for fear of being tainted as dabblers in occultism. Perhaps such researchers were still uneasy with their newly hard won admittance into the halls of Western university life. Virtually the last thing they wished was to be publicly linked to apparently superstitious, unscientific pursuits. For instance, we now know that Freud was more than mildly interested in the Kabbalah, yet deliberately kept this involvement well under wraps throughout his life. Apart from outright ridicule by some Jewish rationalists, this entire tradition was ignored by Western thinkers in modern times.

Recently, though, scholars with clearly impressive creden-

1

tials have all over the globe begun to devote intensive effort to this inquiry. With an attitude of respect at times approaching that of reverence, they have helped to uncover, analyze, and translate the long forgotten writings. Even if the Kabbalah's intriguing doctrines do not conform to modern mainstream thought—so investigators have realized—that hardly makes its ideas unworthy of serious attention.

As a result of modern scholarship, the Kabbalistic system has gradually been made more accessible to contemporary men and women. Manuscripts that have for many decades lain away in dusty library archives are now seeing the light of day in the technological era. For the first time, some, though certainly not all, of the key texts of the Kabbalah, can be read without years of arduous religious training. On college campuses, the rise of Jewish Studies programs in the late 1960s and early 1970s has further awakened curiosity in this ancient Jewish current. With the books of Martin Buber and Gershom Scholem as their guides, students have begun to examine the depth and scope of this fascinating approach. In this way, the study of the Kabbalah has started to penetrate the intellectual mainstream. As one favorable indicator, doctoral theses on various aspects of the Kabbalistic and Hasidic movements have been accepted at major universities for several years now, in fields ranging from literature to psychology. Moreover, at present several professional journals regularly devote space to this previously disparaged subject; their "parent" associations have also sponsored lectures on this topic at national conferences.

Indeed, the Kabbalah is exerting growing attraction upon many persons today searching for a better understanding of the human mind, as well as of the emerging synthesis between science and mysticism. Over the last ten to fifteen years, scientific investigators have again and again found startling insights in the longstanding spiritual traditions regarding our mental and physical makeup. For example, stories of Hindu *yogins* who could at will alter their heartbeat, rate of breathing, or body temperature, seemed almost absurd until very recently. But in today's biofeedback laboratories and clinics, ordinary people sometimes learn to accomplish similar feats in a matter of weeks. The healing properties attributed to Eastern forms of meditation likewise appeared as simply so much superstitious hyperbole. Yet, across the world today, physicians and other health professionals are effectively prescribing variants of classic meditation for people suffering from a wide range of chronic illnesses, such as cardiovascular disease, hypertension, and even cancer. Thus, the ancient spiritual disciplines appear less impractical with each new day.

To many of those interested in the exciting quest for our highest potential, the Kabbalah is as yet only vaguely known. Nevertheless, the Jewish visionary tradition offers us a penetrating understanding into the fundamental nature of the human mind. For instance, its views of dreams antedate modern psychology by close to seven hundred years and in some ways are still ahead of mainstream notions. The Kabbalistic emphasis on song and dance as powerful healing tools has anticipated the contemporary field of music therapy. Its model of daily and altered states of awareness similarly bears an uncanny prescience of the most up-to-date theories on how mind works. Even its seemingly most speculative areas— such as the nature of prophecy and clairvoyance, inner events at the "hour of death," and the continuity of our consciousness after physical mortality—are beginning to be taken seriously by a host of innovative investigators.

At the same time, a major influence on the spread of the Kabbalah today comes from within the Jewish religious ranks themselves. During the founding of Israel, Chief Rabbi of Palestine Abraham Isaac Kook for many years expounded upon Jewish mystical themes. He deemed the desire for the transcendent as a basic human need and its attainment as our worthiest goal. Until his death in 1935, he also preached the unity among our physical, emotional, and spiritual selves, commenting for example, "Melancholy spreads as a malignant disease throughout the body and spirit."[1] In coming years, his doctrines—some of which have recently been translated into English and are now promulgated by his son Zvi

Yehuda Kook in Israel—will no`doubt extend the Kabbalah to more widespread comprehension.

Hasidic groups, particularly the Lubavitcher sect, have in the last few years begun to make concerted efforts to reach out to Jews seeking a firmer spiritual identity and dissatisfied with the pervasive "bagels and lox" approach to Judaism. Such Hasidic organizations seem to hold a special appeal for those persons who have already participated in various forms of Eastern meditation. In *Chabad* (the formal Lubavitcher designation) centers in most large North American cities, classes in "Jewish meditation" and esoteric psychology are increasingly available—in this case, emphasizing the teachings of their founder Rabbi Schneur Zalman of Liady of the late eighteenth century. Other programs require less commitment than that demanded by the Lubavitchers, but similarly stress the unity of the visionary path with mainstream Jewish values.

Thus, relying to varying degrees on the original texts, they seek to teach the initiate how to meditate in the classic Kabbalistic methods. Some Jewish authorities have also begun to relate Jewish esotericism to the current thirst for knowledge about the ecstatic experience and our inward creative states. Ironically, the same Jewish Reform movement which nearly two hundred years ago arose to combat what it viewed as the backwardness of this tradition, is now finding a need to return the Kabbalistic perspective to its rightful place in Judaism. Explicitly recognizing the glitter of the authoritarian cults for some Jewish youth today, rabbis are now openly praising the transcendent revelations offered by the Kabbalah. All this would have been unthinkable only a decade ago.

In short, larger numbers of people than ever before in the technological era—in both the secular world and established Jewish circles—have shown an awareness and respect for this ancient system of knowledge. So far, however, this involvement has yet to fully connect with the wider Jewish culture, or the inward yearning in the West that has embraced Zen Buddhism, Yoga, and a host of Oriental approaches to the higher nature of human capacities. Thus, while there are literally dozens of volumes in print relating such disciplines to modern-day psychology, there is not a single work available at present which deals in this manner with the Kabbalah.

The chief focus of *The Way of Splendor: Jewish Mysticism and Modern Psychology* will therefore be on the psychological aspects of the Kabbalah, as one of the distinguishing features of Jewish mysticism is its emphasis on the day-to-day relevance of the visionary experience. As many scholars have noted, a basic goal of this path is to teach the initiate how to bring the divine element into the stream of ordinary activity. Following a look at the historical evolution and metaphysical assumptions of the Kabbalah, I will explore such topics as its views on human emotions, the mind-body relationship, the nature of our consciousness, and our potential for self-transcendence. Finally, I will share my findings on Kabbalistic notions regarding such intriguing subjects as parapsychology, life after death, and reincarnation.

One of the main themes to emerge from this book—and one which was originally quite unintended—is the amazing correspondence that appears to exist between the Kabbalah and other longstanding spiritual traditions. Indeed, while differences among these world-wide disciplines are certainly noticeable, their commonalities seem far more salient. Though a cross-fertilization of ideas undoubtedly took place, I am convinced, however, that this phenomenon also points to the generalizability and relevance of the conclusions found in these systems of knowledge. Furthermore, I have been repeatedly impressed with the optimism and confidence in the human enterprise that these age-old approaches share. In a difficult and confused time, the importance for humanity of the ancient spiritual traditions looms greater than ever.

The Kabbalah, with its fundamental belief in the sanctity of life, its emphasis on the higher reaches within each of us, and its unswerving ethical basis in Judaism, carries with it a universal and timely meaning.

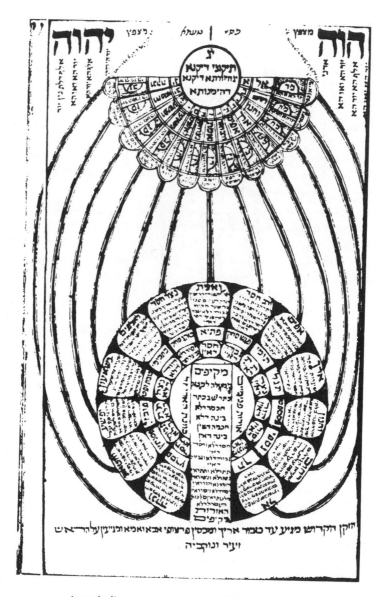

A symbolic arrangement of the sefirot known as "the light surrounding the interior lights."

CHAPTER ONE

JEWISH MYSTICS: SEEKERS OF UNITY

"The Jew has the advantage of having long since anticipated the development of [the study of] consciousness in his own spiritual history. By this I mean the . . . Kabbalah."

—Carl Jung

"Where philosophy ends, there the wisdom of the Kabbalah begins."
—Rabbi Nachman of Bratslav

DATING BACK TO THE MIDDLE AGES, the term "Kabbalah" comes from the Hebrew root-word "to receive." It incorporates a massive, detailed, and coherent world view of our relation to the universe. Metaphysical discourses of immense power are combined with specific methods for how we can go beyond our daily, mundane frame of mind. Yet, its ultimate origins are lost in the ruins of antiquity, as it has

7

become increasingly clear that from its very inception about four thousand years ago, Judaism has nearly always possessed an esoteric side. Sometimes this approach to the divine has gone deep into the underground of the Jewish mind and exerted its strength in hidden, barely discernible ways. At other periods in Jewish history, it has burst into magnificent flower and entranced almost entire generations.

Historians generally demark the primary phase of this recorded discipline as the *Merkabah* or "Chariot" epoch. It spanned the length of the first century B.C.E. through the tenth century C.E. and was centered in Palestine, ruled by a series of world powers. Despite the longevity of this tradition, it was a more or less cohesive body of knowledge, held together by an integrated set of doctrines and techniques concerning higher states of awareness. Shaped by some of the most renowned rabbis of the epoch, it is seen as the direct forerunner of the later emergence of the Kabbalah itself.

The sources indicate that two main branches of inquiry dominated practitioners of this system: *Ma'aseh Bereshit* ("Act of Creation") and *Ma'aseh Merkabah* ("Act of the Divine Chariot"). The former was more theoretical and dealt with the creation of the world and the first divine revelations. The *Ma'aseh Merkabah*, based on the prophet Ezekial's description of the Celestial Chariot, is a study of our connection to the deity. Both of these paths were enshrouded in mystery and kept hidden to all but the most pious Jewish scholars of their day. Many of the great sages who worked on the compilation of the *Talmud* (the major text of Judaic law, commentary, and Biblical exegesis, completed about 500 C.E.) were knowledgeable about this secret tradition, though not all were motivated to practice it. For even then, its adepts warned that very real mental and physical dangers await those who rush into this metaphorical garden, however sincere their goals.

In the archetypal tale to underscore this point, four great Jewish sages, Ben Azai, Ben Zoma, Ben Abuyah, and Rabbi Akiva, are said to have pursued the hidden way to its utmost. Of the four men, each acclaimed as a scholar during the time of the second destruction of the Temple in Jerusalem in the first century C.E., only Rabbi Akiva emerged unshattered from the experience. Death, madness, or apostasy greeted the others. To prevent similar fates from befalling others, adepts therefore kept the teachings largely oral in nature. They were passed down from master to chosen disciples. And when the information was made available in written form, it was virtually always prohibited to the masses of the Jewish people. Indeed, this attitude has been carried forth by the rabbinate to the present day.

Initiates in the visionary tradition were known as *Yorde Merkabah* ("those who descend in the chariot") because they would "descend" ever deeper inward to the recesses of their own mind. In the deepest realms of meditation, the ethereal Chariot was said to be hidden, ready to raise the disciple through all levels of consciousness until Ezekial's heavenly image was beheld. In *Heikhalot* ("Heavenly Hall") writings, the masters of this system chartered like expert cartographers the difficult inner terrain to be crossed by those on the quest. They described what the initiate might be expected to see and feel. For example, the sixth heavenly plane was said to resemble an endless, dazzling reflection of waves like the sea. At each further step inward, more and more confusing and even terrifying visions were depicted as awaiting. In one fragment, characteristically symbolic, that dates from the fourth or fifth century C.E., its anonymous author comments, "From *Makhon* to *Aravot* is a five hundred year journey. . . . What is therein? The treasure houses of blessing, the storehouses of snow, the storehouses of peace, the souls of the righteous and the souls yet to be born, the dreadful punishments reserved for the wicked. . . ."[1]

Yet, the sages hinted, such images are ultimately subordinate to the disciple's own mind. This same literature therefore advised the practitioner not to be overwhelmed by the apparitions that appeared. If adequately prepared through previous training, he would be able to utter the appropriate words at the right time and banish the visions that would shatter his soul, the masters explained. Typically, fasting, special breathing exercises, and rhythmic chants were used

to help guide the initiate into an altered state of consciousness. Interestingly, there are striking parallels between this
approach to higher awareness and those of several other spiritual traditions. In Tibetan Buddhism, for example, disciples
are likewise admonished that the "visions of deities experienced in the *bardo* [nonphysical state] are the reflections of
spiritual processes and experiences on this life."[2]

The other major esoteric trend in Judaism during this era
was more speculative and focused on the structure of the
cosmos and our connection with it. The most significant text
was the *Sefer Yetzirah* ("Book of Creation") believed to represent the first Jewish metaphysical work to appear in writing.
It was composed anonymously during the third and sixth
centuries, while the *Talmud* was being molded into its final
form. Quite brief despite its tremendous impact, the *Sefer
Yetzirah* comprises less than two thousand words, regardless
of edition. Not an ecstatic or meditational treatise, it offers a
terse yet evocative description—a summary statement in
format—of the hidden workings of the universe.

In the *Book of Creation*, thirty-two secret routes to the deity
are discussed (intriguingly, corresponding in number to precisely one half of the sixty-four cosmic situations identified
in the Oriental *I Ching* or *Book of Changes*). These channels
are symbolized by the ten primordial numbers—*Sefirot*, or
energy-essences, as they are termed—and the twenty-two
letters of the Hebrew alphabet. All aspects of the cosmos,
including the nature of space, time, and our interaction with
them, are said to be upheld by the constant interplay of these
vibrational forces. The concept of the ten *Sefirot* became the
foundation for the later Kabbalah, which developed this notion into a formalized system known as the *Tree of Life.*

With its precise and deductive style, the *Sefer Yetzirah*
attracted a great deal of interest from Jewish visionaries from
its first circulation in the sixth century C.E. It provided the
basis for later Kabbalistic inquiry into our makeup as an
energy matrix, as well as our relation to the energies in the
universe around us. Over the years, many commentaries on
the *Sefer Yetzirah* were promulgated, and it was perhaps the

most widely studied esoteric Jewish work prior to the appearance of the *Zohar* ("Book of Splendor") in thirteenth-century Spain.

During this era, the themes of the *Book of Creation* and the *Merkabah* school occupied the central concerns of Jews seeking higher knowledge. Little is known about the lives of these adherents, or even of their motives. For the most part, they were undoubtedly rabbinical scholars who felt a yearning for something not found in the Talmudic laws and ordinary biblical discussions. And, they considered themselves to be following a lofty tradition, which they linked back to the Prophets and indeed Abraham, the alleged writer of the *Sefer Yetzirah*. The authors of the exotic texts were far more concerned with spreading their message than with attaining fame; consequently, only the barest conjectures exist as to who actually composed these documents. In this era, too, the teachings of both Sufi (Islamic) and Christian mystics comingled and, for instance, the classic eleventh-century Jewish work by Bachya ben Joseph Ibn Paquada, *Duties of the Heart*, is highly similar to Sufi writings of the time.

With the appearance of the anonymously written *Sefer Bahir* ("Book of Brilliance") in Provence, Southern France, around 1175, the true period which demarks the Kabbalah was ushered in. This fascinating work takes its title from the opening verse: "And now they do not see light, it is brilliant (*Bahir*) in the skies."[3] Its central premise is that there is a vast, unseen order beyond what we typically experience in everyday life. Perhaps reflecting their assessment of the oppressed Jewish condition in the Middle Ages, these early Kabbalists emphasized repeatedly the hidden aspects of the deity. "People want to see the king," the *Book of Brilliance* declares, "but do not know where to find his house. First they [must] ask, 'Where is the king's house?' Only then can they ask, 'Where is the King?' "[4]

Comprising, then, a treatise and manual on how to find the glory behind the mundane world, the *Bahir* spread rapidly throughout the Jewish world. Some of its methods for attaining higher awareness focus on channeling a life energy that is said to flow through the human body—a notion found in other traditions such as *kundalini yoga*. For the first time, albeit very slowly, esoteric conceptions started to reach a wider audience among Jews. By the year 1200, the Kabbalists had acquired a distinct identity, especially in areas of Southern France and Spain. They were not numerically significant, but the amassing of a movement was far from their aim; their purpose was to enable individuals, not large groups, to rise beyond the misfortunes so common to Jews of the time. Thus, in one of the earliest published Kabbalistic texts, Rabbi Abraham ben David (Raavad) commented that all of these esoteric teachings were transmitted only from "one mouth to the next."[5]

At roughly the same historical period, a somewhat parallel development occurred in Northern European Jewry, particularly in Germany. Around 1150 to 1250, a group known as the Hasidim ("Devout") and not to be confused with the East European movement of the eighteenth century, exerted a long-lasting impact on German Jewry. The major literary work of this circle was *Sefer Hasidim* ("Book of the Devout"), a compilation of various writings from this time and locale.

The German Hasidim focused their speculation on the "mystery of God's unity" and an esoteric analysis of the Torah. They believed—as did the later Kabbalists— that every section and even every word of the Pentateuch contains a secret, hidden meaning. They also explored in considerable detail the nature of altered states of consciousness, such as the phenomenon of automatic or spontaneous writing. Furthermore, this group was highly involved with using dreams as a gateway to higher knowledge. Unlike most Jewish visionaries, though, they advocated an ascetic way of life as a means of liberation from the disappointments of earthly living. Existing in an extremely oppressive atmosphere for sheer Jewish survival, they emphasized bodily self-denial as the best method for attaining true understanding of our purpose in the material world.

Abraham Abulafia: Prophetic Kabbalism and "Jewish Yoga"

Abraham ben Samuel Abulafia (1240–c. 1292) was one of the most important Kabbalists, and perhaps, among the most interesting figures in all of Jewish history. He had a profound influence on the development of prophetic Kabbalism in general and on the greatest flowering of the Kabbalah in Palestine three centuries later. The details of his life—filled with intrigue, religious and political plotting, near death and seeming miraculous divine intervention—make for reading as provocative as any historical novel. Yet, he is scarcely mentioned in most contemporary accounts of Jewish philosophy or history, undoubtedly due to his unique and controversial ideas.

Born in Sargossa, Spain, Abulafia was a highly intelligent and well-read young man. Unlike most Kabbalists of his time, though, he had little formal rabbinical training. As a youth he traveled a good deal, eventually settling in the city of Barcelona. There, he delved deeply into the Kabbalah, as well as Maimonades' *Guide for the Perplexed*, a classic volume of intellectual thought by the twelfth-century Jewish thinker. At the age of thirty-one, from Abulafia's own account, he attained spiritual enlightenment, accompanied by various psychic gifts.

Abulafia proclaimed his prophetic visions in several countries where he traveled, including Spain, Italy, and Greece. Though he relied mainly on oral instruction to spread his methods for achieving higher consciousness, he also broke with Kabbalistic tradition by writing specific manuals on the esoteric path. As he continued to exert a powerful effect on other Kabbalists, he gradually came to view himself as a kind of messianic figure. In 1280, Abulafia amassed the *chutzpah* or audacity to seek to convert to Judaism no less a personage than the rabidly anti-Semitic Pope Nicholas III.

The Jewish religious establishment joined hands with Christian authorities in condemning Abulafia as a needless troublemaker. In his zealous efforts to bring the Kabbalah to the very head of the Christian world, he may have placed his less visionary fellow Jews in real jeopardy: hence, the dispatch with which the rabbinate rejected the venture and his other adventures to follow. Indeed, one reason for the orthodoxy's historical uneasiness with the esoteric discipline is that it has often led to messianic movements or inflated Jewish hopes for a radical turn of events in their earthly status as a people.

Meanwhile, Abulafia and his disciples spent several weeks in intensive preparation for their task. They prayed, fasted, and carried out secret meditative rituals, such as conducting permutations of the Hebrew alphabet, in order for the mission to succeed. Even before Abulafia reached the city of Rome, the Pope condemned him to death. The stake and fire were readied for him. When the impassioned visionary arrived at the city gate, he discovered that Pope Nicholas III had suddenly died during the night. The Franciscans held him in prison, but soon released him, apparently swayed by his charismatic personality.

After this episode, Abulafia resumed his wanderings. In Italy, he continued his teaching and writing, setting forth methods by which, he believed, any person could acquire paranormal abilities. For him, such powers and their related ecstatic mental states are within the grasp of each of us. He caustically accused the rabbinate of overemphasizing the Talmudic law to the exclusion of direct communion with higher forces in the universe. He was also tolerant of other faiths and was on friendly terms with Christian and Islamic mystics whom he met. Similar to masters of kundalini yoga, Abulafia suggested specific body postures, altered forms of breathing, and solitary contemplation as the pathway to the divine. He likewise warned of a "fire" which may arise out of one's body during intense concentration. Paralleling Eastern teachings, he advised his disciples not to try to progress too quickly, lest they experience potentially devastating mental and physical reactions. "Cleanse the body and choose a lonely house where none shall hear thy voice," he wrote. "Sit there . . . and do not reveal thy secret to any man."[6]

After a well-publicized and abortive messianic effort, Abulafia fled in 1290 to the island of Comino, near Malta. He is believed to have died about 1292. He left behind a legacy of twenty-six Kabbalistic manuals and twenty-two prophetic works, nearly all of the latter long since disappeared. Many of his meditative guides, however, are extant and remain popular among Kabbalists to this day.

The Zohar: The Key Kabbalistic Text

During this period of Abulafia's bold prophecies and vehement battles with the rabbinate of his day, there appeared in Spain, in the 1280s or 1290s, a remarkable volume of Jewish visionary lore. Entitled the *Zohar* ("Book of Splendor"), it was published by Moses de Leon (1250–1305) and bore the name of the great second-century Rabbi Simeon bar Yochai, who lived shortly after the destruction of the Second Temple in Jerusalem. Written in an exalted style of Aramaic, the *Zohar* contained a fascinating blend of metaphysics, mythical cosmogony, and esoteric psychology. It aroused immediate excitement among both Kabbalists and non-Kabbalists alike. When asked how the exotic volume had come into his possession, de Leon swore that it had arrived by special messenger, sent by the sage Nachmanides in Palestine, who had found it by accident. Today, nearly all scholars agree that de Leon himself wrote the *Book of Splendor* in the early 1280s; a few years later, an anonymous author composed the last of the *Zoharic* books, namely, *Ra'ya Mehemna* ("The True Shepherd") and *Tikkune Zohar* ("Emendations to the *Zohar*").

While little is known about de Leon's life, he was on close terms with Abraham Abulafia's relatives and studied with one of his most ardent disciples. Yet, there is no evidence that the founder of prophetic Kabbalism and the "author" of the *Zohar* actually met, and neither one was ever mentioned in writing by the other. De Leon's works, published under his own name, first appearing in 1286, were highly speculative in format and focused upon the hidden meaning of the biblical stories. Both of these features are pervasive in the *Zohar*; by attributing this complex work to the illustrious Rabbi Simeon bar Yochai, de Leon probably sought to make his own ideas more readily accepted by his contemporaries.

The *Book of Splendor* is a volume that defies easy analysis. It consists of a variety of parts, among which there is considerable overlap of material. Many of the sections, which vary tremendously in terseness and difficulty of symbolism, appear to record the conversations of Rabbi Simeon bar Yochai, his son Eliezer, and their colleagues. The ever-present backdrop to their provocative discussions is the land of Palestine, then under Roman rule. The Jewish people had just witnessed the ruin of their holy Temple and the massacre of their finest scholars. Yet, the *Zohar* is infused with a sense of awe and mystery, rather than defeat or gloom. Many of its passages are beautifully poetic, describing in symbolic terms the wonders of the universe the deity has fashioned. Its central image is the Tree of Life, the fundamental structure of energy within every living and inanimate object for the Kabbalists.

Perhaps the most basic premise of the *Zohar* is that everything in the cosmos is in constant interplay, with an irreducible order underlying all. Nothing that happens to us is viewed as meaningless or haphazard; what we view as reality (what Alan Watts once called "how the world looks on a bleak Monday morning") is simply one realm of consciousness to which we have become habituated. "Man, whilst in this world," the *Zohar* declares, "considers not and reflects not what he is standing on, and each day as it passes he regards as though it has vanished into nothingness."[7] *The Book of Splendor* also emphasizes that heightened awareness alone is not sufficient for us to live properly on earth. For reasons to be discussed in the next chapter, it teaches that ours is the cosmos of action, where concrete activity is required. This notion aptly echoes the Taoist sentiment expressed by Lao Tse that, "A journey of a thousand miles starts from beneath one's feet."[8]

Like other Kabbalistic texts, the *Zohar* is filled with erotic imagery. It affirms that sexual intercourse between husband and wife is one of the most powerful spiritual practices, capable of shattering and transforming our daily, mundane frame of mind. The *Book of Splendor* also emphasizes the existence of a "female" counterpart to the deity, observing that, esoterically speaking, "the supernal Mother" is present with the man only when the home is prepared and when "the male visits the female and they join together."[9] Indeed, the Zohar even compares the most ecstatic states of sacred bliss to what may be experienced during sexual union with love.

Despite its length and complexity, the *Zohar* spread rapidly. During the fourteenth century, it was carried from Jewish Spanish communities outward, especially to Italy and the Middle East. Now that essential Kabbalistic concepts had appeared in the *Book of Splendor*, numerous works were published before long, providing additional commentary and clarification upon the secret significance of Jewish law, ritual, and the quest for personal transcendence. The excitement that these writings generated was sometimes so intense that its advocates argued, in effect, that Judaism was barren without the germinal force of this exotic current. After all, they insisted, didn't the *Zohar* itself say plainly, "Woe unto those who see in the Law nothing but simple narratives and ordinary words! . . . Every word of the Law contains an elevated sense and a sublime mystery."[10] Without the magnificent Kabbalah, such exponents declared, the Jewish tradition was but an empty shell.

These statements served to arouse enmity among the rabbinical establishment. Strong opposition to the Kabbalah—sometimes flatly condemned as heretical—was therefore often voiced by literalists and mainstream philosophers. These normative thinkers regarded the *Zohar* and similar works as filled with nondualist concepts that denied good and evil, messianic pretensions, and a dangerous downplay of the realities of Jewish survival in a hostile Christian world. Other rabbinic scholars, though, felt that the Kabbalah was permissible to be studied—but only by those already well-versed and even intimately sophisticated with the intricacies of Jewish law. Otherwise, they stressed, many would be led astray by its dazzling allure.

Safed and the Flowering of the Kabbalah

Although the Zohar and other Kabbalistic writings intrigued individual Jews and non-Jews alike for many decades, it was not until the 1500s that the Kabbalah began to amass an international audience of important proportions. Nearly all historians now agree that the critical event was the rise of the Inquisition and the Jewish expulsion from Spain in 1492. Ironically, the tragic circumstances involved—among the most devastating of all Jewish experiences prior to the Holocaust—directly led to the greatest flowering of the Kabbalah in its entire history.

Since the victory of Islamic forces over the Catholic Visigoths in the seventh century, Spain had been a country of three religions. Jews, Christians, and Islamic peoples had managed to maintain a tolerant attitude toward one another, for the most part. While Jewish life in Spain had never been easy, it had for centuries been assured of at least its survival. Indeed, Jews comprised a major part of Spain's middle class of artisans, skilled laborers, physicians, and scholars. By virtue of their learning and sophistication, they rose to positions of prominence. Some, known as Marranos (meaning "swine," the term used by unconverted Jews to describe their former brethren) even embraced Christianity and married into the aristocracy.

Then, in 1469, Isabella of Spain married Ferdinand of Aragon. Soon the liason led to a pact between Church and throne. In 1474, Pope Sixtus IV issued his horrifying proclamation establishing the national Inquisition in Spain. Several years later, the terrible wheels began to turn. Over the next decade, thousands of these former Jews were burned at the stake in the *auto-da-fe* ("acts-of-faith"). In 1492, all Jews were ordered to leave the country within four months, on penalty of death to any who remained or tried to return. For those who refused to abandon their homes of centuries, torture and death were readily delivered.

The blow was truly cataclysmic. It shook the Jewish popu-
lace to its psychological and spiritual roots. If after six hundred years of peaceful residence in Spain, having contributed
so much to the arts, sciences, and trades, this was the reward, there seemed little hope for survival anywhere in the
world. As the Jewish community fanned out across the Middle East and North Africa, the mainstream religious homilies
were no longer very consoling. An apocalyptic mood seized
many. Some considered the Day of the Messiah to be near.
Others viewed the Inquisition and the Spanish expulsion as
clear signs of divine retribution and therefore a call, in a way,
to intensified spiritual devotion.

For instance, one Jewish scholar of the day, speaking for
many colleagues, referred to his contemporaries as an "evil
generation, increasing rebellions and transgressions without
number."[11] As it became apparent that the exodus from Spain
would be accompanied by no immediate messianic intervention, the rigorous inward discipline demanded by the Kabbalah
suddenly possessed a tremendous magnetism. With its prom-
ise of exalted joy and ecstatic visions for the devout, the
esoteric tradition now appealed to many. Furthermore, political and social action was virtually impossible and likewise
helped propel certain numbers of Jews to the mystical way of
life.

The expulsion brought many from Spain into the area around
Palestine for refuge. Before long, the town of Safed, in Palestine's Galilee region, became known as the new center for
Kabbalistic study. For both economic and political reasons,
many Jews preferred this small town to Jerusalem, the holiest
city of Palestine and its historical metropolis. Safed also served
as a magnet for spiritual reasons: the illustrious Simeon bar
Yochai was buried there and his grave was a shrine for pious
Jews around the globe. During the decades that followed the
Spanish expulsion, Safed attracted first one, then another, of
the leading intellectual and spiritual giants of the period.
Curiously, little true historical information is available about
these figures, even though legends sprang about them even
prior to their deaths.

One of the greatest of the Safed Kabbalists was Moses Cordovero (1522–1570), a brilliant scholar and writer. His birthplace and early life are unknown. Cordovero lived in Safed, where he studied under prominent Kabbalists of the time. His first major work was completed when he was twenty-six and aroused immediate interest in his systematic treatment of the hidden nature of human existence. Entitled *Pardes Rimmonim* ("Orchard of Pomegranates"), it discussed the thirteen "gateways" to higher consciousness. Of the many books which he wrote, only one—*Tomer Deborah* ("The Palm Tree of Deborah") is yet available in an English translation.

Cordovero's approach to higher consciousness was a supremely intellectual one. He masterfully synthesized and developed virtually all of the different strands of the Kabbalah up to his time, particularly those related to the *Zohar*. For him, the continual exchange of energies among the various *Sefirot* or divine channels is the key to understanding both our own inner makeup and our relation to the unseen forces of the universe.

This influential Kabbalist also laid the foundations for the important ethical literature of the Jewish esoteric tradition. Rather than urging a passive, retreatist approach to earthly life, Cordovero and his followers accented the significance of our actions in daily, social life. In fact, as late as the nineteenth century, the nonmystical, moralistic *Musar* movement studied his *Palm Tree of Deborah* as an essential guide to ethical behavior. In it, echoing *Zoharic* sentiments, sexuality between husband and wife is prized as integral to a spiritual life. "A man should be very careful to behave so that the *Shekinah* (the female component of the Deity) cleaves always to him and never departs," Cordovero wrote. "Man stands between the two females, the physical female ... and the *Shekinah* who stands above him to bless him."[12]

As a chief member of a group which called itself *Chaverim* ("Associates"), Cordovero drew up a list of moral precepts for the daily life of its members. Some of its interesting principles include: never to be forced into anger, never to harm the body by overeating, always to speak the truth, to accept both the delights and pains of earthly life, and to mentally review one's actions of the day before each meal and before going to sleep at night.

One of Cordovero's teachers and colleagues was Joseph Karo (1488–1575), a major Kabbalist of the time. He was well-accepted, even acclaimed by the rabbinical establishment of his day—largely due to the fact that he kept his exotic interests secret for long years. Indeed, Karo is most widely admired for his two chief legalistic works in Judaism, *Beth Yosef* ("The House of Joseph") and the *Shulchan Arukh* ("The Prepared Table"). First printed in Venice in 1564, his books are still closely read in the study of Jewish law.

Born in Toledo, Spain, Joseph Karo settled in the cosmopolitan city of Constantinople with his family after the great expulsion of 1492. He became renowned as a Talmudic scholar and legal thinker, but eventually found himself drawing close to Kabbalistic circles. Under careful tutelage, Karo experimented with what psychologists today would call altered states of awareness and trance phenomena. After a time, he learned to enter into a mediumistic trance.

In this condition, as described in his life-long diary and confirmed by independent observers, Karo would lose his ordinary frame of mind and speak in a changed voice. He would then proceed to discourse—sometimes freely, at other times in a strange, halting manner—upon such evocative themes as the higher nature of dreams, the right way to meditate, the nature of the deity, and even life after death and reincarnation. Karo and his contemporaries in Safed referred to this as the *maggid* (a technical term indicating an agent of celestial speech) phenomenon and believed that a spiritual entity was actively communicating through the channel created by the human medium. Scholars today are finding that this fascinating occurrence was actually far from rare in the Jewish tradition. "Practically every new publication on the history of Jewish mysticism brings to light new cases,"[13] observed Professor R.J. Zwi Werblowsky in his book, *Joseph Karo, Lawyer and Mystic* (Jewish Publication Society: 1977).

The renowned Talmudic scholar moved to Safed in 1536.

Within a decade he had so distinguished himself that he was appointed chief rabbi there. For the many years he resided in the town—until his death at the age of eighty-seven—Karo served as an elder statesman for younger Kabbalists, helping to keep their visionary enthusiasm within the bounds of Jewish law. Yet, many of the views set forth in his journal of the *maggid*'s pronouncements, *Maggid Mesharim*, bear striking similarities to other spiritual disciplines, such as Yoga and Tibetan Buddhism.

The last of the major Safed Kabbalists to be mentioned here—and unquestionably the most important member of its community of seers—was Isaac Luria (1534–1572). He became an almost mythic figure in his own lifetime and almost solely through the incredible power of his ideas helped elevate the Kabbalah to an exalted position in aspects of Jewish thought. Despite the brevity of his life and activity in Safed, he exerted a tremendous impact for centuries upon mainstream Judaism.

Born in Jerusalem to a German family, Luria displayed a dazzling mind at an early age. Due to financial difficulties, the family moved to Cairo after the father's death. There, young Luria's wealthy uncle took them in and provided for the boy's continued education. At the age of seventeen, two years after his marriage, he began to study the Kabbalah in earnest. He focused upon the *Zohar* and Cordovero's tracts in particular, preferring a monastic way of life in pursuit of higher knowledge. Eventually, upon sustained practice of Kabbalistic techniques, he began to experience visions.

Around the beginning of the year 1570 (there are no details on Luria's prior adult life), he felt the inner call to settle in Safed. Like Joseph Karo, he believed that divine exhortations were telling him to make the move from hundreds of miles away with his family. Immediately, he was welcomed by the Kabbalists there and briefly studied under Cordovero himself, who died later that year. Cordovero is said to have appointed him as his own spiritual successor and Luria became the head of a group known as the Cubs—as he was

ST. PAUL'S CHURCH BOOKSHOP
2728 SIXTH AVENUE
SAN DIEGO, CALIFORNIA 92103

DATE 8/16/85

| NAME | |
| ADDRESS | |

SOLD BY	CASH	C.O.D.	CHARGE	ON ACCT.	MDSE. RETD.	PAID OUT
	✓					

QUAN.		DESCRIPTION	PRICE	AMOUNT
	1	Jung's Typology		11.50
	2	Yoga		9.95
	3			21.45
	4	Plus		92.00
	5	From other side		113.45
	6	tax		6.81
	7			120.26
	8			
	9			
	10			
	11			
	12	Continue		

CUSTOMER'S ORDER NO.   REC'D BY

KEEP THIS SLIP FOR REFERENCE
5H 528 **REDIFORM**

nicknamed the "Ari" or "Lion" in Hebrew, in abbreviation of his title the Ashkenazi Rabbi Isaac.

Luria helped build a special set of living quarters for his disciples and their families. Early each Sabbath morning, he and his followers would form a procession and lead themselves out to the surrounding fields. Dressed in white flowing garments, they would wait to receive the spirit of the "Sabbath Queen," a presence they felt as a personification of the holy day of rest. They would welcome this supposed ethereal being with the song *Lekha Dodi* ("Come, My Beloved"), still part of the Conservative and Orthodox liturgy today. Typically, on these occasions, Luria would lecture upon the hidden workings of human consciousness and the cosmos.

Like many other Kabbalists, his declarations were almost exclusively oral in nature. He readily admitted his inability to write down his teachings, and is reputed to have commented, "It is impossible, because all things are interrelated. I can hardly open my mouth to speak without feeling as though the sea burst its dams and overflowed. How then shall I express what my soul has received, and how can I put it down in a book?"[14]

Therefore, what we know of Luria's ideas comes to us through a filter—namely, his innermost disciples. What he succeeded in doing, by the sheer grandeur and power of his vision, was to recast the whole Jewish experience in a completely new light. His major themes dealt with the fundamental questions of suffering and evil in the world. Not only is the Jewish people in exile from the Promised Land, but the Divine Presence is itself separated from its Source, Luria declared. For in the very act of Creation, this cosmic Exile was set into motion. In order for the material world to come into being, God contracted part of His Light—what the "Ari" termed the *Tsimtsum*—and divine "vessels" were readied to be filled with His Essence. However, unable to withstand the intensity of this energy, the "vessels" shattered and confusion or evil was thereby introduced to the universe. The heavenly sparks from the Light were lodged in all things, Luria preached; it is the task of each of us to elevate them back to their primary Source. When this finally occurs, the divine harmony will be complete once more.

For Luria and his generation of followers, then, even the most seemingly insignificant act carries with it cosmic import. Luria devised special techniques to focus people's thoughts during meditative prayer and required complete mental and physical concentration for such methods. He made extensive use of the *Sefirotic* scheme found earlier in the Kabbalistic tradition. Interestingly, his techniques bear parallels to the complicated visualization efforts long part of the Taoist and Tantric Yogic traditions. Moreover, the doctrine of reincarnation which he espoused at great length is also closely akin to certain Eastern spiritual teachings.

The task for recording the maxims of the "Ari" was seized by Chaim Vital (1543–1620), his chief disciple as well as biographer and scribe. Vital copiously recorded his mentor's nearly every word, or so he claimed in later years. After the "Ari's" death, he vied among several disciples for recognition as the only "official" interpreter of the master's discourses. Vital's works include *Sefer Ha-Etz Chaim* ("Book of the Tree of Life"), *Sefer Ha-Hezoynot* ("Book of Visions"), and *Sefer Ha-Gilgulim* ("Book of Transformations"). They reflect the interests of the Safed group in such intriguing subjects to us today as dreams, meditation, altered states of consciousness, and parapsychology.

With its bold images of exile and return, death and rebirth, Luria's world view spread with astonishing rapidity throughout the Jewish world. His teachings gave a definite answer to thousands as to why such events as the Spanish Inquisition and Expulsion had occurred. Physical mortality was not the end of a person's existence and each individual was here on earth for a specific purpose, the "Ari" had indicated. His forceful ideas gave the Jews renewed hope and a sense of purpose amidst a hostile Christian world. His message was carried first to Turkey and the Near East, then to Italy, Holland, and Germany, and eventually to Poland and Eastern Europe. With their undeniable poetic power, as well as respect for the Jewish legal tradition, Luria's discourses became popularized in numerous works in the late sixteenth and seventeenth centuries. In particular, they formed the basis for books designed to impart ethical conduct from an esoteric vantage point. New prayer books, derived from the practices of the Safed community, were freely circulated. The ideas of Luria and his disciples also inspired new generations of poets. Great religious writers like Moses Zucato (c. 1620–1697) and Moses Chaim Luzzatto (1707–1746) drew directly from Kabbalistic images as their poems evoked regained inner strength among thousands of Jews. Luzzatto was himself an ardent Kabbalist and trance medium, writing several works on esoteric psychology.

Nevertheless, actual study of the Kabbalah became forbidden to all but the most erudite Jewish scholars. Partly as a result of a demoralizing messianic movement around the years 1660–1670 in Turkey and surrounding nations, the rabbinate declared emphatically that the Kabbalistic texts—the *Zohar*, works by Cordovero, Vital, and others—were absolutely "off limits" to everyone except the greatest Talmudic thinkers of their time. The orthodoxy's dictum became—and still is to this day—that pursuit of the Kabbalah is forbidden until one is over forty years of age, married, and has already achieved a "full belly" of knowledge with the Talmud and other essential aspects of normative Judaism. The leading rabbis throughout the Jewish world had great respect, even awe for the Kabbalistic tradition, but believed that it was too easily misinterpreted by the masses to be permitted simple access. Its doctrines, the religious establishment felt, simply led too often to messianic delusions, apostasy, or even madness, if blindly seized by the untrained.

In this same era, the Kabbalah became studied by growing numbers of educated Christians. For instance, in 1587, a landmark volume, *Artis Cabalisticae Scriptores*, was published. It contained a variety of articles by Christian scholars on Kabbalistic works and sought to prove, for example, that the *Zohar* actually affirmed the divinity of Jesus of Nazareth. In 1651, the French bibliographer Gaffarel published an index of the codices of the *Zohar*. And in 1677–1678, Knorr von

Rosenroth translated the teachings of the *Book of Splendor* into Latin for scholars unable to read the original Aramaic and Hebrew texts. This work became the standard for Christian theologians for centuries and in our own time was attentively read by the Swiss psychoanalyst Carl Jung. Of particular interest to Christian thinkers in this period, it seems, was the *Sefirotic* system, which they viewed as shedding light on their own exotic interpretations of the New Testament, such as on the nature of the Trinity.

THE KABBALAH IN THE AGE OF REASON
AND TECHNOLOGY

Hasidism: Kabbalah for the Masses

While individual Christian scholars quietly explored the Kabbalistic tradition, Jewish communities throughout Eastern Europe had been thirsting for a new vision. In the mid-seventeenth century, a series of pogroms and massacres led by the Cossack chieftain Bogdan Chmielnitzki murdered an estimated three to five hundred thousand Jews in Poland alone. Indeed, it was not until the Holocaust three hundred years later that such devastation would again be wrought upon the Jewish people. Within a generation, an abortive Jewish messianic movement, under the sway of Sabbatai Zevi (1625–1676) caused even further despair.

Most East European Jews were poor, uneducated, and completely barred from participation in the wider political and economic system. Feudalism still flourished until well into the late nineteenth century. As recently as the turn of the twentieth century, in fact, a Russian Jew was publicly accused and tried for ritual murder (allegedly slaughtering a Gentile boy for the purpose of making Passover *matzoh*), in a case that later formed the subject of novelist Bernard

Malamud's *The Fixer*. Without the slightest hope of even physical security in an antagonistic milieu, the Jewish people had little to trust in except their religion. Yet, it lay dominated strongly by stern literalists and Talmudic intellectuals, and was therefore unable to really satisfy their longing for solace and a sense of purpose.

It was against this historical backdrop that the Kabbalah rose to its greatest influence, under the charismatic leadership of an obscure man without formal education about whom almost nothing is known for sure: Israel ben Eliezer (c.1698–1760), who came to be known as the Baal Shem Tov ("Bearer of the Good Name") or Besht, in abbreviation. The movement that he founded became known as Hasidism ("Devout" in Hebrew). It is unquestionably the most widely recognized phase of Jewish mysticism, thanks to the popular writings of Martin Buber and other twentieth-century philosophers. But it has also been subject to gross misinterpretation, some sources depicting the early Hasidim as little more than carefree pantheists romping through the fields In actuality, we are finding increasing evidence of just how thoroughly the Hasidic leaders were affected by classic Kabbalistic doctrines.

Scholars today generally agree that Israel was born in the small Ukranian village of Ukob, near the Carpathian mountains. He apparently came from a family distinguished by neither social position nor education. While he was still young his parents died, and most probably someone in the community took him in and gave him a home. As a youth, he is said to have displayed far more interest in solitary wanderings through the forest outside the village than in formal religious study. He was hired as a teacher's aide, his duties consisting largely of transporting the village children to and from school. Later on, he performed manual chores for the synagogue sexton. Secretly, at night, however, he would return to the synagogue, where according to legend he would devote long hours to study of mainstream and esoteric Jewish writings.

Israel kept his far-reaching studies to himself, and no one it appears, suspected the young man of being anything more than a rather simple and coarse-featured fellow. In fact, his brother-in-law, a prominent rabbi, was so disgusted with the seeming ignorance of his sister's new husband that he urged her to divorce him. When she declined to do so, her brother bought them a horse and cart and told them to move and settle elsewhere.

Eventually, the newlyweds settled in a remote village in the Carpathian Mountains, where they eked out a meagre living close to nature. After some time, they achieved a reconciliation with her family and the couple ran an inn in a larger town, Miedzyboz. Israel gradually became known there as something of a wonder-worker or "Baal Shem." The tales say that he was already well versed in Kabbalistic healing methods by this time; there is no record of his having been taught by any living Kabbalistic teacher.

In about 1734, according to tradition, at the age of thirty-six, Israel revealed the full extent of his spiritual mastery. The first person to whom he openly confided was allegedly his brother-in-law, who immediately became a close supporter. A highly respected rabbi and Kabbalist of his time, he was to serve as an important link between the religious establishment and the village folk in the burgeoning movement that Israel had begun to spark.

The teachings of the Besht spread rapidly among the uneducated Jewish majority, but before long, he had also attracted some of the finest scholars of the day. Many of them were far more learned than he in the subtleties of the Talmud, yet found his charismatic personality irresistible. The multitude of legends which sprang up shortly after Israel's death tell us that his mastery of the Kabbalah was incomparable and convinced his more erudite contemporaries that he indeed convened with higher powers. Like Isaac Luria two hundred years earlier, the Besht transmitted his teachings by strictly oral means. Of the hundreds of sayings, homilies, and interpretations that have come down to us from him, not one word issued directly from his pen. However, while he wrote no books, he carried out an active correspondence and four letters attributed to the Baal Shem Tov are extant today.

In effect, the Besht took the Kabbalah's abstruse notions and by the sheer power of his presence—relying upon stories and legends—made them accessible to the impoverished Jews of Eastern Europe. His message of hope and passion came as a cleansing breath to tens of thousands of Jews who had come to experience the orthodoxy's emphasis upon Talmudic scholarship as heavy and oppressive. The Baal Shem Tov stressed that book learning is fine, but ultimately useless unless wedded to the way of the heart. "No child can be born except through pleasure and joy," he is credited with saying. "By the same token, if one wishes his prayers to bear fruit, he must offer them with pleasure and joy."[15]

The Besht instructed his followers to pray as fervently as possible, so that the very walls and doors of the synagogue might seem to dissolve into nothingness. He also urged his disciples to accept and enjoy the delights of the physical world. Life on earth is meant to be joyful and extolled, not denigrated, he insisted, declaring that, "Without the feeling of love, stimulated by pleasures, it is difficult to feel true love of God."[16]

Furthermore, Israel disseminated specific meditative techniques, consistent with Isaac Luria's, for attaining higher consciousness. Echoing the teachings of the sixteenth-century sage, the Baal Shem Tov preached that it is our mission to liberate the innumerable fallen sparks in the material world. Every act, the Besht is reputed to have emphasized, if carried out with the right intention or *kavvanah*, helps in the redemption of the cosmos from darkness and confusion. No matter how powerless we may feel, all paths lie open to the presence of the divine. The Baal Shem Tov thus observed, "No two persons have the same abilities. Each man should work in the service of God according to his own talents. If one man tries to imitate another, he merely loses his opportunity to do good through his own merit."[17] This idea was central to his teaching.

Several years before his death, the Besht carefully chose and trained disciples who would succeed him in extending the Hasidic movement. Within fifty years of his passing in 1760, it had spread with such astonishing rapidity—though not without strong opposition among certain Jews—that it had won over half the Jewish population of Russia and Poland, the great centers of Jewish life in the eighteenth and nineteenth centuries. Without doubt, the message of the Baal Shem Tov had touched something very, very deep in the Jewish communities.

Heirs to the Besht: the Great Maggid

The mantle of Israel's leadership fell to Rabbi Dov Baer of Mezritch (1710–1772). Known as the "Maggid" or spiritual master, in his early life he was well known as a brilliant but overly ascetic scholar. According to the classic legend, in meeting for the first time with the Besht, he was challenged to interpret a difficult portion of the *Zohar*. After the Maggid concluded, Israel proceeded to explain the passage and as he did so the room reputedly became filled with the dazzle of celestial beings. "Your interpretation was correct," the Baal Shem Tov quietly said to the other, "but your way of studying lacked soul." Soon after, the Maggid became a close colleague of the Besht and organized his discourses into a more academic style.

Like his mentor, Rabbi Dov Baer of Mezritch wrote no books. He would give his discourses on the Sabbath and on the following day his disciples would record his views. His doctrines are to be found in their works as they quoted him frequently. Interestingly, the Maggid apparently lectured in a form of "automatic speech," in which—according to testimony from his many followers—he spoke from a visibly altered state of consciousness or trance. Indeed, the Maggid taught that the cultivation of this frame of mind is an important aim of meditation. In an article in 1960 in *The Journal of Jewish Studies*, J.G. Weiss observed of this doctrine, "The speaker must have no power over his diction, which bursts forth from him uncontrolled and impulsive. . . . His duty is not to preach but rather to withdraw, by mystically annihilating himself, and allow God to make use of his lips."[18]

The Maggid gathered around him a gifted group of teachers, who later became Hasidic masters in their own right. For this reason, there is little doubt that the rapid spread of Hasidism was largely due to the Maggid's brilliant organizing efforts. Philosophically, he insisted that our normal, waking consciousness is but one way—and a pale way at that—of experiencing the world. He stressed that through the diligent training of our attention, each of us can become more closely aware of the divine pattern of the cosmos. "When a man . . . strips away the material aspect which envelops [him] . . . he will depict in his mind only the divine energy which derives . . . from the supernal root so that its light will be of infinite greatness."[19]

Rabbi Dov Baer of Mezritch also spoke extensively about the proper way for us to meditate. He believed that it is a process that requires patience and commented, "To do this, man must concentrate his thought upon certain details. This is oftentimes arduous labor, but success brings joy."[20] Similar to masters of several other spiritual disciplines like Tibetan Buddhism and Yoga, he insisted that we should not struggle to banish troubling thoughts from our mind, but rather, we should strive to elevate the ideas and feelings that flit across consciousness. His most important sayings were recorded by one of his disciples in a work entitled *Maggid Devaray Le-Yaakov* ("He Telleth His Word to Jacob") or *Likkutey Amarim* ("Collected Sayings"). Written with the Maggid's approval, it was first published in 1784.

While Rabbi Dov Baer of Mezritch, as a masterful scholar, did much to secure the growing Hasidic movement as a valid Jewish approach, the rabbinical establishment nevertheless grew increasingly disturbed over Hasidic activities. The orthodox leaders were not merely irritated by the anti-intellectual tone that seemed to them associated with the new movement. Even worse, they felt, was the emphasis the Hasidim placed on the role of *zaddik*, the supposed intermediary between human and God—a religious figure that came to be popular among the disciples of the Besht. The Baal Shem Tov had encouraged his myriad followers to look to the *zaddikim*, his chosen proselytes, for spiritual guidance in everyday affairs. But over the years, *zaddikim* bloomed like wildflowers all over Eastern Europe. Some possessed obvious wisdom. But others, claimed the Hasidic adversaries or *Mitnaggedim* ("opponents") as they came to be known, were charlatans and fools.

Furthermore, the *Mitnaggedim* condemned other Hasidic practices—such as substituting the Lurianic Prayer Book for the traditional one, wearing special clothing, meditating and praying in certain variant ways—as heretical. Especially in Lithuania, the stronghold of traditional rabbinical study, opposition to Hasidism was extremely bitter. In 1781, Elijah *Gaon* ("Great Scholar") of Vilna (1720–1797) issued an interdict which forbade pious Jews to marry Hasidim. In several towns, Hasidic writings were publicly burned by the *Mitnaggedim*, who felt the very future of the Jewish people was at stake. Yet, the burgeoning movement could not be stopped.

It is important to realize that the dispute was *not* between Kabbalists or mystics *versus* rationalist interpreters of Judaism. In the past, some scholars have erroneously arrived at this view, since the Hasidim were enthusiastic Kabbalists. Rather, the *Mitnaggedim* were Kabbalists, too, though they regarded the esoteric discipline as better left for only the most learned. Essentially, they looked upon the Hasidim as vulgarizers of an awesome, potentially explosive sacred tradition. for instance, the Gaon Elijah was so immersed in the Kabbalah that his writings on this subject alone surpass in volume all those of his Hasidic contemporaries put together. Even more interesting, this towering intellectual was also a trance medium. Like Joseph Karo of the sixteenth century, the Gaon Elijah is said to have regularly experienced paranormal trances since before the age of thirty.

The Lubavitcher Founder

As the Hasidic movement grew despite the antagonism of the *Mitnaggedim*, the power and vigor of its original vision slowly declined, perhaps inevitably. New generations of Jews, who had never met the Baal Shem Tov or his chosen disciples, were bound to distort or even subvert the early teachings. For instance, various doctrines about prayer and meditation became progressively more diluted. The Kabbalistic underpinnings of fundamental Hasidic thought steadily weakened to the point where some twentieth-century scholars have even doubted the connection.

One of the great Hasidic masters who sought to preserve the purity of the original message was Rabbi Schneur Zalman of Liady (1747–1812), the most influential of the Maggid's many disciples. Born in central Russia, he was a child prodigy in his mastery of the Talmud, then chose to continue his studies under the wing of Rabbi Dov Baer of Mezritch. The older teacher encouraged his young disciple—more than thirty-five years his junior—to develop a new Code of Law which would update the work of Karo.

Rabbi Schneur Zalman was drawn to a more organized approach to a higher consciousness than that favored by many *zaddikim* across the countryside. He was especially interested in explicitly relating popular Hasidic precepts to classic Kabbalistic ideas. Encouraged by his mentor, he published in 1797 the first part of his *Tanya* ("It Has Been Taught"). The meaning of the title derives from the book's opening word, *Tanya,* as Hebrew books were frequently called after their opening phrase. Another name for the complex work is *Likkutey Amarim* ("Collected Sayings"), with the final parts added in 1806 and 1814 respectively. Its author called his system *Chabad*—in abbreviation of the first letters of the highest three *Sefirot* in the formalized Kabbalistic system— *chochmah* (wisdom), *binah* (understanding), and *daath* (knowledge).

In the *Tanya*, Rabbi Schneur Zalman wrote compellingly on a variety of interesting topics, from metaphysics to human motivation and personality. He emphasized our capacity for inner growth and the importance of free will in determining our lives. The founder of Lubavitcher Hasidism also stressed the necessity for activity as an antidote to depression, commenting that, "There is no other way of converting darkness

into light except through action."[21] His model of our emotional makeup focuses extensively on our highest nature, which
he believed is linked step-by-step all the way up to the divinity. Yet, he also recognized the power of our lower emotions,
like fear, anger, and sadness. Such feelings, he declared, must
be confronted and overcome through honest self-examination.

The proponent of *Chabad* Hasidism likewise taught his disciples that a basic human desire is to merge with the *Ein Sof*
("Infinite"). The human soul, he wrote, "naturally yearns to
separate itself and depart from the body in order to unite
with its origin and source . . . the fountainhead of all life."[22]
This kind of viewpoint is found in various Eastern religions.
But the Jewish orthodoxy has always been very uneasy with
such references to our specific, individual relationship with
the divine. To them, Rabbi Schneur Zalman seemed to be
urging a new religion that would destroy Judaism. After all,
they reasoned, he had clearly announced, "I come now to
recall you to your duty, to awaken those who sleep the heavy
slumber of vanity . . . to open the eyes of the blind that they
should see."[23]

Twice the *Mitnaggedim* actually denounced him to the Russian government for alleged treason to the Czar. The Hasidic
opponents claimed that Rabbi Schneur Zalman's group was
secretly plotting to overthrow the official state rulers. The
author of the *Tanya* was imprisoned both times, but the Czar's
police could find no evidence to support these charges. After
his second release, in 1801, it was apparent to even his most
bitter foes among the orthodoxy that he was not going to stop
preaching and this movement could not be eliminated. Ironically, before long, both *Mitnaggedim* and Hasidim would find
themselves united against a common enemy— namely, the
new Jewish secularists or *Maskalim*.

Rabbi Schneur Zalman of Liady not only had the genius to
offer a lucid account of the Kabbalah for large numbers of
Jews, but also possessed superb organizational skills. He
founded the Lubavitcher sect, which planned and established
schools, community programs, and social services, especially

for Jews in out-of-the-way places. Today, there are several hundred thousand Lubavitcher Hasidim throughout the world in tightly knit communities.

Rabbi Nachman of Bratslav

Contemporary to the Lubavitcher founder was another Hasidic giant, Rabbi Nachman of Bratslav (1772–1810). His intriguing teachings contain a veritable storehouse of information on dreams, altered states of consciousness, the mind-body relationship, and other topics of considerable interest to us today. Born in a small village of the Ukraine, he was a great-grandson of the Baal Shem Tov and while still a youth is said to have been drawn to the visionary life.

In 1798, Rabbi Nachman of Bratslav, at the age of twenty-six, journeyed to Palestine. He sought to make the pilgrimage to Safed to visit the graves of such great Kabbalists as Simeon bar Yochai, Isaac Luria, and others. In his later years, Rabbi Nachman dated his real spiritual life from this voyage on. Though the details of his months in the Holy Land are scanty at best, it seems that he contacted Sufis as well as fellow Kabbalists there. Shortly after his return, he settled in Bratslav, where he lectured upon the Kabbalah before small groups of loyal followers. Though he transmitted his provocative message orally, much of his word was fortunately recorded by one of his disciples and published about 1805. It is entitled *Likkutey Moharan* ("The Collected Sayings of our Master Rabbi Nachman"), with another series published after his death, in 1811.

After only five years in Bratslav, Rabbi Nachman contracted tuberculosis. Aware that his death lay near, with a calm heart he moved to the city of Uman. According to Martin Buber, Rabbi Nachman sought to "raise upward" what he felt were the trapped souls of the many soldiers who had died there in battle years before. This Kabbalistic thinker also believed that our thought can influence events in the physical world; he is said to have been clairvoyant and to have possessed psychic abilities. As was true for Isaac Luria and other great

Kabbalists, he was convinced of the survival of human consciousness after physical mortality, and like other Hasidic leaders he preached that the moment of bodily death is a critical one for that transition.

Rabbi Nachman taught that each of us can attain higher spiritual awareness through individual efforts. He emphasized emotional vitality, especially joy, as the gateway to the divine, repeatedly condemning asceticism and bodily denial. Such punishing of our physical aspect, he stressed, has little to do with a spiritual way of life. "The general rule is that a man must try always to be joyful," he declared, "even if he has to resort to silly things."[24] For him, our mind and body are closely intertwined. Nearly two hundred years ago, he described with an uncanny accuracy the vital link between emotions such as chronic fear, anger, or depression, and the onset of physical illness.

Rabbi Nachman of Bratslav also stressed the significance of solitary meditation, in sharp contrast to the mainstream Jewish emphasis on communal prayer. Through this private experience, he contended, we can best attain a more lofty state of consciousness. To be in solitude is the highest ideal and the doorway to exalted perceptions of the universe, he taught, advising his followers to each set aside at least an hour per day for individual communion with the divine. Whether we are alone in a room or outside in a field, the Bratslav Hasid commented, "You must make sure—set aside a specific time each day to calmly review your life."[25]

This masterful Hasidic leader is best known today for the many parables and stories with which he gave shape to his brilliant ideas. His tales have been compared to the works of Kafka more than a century later. Rabbi Nachman's themes—of lost kings and shipwrecked voyagers, madmen and dreamers, hidden treasures and sudden coincidences—illustrate many classic Kabbalistic concepts in symbolic form, yet defy simple categorization. Most of the stories were recorded in a garbled and fragmented manner, for their author did not write any of them down. In 1815, thirteen of them were published in Yiddish with a Hebrew translation.

Today, a Hasidic sect still looks to his teachings for inspiration in daily life. Known as the "dead Hasidim" in other Hasidic circles, their chief synagogue stands in the orthodox, Meah She'arim section of Jerusalem. Following Rabbi Nachman's statement, "My light will glow till the days of the Messiah,"[26] the Bratslavers still speak of their founder in the present tense and have never appointed an heir to his spiritual mission.

The Decline of the Kabbalah in the Industrial Age

Despite the valiant attempts of the great Hasidic masters of the late eighteenth century, the Jewish people continued to abandon interest in its esoteric tradition. The times were rapidly changing. With the advent of the revolutions in the American colonies and then in France, a new era of liberal democracy and political reform was dawning in the West. After countless years of having been systematically denied access to the universities and forced to live in cramped and demeaning ghettos, many Jews were more than eager to participate in the general cultural advance.

The Jewish Enlightenment or *Haskalah* movement first arose in Germany, about the same time that the *Mitnaggedim* fought the Hasidim in Eastern Europe so vehemently. Under the leadership of Moses Mendelssohn (1729–1786), a nucleus of Westernized disciples began to establish secular Jewish schools— the first in Berlin in 1781. Their goal was to crush the superstition that they felt enslaved their less cosmopolitan brethren. In particular, they regarded the Hasidim, with their Kabbalistic concepts, as the most backward, ignorant, and foolish of contemporary Jews. Many *Maskalim* ("Enlightened") wrote diatribes against the Hasidic groups, accusing them of trying to drag the Jewish people down into a perpetually medieval way of life. As the Haskalah movement spread, Jews began to gain entry into various professions. They increasingly prospered as merchants, bankers, brokers, agents, manufacturers, doctors, teachers, journalists, and government contractors. For many, there seemed little reason to cling to centuries-old customs; it has been estimated that during the first decades of the nineteenth century, perhaps half of the Jews of Berlin converted to Catholicism.

At the same time, also in Germany, the Jewish Reform movement was born. Backed by the local governments in the country, it succeeded in defusing traditional rituals and prayers. Israel Jacobson, a philanthropist and leader of this movement, established a Reform school in 1801 and in 1808 issued a proclamation which banned discussions on the Kabbalah in Reform synagogues. In the decades that followed, various new prayer books were introduced, shifting the tone and content of worship. For example, in 1819, the long favored Kabbalistic prayer, *Lekha Dodi* ("Come, My Beloved") was replaced by a Lutheran choral in the newly published Hamburg Temple prayer book.

To be sure, such efforts were combated vigorously by the Jewish orthodoxy. They regarded assimilation as the certain path to apostasy. The *Mitnaggedim* and Hasidim both realized that they had more in common with one another than with the *Maskalim*, who smugly viewed them as blindly clinging to outworn beliefs. Another reason for the eventual rapprochement between the Hasidim and their erstwhile rabbinical opponents was the Hasidic downplay of their original Kabbalistic ideas. For instance, by the mid-nineteenth century, the important techniques of Kabbalistic prayer and meditation that the Baal Shem Tov had taught were all but extinct among the Hasidim. The Besht's suggestions for transforming disturbing thoughts during prayer was gradually minimized and later dropped altogether. This same pattern repeated itself for other tenets of the Hasidic founders, more and more viewed as almost mythic supermen by later generations of followers. The Hasidim did not altogether eliminate the Kabbalah from their teachings, but like the *Mitnaggedim*, increasingly argued that such esoteric knowledge was better left to only the most learned of Jews.

Finally, devastating blows to popular acceptance of the Kabbalistic viewpoint were leveled by the newly emancipated Jews in attendance at Western universities. The leader of this intellectual movement was Professor Heinrich Graetz (1817–1891) who in 1854 first joined the faculty of the Jewish Theological Seminary in Breslau, a moderately Reformist organization. Graetz's influence was unparalleled. In his recent book, *Ideas of Jewish History* (Behrman House: 1975), Michael Meyer noted that, "The figure dominates the Jewish historiography of the nineteenth century. Though frequently criticized by other scholars, his work has enjoyed a tremendous and lasting popularity."[27]

Graetz's magnum opus was his *History of the Jews*, published in eleven volumes from 1853 to 1876. Translated and often reprinted, its approach to Jewish history became "the norm during the latter half of the nineteenth century and secured its continuing influence up to the present time."[28] In this set of volumes, Professor Graetz's portrayal of the Kabbalah was negative in the extreme. Not only did he view the Kabbalistic system with the utmost disdain, but he also depicted its most vaunted figures as ignoramuses and madmen. For instance, of the *Zohar*, he wrote, "Its contents are just as curious, confused and chaotic as its form and external dress."[29] He referred to the sixteenth-century Safed thinkers as "having an evil influence" upon Jews throughout the world. He even attacked the revered masters of the Hasidic movement in vicious terms, commenting, "As ugly as the name, Besht, was the form of the founder and the order that he called into existence . . . his brain was so filled with fantastic images that he could not distinguish them from real, tangible beings."[30]

In short, the most authoritative Jewish historian of his era—with an impact that continued for generations— viewed the Kabbalah as a foul and errant stream in the Jewish current. He succeeded in portraying the Kabbalistic tradition as an aberration, an error—and even worse—as antithetical to the true meaning of Judaism. It is little wonder that under this onslaught the Kabbalah soon became ridiculed and then forgotten in dominant Jewish thought and practice, especially among the most worldly Jews in the West. In the new age of the steam engine and the locomotive, the ancient symbols seemed absurd, and so, their underlying significance passed from historical memory.

In the Middle East, though, the Kabbalah was still popular among Jewish communities. As late as the twentieth century, in the old section of Jerusalem, a tightly organized band of students continued to explore the *Zohar*, Isaac Luria's meditative techniques, and other Kabbalistic aspects. Based in the Beth El Yeshiva there, they served as the chief center for the esoteric Jewish tradition throughout the Orient and North Africa. Yet, until the modern formation of Israel, the Sephardic culture itself, in its near entirety, was almost wholly isolated from Western Judaism.

By the mid-nineteenth century in Western Europe and the United States, the Kabbalah had thus become a virtual relic. At best, it was viewed as an outmoded repository of once-relevant speculation. At worst, and this was by far the dominant appraisal for nearly a century—it was regarded as simply an embarrassing reminder of a medieval outlook that modern Jews were eager to leave behind.

But times change and perhaps for many reasons the Kabbalah is once again beginning to resonate with wide appeal. It is time for a close look at its message for humanity in the late twentieth century.

CHAPTER TWO

WE ARE THE COSMOS

"As man's body consists of members and parts of various ranks all acting and reacting upon each other so as to form one organism, so does the world at large consist of a hierarchy of created things, which when they properly act and react upon each together form literally one organic body."

—the Zohar

"All things have one root."

—Rabbi Nachman of Bratslav

THERE IS AN EXCITING REVOLUTION occurring today in the way in which we are viewing our relation to the cosmos. In diverse fields ranging from cellular biology to environmental psychology to astrophysics, innovative explorers are converging on a new model to explain how the universe operates. Going beyond the mechanistic perspective that has previously limited orthodox science, this approach is known as "holism." It insists that we can best understand the world around us as a web of meaningful wholes in vital interconnection, not as a machine-like structure of isolated parts.

Thus, concerning the realm of the human body, there has arisen a popular movement advocating what it calls "holistic health," or the unity between mind and body. This orientation—increasingly articulated by professionals themselves—emphasizes that our physical processes cannot possibly be separated from our emotions. Our mental and bodily aspects constitute a totality. Each must be taken into account to truly comprehend the other, insist exponents of this compelling approach. However, the values that underlie this conception are common to a growing number of other disciplines, which are similarly undergoing a powerful reexamination of their fundamental premises.

Interestingly, in the last few years, many investigators are discovering to their surprise that the holistic model is actually far from new. In fact, they have begun to realize, the idea that the universe is an organic totality, with everything in constant interplay, has been taught for centuries by spiritual traditions around the globe. That is, central to nearly all of these ancient systems of knowledge is the message that nothing is truly divided from the rest of existence; an irreducible harmony, of which we are a basic aspect, rules all.

Perhaps reflecting their status as heirs to the oldest and most well-established area of science, physicists have been the most ready to recognize the parallels between this twentieth-century view of the cosmos and the notions found within various age-old religious doctrines. For example, in his well-received book, *The Tao of Physics* (Shambhala: 1975), Dr. Fritjof Capra drew a fascinating set of comparisons between contemporary quantum mechanics and such inner paths as Buddhism, Hinduism, and Taoism. Arguing persuasively that the ways of the scientist and the mystic may not be as antagonistic as we have thought, he demonstrated the remarkable consensus about the universe shared by today's physicists and historically prominent spiritual masters of the East. "The further we penetrate into the submicroscopic world," Capra observed, "the more we shall realize how the modern physicist, like the Eastern mystic, has come to see the world as a system of inseparable, interacting, and ever-moving components, with man as an integral part of this system."[1] Since he penned these cogent words, an accelerating number of books in the physical sciences have appeared, articulating virtually this precise perspective.

Within the field of psychology, though, this unified model of life has been slower to emerge. Some commentators have attributed this fact to the relatively young and self-conscious status of the discipline. For instance, there are still persons alive who studied directly with Freud himself, the founder of modern personality theory and psychotherapy. Many others currently in active practice were trained by his direct disciples. It would be as though some of Sir Isaac Newton's pupils were currently walking about, pursuing their illustrious teacher's notions on mathematics and physics.

Out of the need, therefore, to appear as intellectually mature as possible, many mainstream psychologists have tended to cling erroneously to the nineteenth-century view of the world—in which we are all isolated like billiard balls, independent of one another. Furthermore, until quite recently, the social and behavioral sciences have paid little attention to such significant breakthroughs in physics as the discovery that the experimenter cannot help but influence the results of his or her inquiry—and therefore, that there can be no ultimate "objectivity" in the investigation of our mental nature.

To be sure, critics have long insisted on a more integrated perspective. At the dawn of the atomic age, William James urged in the very early 1900s that the budding field of psychology shed its cultural biases. The brilliant Harvard professor was extremely interested in mysticism, Oriental religion, and even spiritualist phenomena for their possible contributions to our understanding our full human capacities. Later, iconoclasts such as Carl Jung and Wilhelm Reich outraged their colleagues by calling for a sweeping new approach to the study of people—one which would recognize that each of us moves through life in constant interrelation with diverse aspects of the universe. They argued that mainstream psychology was far too narrowly focused on a provincial outlook that denied our higher potential. Yet, these gifted figures, like others who shared their beliefs, were dismissed as impractical dreamers by more conservative members of their profession.

Beginning in the 1960s, though, the relevant climate of thought began to change. In his small but provocative book, *The Psychology of Science* (Harper & Row: 1966), Abraham Maslow condemned orthodox science for its "unproved articles of faith, taken-for-granted definitions, axioms, and concepts."[2] He envisioned a new psychology, one which refrained from pigeonholing people and "atomizing" them into meaningless statistical entities. He declared, "It is my impression that the weaknesses of classical science show up most obviously in the fields of psychology and ethnology. Indeed, when one wishes knowledge of persons or of societies, mechanistic science breaks down altogether."[3]

The time was now right for such incisive commentary. Before long, Maslow was elected president of the American Psychological Association, the national professional organization. His books on psychology, religion, and the visionary experience became popular throughout the West and helped spark the creation of two new movements—humanistic and transpersonal psychology. Both of these approaches emphasize the uniquely creative and intuitive functions of our mind. They reject the view that the purely statistical orientation is the only valid means to comprehending human cognition and behavior.

Furthermore, explorers in these movements harbor an open respect now for humanity's great spiritual traditions. Farsighted researchers are avidly searching the ancient disciplines for their compelling insights concerning our inner makeup. Such psychologists are glimpsing just how much of the established field has been dominated by unsubstantiated, unchallenged, and even unexamined assumptions. As a result, we are all starting to see the blinders that have restricted the scope and depth of the search for our intrinsic nature, as well as our links to the surrounding universe.

One of the most comprehensive and fascinating of these pathways is the Kabbalah. Today, it is beginning to attract the full attention it deserves, for it offers a clear and alternative set of values to those that have ruled mechanistic science. The Kabbalistic system provides a detailed, consistent picture of our personality and presents an all-inclusive view of our tendencies, weak and strong. Moreover, its perspective on the human relation to the cosmos shows some striking parallels to what several other spiritual disciplines have long taught. Jewish mysticism has even anticipated many of the latest theories of modern biophysics. Thus, by examining the Kabbalah's chief assumptions, we may not merely gain a fresh perspective of our own cultural biases, but also sight new direction for our contemporary quest for knowledge.

The Cosmic Harmony

Undoubtedly, the most fundamental principle of Judaism's entire visionary way is that the cosmos is a coherent and meaningful whole. The major teachers of this longstanding body of knowledge have insisted repeatedly that each aspect of creation is vitally connected to everything else. Works like the *Zohar*, the "bible" of Kabbalistic lore, stress over and over that all the various dimensions of existence—encompassing the most infinitesimal creatures as well as the most far-flung reaches of space—are intimately interwoven. The world is constructed on this precept, the *Book of Splendor* explains, "upper and lower, from the first mystic point up to the furthest removed of all the stages. They are all coverings to one another."[4]

Indeed, perhaps the most central message of this evocative and complex volume is its often mentioned dictum that "As above, so below." A vast unseen web is said to link each of us. In its time-honored metaphor, we are all individual buds of being on the great Tree of Life, whose roots lie in heaven. In countless, subtle ways in which we ordinarily may be wholly oblivious, what we do, say, and even think is regarded as having a very real influence on the whole. Jewish visionaries have stressed that all the "thousands of worlds" that permeate the universe are bound together in the closest harmony.

Yet, the Kabbalists have been realists enough to also recognize that this optimistic viewpoint directly conflicts with much of our experience in day-to-day living. At one time or another, virtually all of us have felt cut off from friends and family, and longed for a greater sense of companionship. In fact, the apparent separateness of everything that breathes and moves seems to be a basic characteristic of life itself. After all, does not each person feel only his or her own pain?

However, the Kabbalah emphasizes, this image of the world is ultimately an illusion, borne of our quite limited perceptions. The lower an individual's spiritual attainment, the more divided one feels from the rest of existence, even from his or her own inner Source. However, the Kabbalists stress, as we begin to achieve higher states of awareness, we will increasingly see the unity among the apparently haphazard events around us. As will be discussed in Chapter 8, more and more "coincidences" in fact become manifest.

Thus, the Jewish esoteric system sharply differs with the mechanistic view of the universe as simply a random jumble of chaotic forces. Rather, the cosmos is described as ordered into a dazzling array of perfectly integrated functions. Everything that we see has its own distinct role to play, whether or not we can easily discern it. No matter what our degree of understanding, the Kabbalah indicates, we must always remember that no event in the universe lacks a specific purpose. In language and content that remarkably mirrors that of contemporary physicists, Rabbi Moses Chaim Luzzatto of the eighteenth century observed, "The patterns and systems of all existence [are set up] in such a fashion that all of them are interconnected."[5]

Furthermore, Jewish mysticism asserts that the world we behold through our physical senses—as well as through scientific instruments—intrinsically accords at best only a crude picture of the splendors that surround us. Material devices, however sophisticated, simply cannot measure the transcendent. Beyond a certain point, the key Kabbalistic texts suggest, even the most powerful tools fail us. For they too depend on gross matter for their structure. They are unable to really penetrate what lies in other, more subtle, planes of being.

Ironically, this notion, which appeared as superstitious nonsense to most nineteenth-century thinkers, is now almost a truism in the physical sciences. Not very long ago, scientific faith in the ability of our machines to unravel the universe's mysteries was supreme. In the late 1800s, for example, many researchers seriously believed that they were close to basically understanding the workings of the whole cosmos. Such investigators were confident that telescopes, microscopes, and other tools would provide all the answers. Then came the quiet revolution heralded by Albert Einstein and his colleagues.

It has since become very clear that our technological instruments have merely opened up new vistas of unexplored territory. They have obviously brought us no closer at all to solving the central enigmas of space, time, and energy. In fact, the Heisenberg Uncertainty Principle a cornerstone of modern theoretical physics— specifically indicates that our very efforts to probe the structure of the cosmos unalterably affects what we observe. Consequently, the scientific quest as it has traditionally been defined—stressing "objectivity" as the only valid road to knowledge—appears to have definite methodological limits. Nearly seven hundred years ago, the *Book of Splendor* aptly commented, "There is a certain point which is the beginning of number and which cannot be further analyzed."[6]

Through visionary experience, though, Kabbalists have much to offer about our relation to the universe. Significantly, they tell us that the world is ultimately composed of a unity of apparent opposites. Such qualities as activity and passivity, male and female, light and dark, seem separate and indeed mutually contradictory to our normal frame of consciousness. Yet, the Kabbalah insists that all are in fact one. Thus, in one acute commentary on the biblical line, "And God divided the light from the darkness," the *Zohar* explains:

> Up to this point the male principle was represented by light and the female by darkness; subsequently they were joined

together and made one. The difference by means of which
light is distinguished from darkness is by degree only; both are
one in kind, as there is no light without darkness and no
darkness without light.[7]

This intriguing, nondualist concept is, of course, highly
similar to that of Taoism and other Oriental philosophies. For
example, the terms *yin* and *yang* originally represented two
sides of a mountain, both terms compounded with the Chinese character for "mound of earth." Eventually, these terms
came to be associated with the two pulses of the Tao as it
moves in the world—one active and thrusting (in Kabbalistic
writing known as the "King"), the other receptive (called the
"Queen" or "Shekinah").

According to the Kabbalah, then, all aspects of creation,
from the origin of the physical universe to the simplest human
act, involve a balance between these two forces. To effectively convey this idea, many Jewish mystics have used sexually charged imagery of the most bold nature. The next chapter
will focus in more detail on this provocative feature of their
teaching. Suffice it to say here, however, that particularly the
thirteenth-century *Book of Splendor* is replete with references
to the joyful lovemaking of the celestial "King" and "Queen"
to give birth to new energies in the cosmos. In fact, some
sections of this sacred volume actually make use of the metaphor of sexual orgasm to describe the interplay of these polar
but complementary forces. For instance, one passage vividly
relates that, "The seed [of the Righteous One] does not flow
save when the Female is present and their mutual desires are
blended into one indissoluble ecstasy."[8]

The Kabbalists add that not only does the universe as a
totality consist of a union of active/passive aspects of being;
each living and nonliving entity does likewise. Every person
is seen to incorporate what are commonly stereotyped as
masculine and feminine qualities. None of us solely possesses
the personality traits supposedly belonging to only men or
women. Thus, the *Zohar* comments that the primal "Man of
Emanation" was both male and female, and even more ele-

gantly states, "Every figure which does not comprise male and female elements is not a true and proper figure."[9]

Therefore, Jewish visionaries have always advised their initiates to seek an inner balance between these two tendencies. To best develop within, we must learn to embrace both assertive and nuturant traits. The Kabbalists would also suggest that a completely analytic approach to knowledge inevitably leads to a fragmented view of both human nature and the universe's structure; a complementary,. holistic orientation is also necessary, incorporating subjective experience. In this vein, recent research on human brain hemispheres highlights that both intuitive and rational processes are central to our ability to respond meaningfully to the world around us.

Furthermore, the Kabbalah tells us that even time and its various subcomponents are composed of "King-like" and "Queen-like" attributes. For example, the *Book of Splendor* reports that particular seasons of the year, hours of the day, or solitary moments, are rhythmically "ruled" to subtle degrees by either of these forces. In other words, external cycles of which we may be little aware are seen to influence us to more active or receptive moods. In the late eighteenth century, the Hasidic leader Rabbi Nachman of Bratslav insightfully observed that "All creation is like a rotating wheel, revolving and oscillating . . . everything revolves in cycles."[10] The better able we are to discern the recurrent characteristics in nature, the more in tune with the divine stream within us we become, he indicated. The entire universe is in a constant flow of change that inextricably affects our daily life, Rabbi Nachman emphasized.

Here again, the Jewish esoteric tradition seems to have show astonishing prescience. In laboratories around the globe today, investigators are discovering the great extent to which living organisms are regulated by complex internal and external rhythms. Life processes appear to be quite cyclical, whether in simple one-celled creatures or humans. In her interesting book, *Body Time* (Pantheon: 1971), Gay Luce summarized much of the research prior to the past decade in this burgeoning field. More recently, even as unlikely an object as the moon has been scientifically studied to evaluate its effect on animal behavior. In *The Lunar Effect* (Doubleday: 1979), Dr. Arnold Lieber has documented how the recurrent appearance of the new and full moon significantly correlates to increased rates in homicide; his earlier articles on this subject appeared in the prestigious *American Journal of Psychiatry* and *Journal of Clinical Psychiatry*. The precise way in which the moon and other cosmic forces affects biological cycles is certainly not fully understood. But this age-old Kabbalistic viewpoint—which recommends for instance that our fasts be timed with lunar phases—no longer seems so superstitious after all. For optimal mental and physical well-being, we might profitably monitor our activities with those of daily, monthly, or seasonal cycles in our environment.

Interestingly, validation for the relevance of the Kabbalah's ancient assumptions has come not only from the realm of the life sciences. The modern field of quantum mechanics is now converging on some of the seemingly most exotic notions found within the Jewish esoteric system. That is, through repeated experiments concerning the subatomic world, physicists are postulating that the cosmos may operate by laws that go beyond ordinary reason. One major theory is specifically that the universe is composed of a unity between fundamentally opposite but reciprocal aspects. For instance, subatomic particles are regarded as both destructible and indestructible; matter is both continuous and discontinuous. Energy and matter are seen to be but different functions of the same phenomenon. Space and time themselves are two concepts which have appeared completely different, but have been combined in relativistic physics. Dr. Fritjof Capra comments:

> Force and matter, particles and waves, motion and rest, existence and non-existence—these are some of the opposite or contradictory concepts which are transcended in modern physics.... Faced with a reality which lies beyond opposite concepts, physicists ... have to adopt a special way of thinking ... where the mind is not fixed in the rigid framework of classical logic.[11]

Of course, for many centuries the Kabbalah's chief thinkers have been saying exactly the same thing. They have stressed that our day-to-day consciousness, with its inflexible "either/or" categories, is simply not equipped to comprehend the true nature of the cosmos. We must learn to enter into higher mental states, which carry us past the confines of mundane logic and rationalism. In that exalted frame of mind, we will better understand—and experience—the brilliance of the vast celestial harmony.

The Tree of Life

Perhaps the most central feature of Jewish mystical speculation about the universe is the concept of the Tree of Life. Since the Kabbalah's inception, its adepts have devoted tremendous attention to elaborating this complex and imagina-tive topic. Controversies have raged for centuries over its many interpretations. While some modern day teachers of the Kabbalistic way have glossed over these differences of opinion, it is important to realize that they have always surrounded this already intricate subject. In the space available here, it will therefore be possible to sketch only the broad outlines of what is actually an extensive and at times an admittedly confusing body of material.

Jewish mystics have always preached that for the cosmos to exist, some of the primordial divine force had to be withdrawn into itself. What was manifested "before" Creation is not something they have discussed at length, but wisely insisted is simply beyond all powers of human intellect to grasp. In fact, they have explicitly advised that both spatial and temporal qualities—words like "where," "when," "before," and "after"—are utterly meaningless as applied to this question. In any event, the deity—transcending any of our attempts at verbal description—is said to have contracted inward the divine essence, so as to form a primal space or vacuum for matter to come into being. The Kabbalists do not say so directly, but rather intimate that this process—known as the *tsimtsum*—was in itself a kind of primeval exile or self-banishment of the ineffable Splendor.

In the *tsimtsum*, the Essence was concentrated into a single point, from which all the visible and unseen components of the universe originated. In a passage that has entranced many people for centuries, the *Zohar* declared:

> At the outset the decision of the King made a tracing in the supernal effulgence . . . and there issued within the impenetrable recesses . . . a shapeless nucleus enclosed in a ring . . . [not] of any color at all. The most mysterious Power . . . clave, as it were, without cleaving its void . . . until from the force of the strokes there shone forth a supernal and mysterious point."[12]

From this point, there emanated various heavenly attributes, the Kabbalah teaches, giving shape and energy to the universe we know. As to precisely how this occurred, though, Kabbalists have often differed. The *Zoharic* viewpoint was later eclipsed by Isaac Luria's dazzling scheme, first promulgated in the sixteenth century. Two hundred years later, the early Hasidim made other modifications in the doctrine. But the absolutely crucial element to nearly every Kabbalistic approach—in fact, what in some respects distinguishes Jewish mysticism from other spiritual systems—is the concept of the ten *Sefirot* that underlie all aspects of the cosmos.

The term *Sefira*—which has no direct counterpart in other languages—dates at least as far back as the appearance of the *Sefer Yetzirah* ("Book of Formation") between the third and sixth centuries C.E. The word is a derivate of the Hebrew demarking "to count" or "to number." The *Book of Formation* tersely relates, "Ten *Sefiroth* alone: ten and not nine, ten and not eleven. Understand with wisdom and be wise with understanding. Examine with them and search among them. Know, think, and visualize."[13] However, this ancient volume does not explain what the *Sefirot* are, or how they were created. This feature of the Kabbalah came later. We are simply told that they are in some manner, together with the twenty-two Hebrew letters, representations of the vital forces of the universe.

In most Kabbalistic systems, then, the act of *tsimtsum*—out of the incredible radiance of the formless *Ein Sof* ("Infinite")— led in a step-by-step fashion to the distribution of ten primordial energies. Historically, these have been depicted in various diagrams, the most favored being the Tree of Life. Each of the *Sefirot* is associated with a huge array of symbols, whose nature has often changed over the centuries—one reason why this format has been such a challenging one to master. The illustration presented (figure 1) is one of the most common portrayals of these cosmic influences.

The top *Sefira* is known as *Keter* or "Crown," signifying the highest of the forces. So lofty has it been regarded that later generations of Kabbalists sometimes elevated it out of the *Sefirotic* arrangement entirely. *Keter* has traditionally been viewed as the primary generative force. Below, on the right and left respectively, are *Hokhmah* ("Wisdom") and *Binah* ("Understanding"). These are seen to correspond to the qualities of active and receptive intelligence. Directly below *Keter*, positioned in the middle, is a "shadow" vessel of energy known as *Daat* ("Knowledge"). It has often been depicted as an intermediary between the triad above it, and may be understood as the synthesis between those qualities.

The second holy triad consists of *Hesed* ("Mercy") on the right, *Gevurah* ("Judgment") opposite it, and *Tiferet* ("Beauty") centered below them. The polar attributes of both mercy and judgment or limiting strength are deemed necessary to sustain the universe in equilibrium. Beauty is the key sphere of energy—described as the highest presence of the divine we can glimpse during earthly life—that underlies several interactive patterns of the *Sefirot*.

The third triad is composed of *Netzah* ("Victory") on the right, *Hod* ("Glory") on the left, and *Yesod* ("Foundation") in the middle below. While *Yesod* is typically viewed as the generative power of the most material universe and also corresponds to our sexuality, these other two *Sefirot* seem far less well defined in many Kabbalistic discussions. One orientation is that *Netzah* refers to eternal aspects of form and *Hod* to their specific appearance and shape.

The Tree of Life

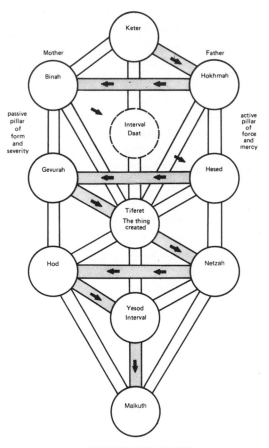

THE LIGHTNING FLASH

Figure 1

Here the impulse of the Will manifesting in Keter passes in an alternating progression from active to passive pillar as it descends through all the Sefirot and Worlds. To quote the Sefer Yezirah: 'The ten Sefirot appear out of Nothing like a Lightning Flash or scintillating flame, and they are without beginning or end. The Name of God is with them as they go forth and when they return.'

Finally, the *Sefira* of *Malkuth* ("Kingdom") completes the structure. This energy-essence often symbolizes the physical realm, as well as humanity. Moreover, it refers to the *She-kinah*, the feminine counterpart of the deity, said to dwell in exile in our universe. Whenever we act with the right intention and devotion, Jewish mystics have long taught, we convene this divine presence around us.

Kabbalists have literally written volumes about this celestial Tree. It is worth noting that its roots are seen to lie in the most transcendent reaches beyond our comprehension. With the appearance of each *Sefira* in the cosmos, some of the divine energy was diluted, until the world around us was created. But link by link, the Kabbalists stress, we are inseparably connected to the most hidden and exalted dimensions of being. In fact, as Chapter 4 will indicate, the Kabbalah has incorporated specific meditative devices to help us "climb back up" the sacred Tree to its Source. "By virtue of the descent and flow of the life-force to the lower planes, by means of many and powerful contractions of various kinds,"[14] do living creatures exist, explained Rabbi Schneur Zalman of Liady.

The Kabbalah further emphasizes that the complex scheme of the Tree is not merely a distant abstraction about the cosmos. Rather, basing their concept on the Biblical passage that we were fashioned in the deity's image, Jewish mystics stress that in the form of *Adam Kadmon* (the primordial human) the powers of the divine *Sefirot* also flow within each of us. Though adepts have differed on the precise correspondence between each *Sefira* and the appropriate part of our body, they have always stressed that this relationship exists—and that it is a crucial one. Thus, the twelfth-century *Bahir* comments, "The Blessed Holy One has seven Holy Forms. . . . All of them have a counterpart in man."[15]

Over the years, several types of diagrams have been drawn to show the connection between our physical aspects and the transcendent. One interesting format is depicted in the accompanying illustration (figure 2). The top of the head corresponded to the crown, the left and right sides of the brain

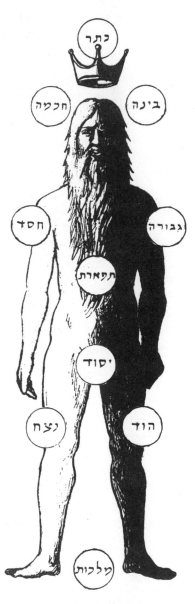

ADAM KADMON

Figure 2

to the next two *Sefirot*, the second triad to the arms and heart, the third triad to the genitals and legs, and the lowest *Sefira* to the feet. At other times, the *Sefirot* are portrayed as concentric circles of bioenergy, with the upper ones closest to the inner core. The lower *Sefirot* are then represented by outer circles.

Jewish visionaries teach that the divine force circulates too through the human *Sefirotic* system. In a striking parallel to various Eastern viewpoints like Tibetan Buddhism, Kabbalistic thinkers have insisted that this flow of energy underlies our mental and physical health. They have taught that through conscious exercises, we can channel this flow to awaken higher potentialities. However, this process is deemed a potentially dangerous one, as our *Sefirot* are regarded as ordinarily in a constant state of dynamic balance. Through inadvertent means—such as misusing the meditative devices to be later discussed—we can upset this harmony and cause ourselves substantial harm.

In a related approach to the Tree of Life, Isaac Luria and his adherents in sixteenth-century Safed taught that the seven lowest *Sefirot* were unable to contain the awesome might of the light of Creation. Like glass beakers too weak to contain strong acid, they therefore shattered. As a result of this *shevirah*—known for centuries as the "breaking of the vessels"—the sacred sparks of splendor became intermixed with *kelippoth*, "shells" of impurity. It is the central task of each person to help restore the holy shards back to their original Source, Luria preached. We can do this through performance of good deeds, as well as meditative prayers; in this process (*tikkun*), each person thus participates in the restoration of the universe to its primal wholeness before any matter existed. Some Jewish mystics, though, have argued over the years that the Lurianic doctrine of the *shevirah* is only a description designed for our limited, earthly perceptions. In the divine reaches of the world, such thinkers emphasize, there has always resounded an unending harmony.

Modern-day proponents of the Kabbalah have often sought to relate twentieth-century knowledge about our inner processes to its longstanding beliefs. For example, some recent books have found analogies between the *Sefirotic* scheme and such diverse contemporary approaches as Jungian psychology and theories of human neuro-anatomy. In one such psychological format, the highest triad corresponds to the ineffable dimensions beyond us, the second triad to our own latent spiritual powers, the third to our ego, and the lowest *Sefira* to our involuntary bundle of instinctual drives.

Moreover, the Jewish esoteric discipline has several other insights to offer us through the Tree of Life. In its conceptual division of our mental abilities into two polar camps, the Kabbalah thereby suggests that each of our attributes must be tempered by its opposite. Direct, intense intellectual activity is inefficient without the capacity to reflect and integrate what we have learned. In fact, the late Swiss psychologist Jean Piaget named these twin characteristics *assimilation* and *accommodation*, considering them essential to our maturation. Similarly, our capacity to dream and imagine the unknown needs to be countered by the use of logic. Neither alone is complete without the other.

The Kabbalah also serves to remind us that like the wider universe we too contain several distinct but interrelated realms of being. One part of us is indeed linked to transcendent dimensions of brilliance, we are told; yet, we also comprise needs and desires that are extremely physical in orientation. At times, one or another of our inner aspects may predominate, but our objective must be to integrate all of them into a harmonious whole. As earthly creatures, we can never completely ignore our instinctual qualities. But nor should we forget that we possess more exalted capabilities. In this vein, some modern Kabbalists have drawn a close parallel between the traditional scheme of the Tree of Life and contemporary biological research, which shows that we have within us a reptilian and mammalian brain, in addition to our abstract reasoning. The crucial concept, though, is that we must recognize and embrace our entire human makeup. In this way, we may better understand the workings of the cosmos as well.

The Four Worlds of Being

Jewish mystics have intriguingly speculated too that four separate but interconnected universes exist. The key to comprehending this initially abstruse notion is found in the Tetragrammaton, the ancient Hebrew name of God. Composed of four letters, it has long signified for Kabbalists the multifaceted process by which the cosmic qualities of Force (*yod*), Pattern (*hay*), Energy (*vav*), and Substance (*hay*), are promulgated. Each of the four realms corresponds in Kabbalistic theory to one of these specific attributes.

The highest dominion of existence is called *Aziluth* or "Emanation." It is said to encompass the pure dimension of the names or "forces" of the divine, specifically mentioned in the *Torah*. Each of the ten names of God is therefore viewed as referring to a different emanation or quality of the transcendent. *Aziluth* corresponds to the Tetragrammaton's first letter, *yod*, which represents the idea of primal force. Since force is defined as the ability to do something, this highest universe is supposed to hold the forces implicit in all the rest. In Kabbalistic theory, it also relates to our deepest inner Source, which we are ordinarily most oblivious to.

Beriah or "Creation" is the second dimension. It is represented by the next letter of the Tetragrammaton, *hay*, said to indicate the attribute of pattern. In the universe of "Creation," the evanescent archetypes of the first are regarded as organized into a coherent order. Corresponding to the human, this realm incorporates our personality and its structure of ideas, concepts, and viewpoints.

Yetzirah or "Formation" is the third universe. The letter *vav* signifies this world, which encompasses the quality of activity or energy. Here, the potentialities built up in the other two are activated. *Yetzirah* also relates to the biological realm of the human body and its many life functions, such as metabolism, digestion, and so forth.

Finally, there is the universe of *Assiyah* or "Action." This is the dimension of matter in all of its myriad expressions, from molecules to the stars. This universe is considered the lowest and most dense of the four; it includes both the corporal pains and sensual delights that we experience in everyday life. Jewish visionaries view it as the dominion of concrete behavior, where actual deeds are of chief importance—a major reason why this tradition has always emphasized engaged activity over quietist contemplation as the way to the sacred. Indeed, there are no monks or monasteries in Kabbalistic history.

Thus, in the Kabbalah's intriguing theory, every form in our universe has previously passed through these three others. For example, a chair must have first existed as a transcendent image, then a specific pattern, and lastly been infused with focused energy before assuming its physical shape in your present room. According to some Kabbalists, in each of the four dimensions the ten *Sefirot* appear, their potencies diminishing as they approach their final manifestation in the world of *Assiyah*. In the second, alternative scheme, the *Sefirot* are depicted as distributed in clusters throughout the four realms. The accompanying diagram (figure 3) should make these viewpoints clear.

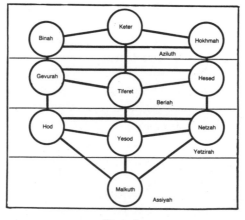

Figure 3

The Distribution of the Ten *Sefirot* Through the Four Worlds.

If you find all this a bit hard to visualize, you are not alone. Some of the greatest Kabbalists explicitly commented on the complexity of this system. Yet, it is crucial to realize that they have often stressed that such descriptions of the cosmos must not be taken wholly literally. They are rather designed to give us merely the framework for understanding the divine order, which far surpasses the capacity of our ordinary senses and intellect to comprehend. Only during those revelatory experiences reported by mystics can we even begin to intuit the full splendor of the divine symmetry, we are told.

While pondering this longstanding model of the universe, it is possible to discover another fascinating parallel to what exponents of modern-day physics have been speaking about for some time now. Albert Einstein, the key founder of this field, often declared that his puzzling and initially unfathomable theories of space and time were simply beyond our day-to-day perceptions of life. He repeatedly explained to lay audiences that his notions ultimately existed as mathematically valid principles, but not as "logical" portrayals of everyday reality. Thus, in his provocative but little-known book, *Cosmic Religion* (Covici, Friede: 1931), this genius wrote:

> I see a pattern. But my imagination cannot picture the maker of that pattern. I see the clock. But I cannot envisage the clockmaker. The human mind is unable to conceive of the four dimensions. How can it conceive of a God, before whom a thousand years and a thousand dimensions are as one?[16]

Regarding Einstein as a kind of twentieth-century Kabbalist *par excellence*, some theoretical physicists by formal training suggest that the Kabbalistic scheme of the *Sefirot* and the four worlds may be perfectly possible. Such scientists have boldly suggested that each of the four universes described in the Kabbalah may indeed exist, vibrating at differing rates of speed, interpenetrating everywhere at the same time. Other scientists have theorized that each universe may fluctuate in its vibrations so that when one is active and "on," the others lie dormant or "off." Yet, because our clocks and all else in our own dimension would "wink" on/off together, we would not observe any measurable gap in its continuity. Though such ideas may seem the sole province of science fiction, a growing number of physicists with impeccable academic credentials are taking them quite seriously indeed. In fact, even a casual perusing of current publications in the field reveals that contemporary researchers are attempting to grapple like mystics with the fundamental attributes of time and matter.

Moreover, some innovative investigators, as Bob Toben highlights in *Space-Time and Beyond* (Dutton: 1975), are converging on the elusive nature of our own consciousness as the key to it all. Our own mental framework may actually hold the secrets to the most distant galaxies. Interestingly, in the foreword to his stimulating book, Toben explicitly mentions the influence of Kabbalistic conceptions on his efforts to integrate today's visionary physics for the interested public.

Thus, we return full circle to the ancient Kabbalah. The boundaries between science and mysticism have become blurred, and in fact may be disappearing altogether. Perhaps they were never as clearly divided as we had been led to believe. In this light, the sentiments of Albert Einstein may be appropriate. In *The World as I See It* (Covici, Friede: 1934), the great mathematician rejected as immature the idea of a "God-the-Father," who bestows favors upon men and women like some celestial Santa Claus handing out sweets. But he spoke of another spiritual perspective, one which— almost word for word—echoes the major, daring teachers of the Kabbalistic way. Not only for its evocative imagery, but also for its exalted mood of yearning, it offers a remarkable glimpse into the man who more than anyone else utterly transformed our understanding of the cosmos. He commented:

> There is a third stage of religious experience which . . . I will call cosmic religious feeling. It is very difficult to explain this feeling to anyone who is entirely without it, especially as there is no anthropomorphic conception of God corresponding to it.
>
> The individual feels the nothingness of human desires and aims and the sublimity and marvellous order which reveal themselves both in Nature and in the world of thought. He looks upon individual existence as a sort of prison and wants to experience the universe as a single significant whole.[17]

In philosophy as well as mathematics, Einstein may well have been years ahead of his time. No doubt, however, the coming years will witness the continued search of modern-day explorers to comprehend the vast celestial harmony. The Kabbalah will be a valuable guide to those on this exciting quest.

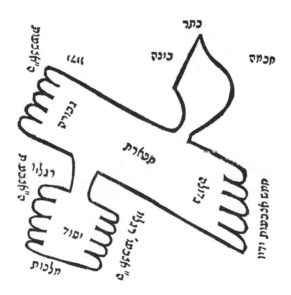

The letter *aleph*. The extremities of the letter represent the hands and feet, each corresponding to the ten sefirot.

CHAPTER THREE

THE SACRED
REALM OF
THE BODY

*"The desire of the female produces a vital spirit and is
embraced in the vehemence of the male, so that soul is joined with
soul and they are made one, each embraced in the other."*

—the *Zohar*

"Strengthen your body before you strengthen your soul."

—Rabbi Nachman of Bratslav

IN THEIR SEARCH for a greater sense of inner wholeness,
many people today are rediscovering the primacy of their
physical bodies. Though our modern industrial society has
long suppressed our capacity to be intimate with or even
much aware of our sensual needs, this situation has fortunately begun to change markedly. There are hopeful signs
now appearing nearly everywhere on the horizon.

For example, the worldwide environmental movement, despite political pressures against it, has succeeded in drama-
tizing the way in which our health is affected by the air and
water around us. Millions of persons in recent years have

adopted an exercise regimen on a daily basis; sports like jogging and bicycling have in fact taken on for some the aura of a frenzy. While large numbers of individuals still consume junk foods, here too an encouraging new awareness has emerged.

One outgrowth of this development currently sweeping the West is a lively interest in Eastern approaches to the mind and body. The appeal of these ancient disciplines has undoubtedly been accelerated by scientific validation for many of their insights. It is becoming readily apparent that their emphasis on the link between our mental and physical health—as well as on simple bodily pleasure and day-to-day vitality—has a great deal of relevance to us today. Through such approaches, people are finding how in countless ways they unconsciously deny themselves the joys that may have been taken for granted in other times.

Thus, private institutes teaching Oriental methods of healing like acupuncture and zone therapy have attracted many adherents. Programs offering instruction in the martial arts, such as karate, *aikido*, and *t'ai chi*, are flourishing across the continent. In nearly every large North American city, established and conservative organizations—including the YMCA-YWCA and publicly funded adult education courses—are likewise providing classes in these various practices. Even local Jewish community centers are regularly sponsoring workshops on *hatha yoga* and related techniques for those wishing to enhance their emotional and bodily well-being.

This fact is rather ironic. To be sure, mainstream Judaism has historically been quite intellectually oriented, with a tremendous respect for scholarship. The achievements of the mind have always been given the highest praise. Other than in Israel, where a pioneering ethos has predominated, the Jewish tradition in the modern era has certainly downplayed the importance of our physical strengths and needs. Yet, one doees not have to seek exotic Eastern ways for obtaining insights on our nature as biological creatures. That is, the Kabbalah has for centuries been profoundly concerned with

the mind-body relationship. Its chief thinkers have focused at
length on the cause of sickness and methods for improving
our overall health.

To those who mistakenly still associate the Kabbalistic path
with idle superstition, it should prove enlightening to discover that nearly seven hundred years ago the *Zohar* detailed
the precise connection between our personal hygiene and
disease. Moreover, this brilliant esoteric work, like others
that have followed it, keenly pointed out the manner in which
our physical processes and emotions are tightly interwoven.

Perhaps even more intriguing is the Kabbalah's venerable
interest in human sexuality—as an integral aspect of our life
on earth and as a potentially awesome power to transform our
inner state of being. It seems no historical accident that many
of the great twentieth-century trailblazers of the mind and its
fiery desires have nearly all been of Jewish heritage. It seems
quite consistent that such thinkers have emerged from a religious background that even in its mainstream valued lovemaking within marriage as a hallowed act. Though Freud, the
first researcher of the modern age to scientifically study sex,
was not an observant Jew, he was no stranger to the Kabbalah.

Similarly, his influential disciple Wilhelm Reich—who first
predicted the "sexual revolution" back in the 1930s—denied
that any specifically "Jewish" sentiments had contributed to
his own bold theories. Nevertheless, his seminal notions on
body language, emotional repression, and the importance of
sexuality in adult daily living all have direct parallels to
traditional Kabbalistic concepts. In Reich's later emphasis on
the transcendent powers of sex with love, he likewise seems
to have unconsciously echoed longstanding esoteric Jewish
beliefs.

The focus of this chapter, therefore, will be on some of the
most interesting and salient features of the Jewish visionary
system as it has looked at the human body. In keeping with
its fundamental principle that "man is fashioned as a micro-
cosm of the world," this age-old tradition has always viewed
our physical makeup as sacred ground.

The Way of Health

We often pride ourselves on the notion that contemporary science has the latest, most up-to-date knowledge on health and disease. After all, ours is the age of the electronic pace-maker, brain scans, kidney transplants, and even the artificial heart, now being tried on an experimental basis. Such inventions of modern medicine are truly impressive testimonies to the achievements of human intelligence. And yet, in the twentieth century, a host of illnesses continue to afflict men and women. Cardiovascular disease, cancer, hypertension, and other serious health problems have attained near epidemic proportions. It seems that while science has succeeded in obliterating many formerly devastating, infectious kinds of sickness, like diphtheria, smallpox, and tuberculosis, it has not proven very effective against these non-infectious illnesses.

In fact, many of the most common, technologically oriented types of treatment, such as radiation and medication, have been found to be often more dangerous than the diseases they are aimed at alleviating. As Ivan Illich reported in his provocative book, *Medical Nemesis* (Pantheon: 1976), the United States government itself has calculated that seven percent of all patients suffer compensable injuries while hospitalized, though few of them press the matter. In another recent study he cited, a million Americans per year were estimated to require hospitalization primarily because of an adverse reaction to drugs.

As a result of this alarming situation—which has steadily worsened in the last few years—innovative health professionals are turning to alternative approaches. A wide spectrum of perspectives currently exists, but basic to nearly all of them is the belief that our mind and body constitute a unity. Our emotional and physical aspects are simply two facets within the same organism; they are inseparable. In the most subtle manner possible, our bodily processes—from respiration to digestion—are affected by our moods. The more chronically tense or unhappy we are, the greater the likelihood we will develop physical symptoms of illness. Conversely, for optimal bodily pleasure and well-being, we need to feel at peace, content within. In a nutshell, this philosophy can be said to comprise the foundation for the rapidly expanding movement in "holistic health," as it has come to be known.

Yet, this orientation to daily life is hardly as recent as some of its more fervent exponents—and critics—would have us believe. It seems clear that virtually every culture in recorded history has possessed at least a rudimentary notion regarding the mind-body relationship. Without the mixed benefits of modern medical specialization, shamans and tribal healers have effectively responded with both psychological and somatic techniques to aid suffering individuals. Thus, for example, in many industrially primitive societies, herbal remedies have traditionally been combined with some form of psychotherapy—such as requiring the patient to "confess" pent-up feelings to family and friends—to alleviate personal distress. Some Eastern cultures, notably China and Tibet, have historically practiced quite sophisticated methods of diagnosis and treatment that are now being closely examined by Western investigators.

The Jewish mystical way represents another age-old body of knowledge which has long dealt with human vitality and affliction. Though frequently dismissed in the modern era as merely an outmoded repository of medieval conjectures, in several respects it has anticipated some of the most contemporary approaches in behavioral medicine. Its chief teachers have indeed been thinking "holistically" for more than a half-millenium.

Perhaps the central Kabbalistic premise concerning our health is that it is a positive state of well-being, not merely the absence of gross disease. Mainstream Western medicine, guided by an emphasis of identifying and labeling stricken tissue, has taken the reverse stance; people are presumed to be "well" if their vital signs are within the normal range and if they voice no specific, localizable complaints of pain. But for the Kabbalists, this viewpoint is extremely shortsighted, for they have asserted for centuries that well-being is an active condition, encompassing such mental qualities as clear thought, a sense of purpose in life, and an openness to higher experience. Of course, they have also deemed health to include a physically vibrant and energetic body. Furthermore, the Jewish esoteric system stresses that health is a condition of dynamic equilibrium among our various inner aspects. Each part of us is fully alive and in balance with the others. As the *Zohar* comments, "These three grades (*nefesh, ruach, neshamah*) are harmoniously combined in those men who have the good fortune to render service to their Maker."[1]

Jewish visionaries have also taught that it is impossible to wholly separate our mental ailments from our bodily ones. Adepts have insisted that no matter how strictly physical a discomfort may feel, it undoubtedly has an important emotional link. Conversely, disorders like severe depression—in which persons may literally stop eating and withdraw from all relations with others may be ameliorated through physical means, we are told. The Hasidic leader Rabbi Schneur Zalman of Liady often remarked that activity is the only way to deal with depression. For the mind and body are intimately interwoven.

This idea, now gaining increasing acceptance even in the health care establishment, was especially emphasized by the early Hasidic leaders of the eighteenth century. Through their many homilies and folk sayings, they revealed an uncanny prescience for the precepts of modern psychosomatic medicine. Figures like Rabbi Nachman of Bratslav—who constantly reiterated the mind-body unity—bore an unstinting opposition to the medical dogmas of the day, particularly their failure to relate our feelings to our physical health. It was not until nearly a century later, in the early 1900s, that scientists would start to recognize emotional influences on bodily symptoms. Indeed, this was one of Freud's first contributions to the budding field of psychopathology.

Among a galaxy of outspoken thinkers, Rabbi Nachman of Bratslav was among the most caustic Hasidic critics of mainstream medicine as it was then practiced. Recoiling from its refusal to acknowledge the inner causes of health and disease, he frequently denounced doctors in the most extreme terms. Once, speaking half in jest, he told a group of followers that the "Angel of Death" who dispatches people to their earthly demise cannot do this entire job by himself. Rather, explained Rabbi Nachman, he appointed helpers in each locality to assist him. "These agents are the physicians."[2]

But the Kabbalists have not simply criticized medical treatment, without offering any constructive guidelines. For hundreds of years, they have emphasized visual diagnosis as a hidden technique for unraveling our degree of well-being. Though many of the great spiritual masters—figures like Isaac Luria, the Baal Shem Tov, and Rabbi Nachman of Bratslav—were described as "psychic" by their admirers, it seems that these leaders possessed a powerful sensitivity to gauging one's physical condition through an analysis of his or her body language. Thus, the thirteenth-century *Book of Splendor* has numerous references to the ways in which we can discern a person's health by looking at bodily indicators.

Some of these, such as the shape of the forehead and the lips, may still seem like superstition to us today. Yet, Oriental medicine stresses precisely these sorts of criteria for judging one's physical status. Other Kabbalistic indicators, including the texture of the hair and facial features, have a readily apparent utility. For instance, abnormal thyroid conditions may be detected through the appearance of the eyes. Flabby, sagging facial and neck muscles may signal the presence of a dangerously under-exercised heart. Commenting on the person who is suffering from mental depression, the *Zohar* observes, ". . . his eyes do not sparkle even when he is joyful."[3] In a more general manner, this work explains that when people's faces are in their ordinary state, "their shapes and lineaments reveal to the wise the inner thoughts and propensities of the mind."[4]

This notion—that our faces loudly speak our hidden emotional state—has been a basic one for Kabbalists. Paralleling the concepts of both traditional Oriental medicine and twentieth-century *iridology* (the study of the iris as a diagnostic indicator), the Kabbalah has emphasized that the form and color of our eyes has definite diagnostic implications. The general appearance of our face—its degree of youthfulness, rigidity, warmth, and so forth—has been seen as a critical guidepost to our underlying mental and physical health. Our face is probably the most individual part of our external makeup and the most resistant to marked change. Typically, with the onset of sexual maturity, it begins to assume a shape that will continue, more or less, for our whole lifetime. This fact often explains how we are able to recognize someone we may not have seen for twenty years or longer—sometimes not even since childhood or adolescence. But to those gifted or trained in "reading" facial expressions, our personality becomes something of an open book, revealing our supposedly hidden feelings. Hinting at this ancient approach to diagnosis, Rabbi Nachman of Bratslav taught his disciples, "One's true face is his mind which illumines it from within."[5]

More broadly for the Kabbalists, our entire array of nonverbal signs are interpreted most closely. In the way in which we speak, walk across a room, or sit at a table, we proclaim our fears and desires. Rabbi Nachman made especial use of the person's handshake and tone of voice as central indicators. Though we can rather easily control what we verbally say to others, it is far more difficult to disguise the meaning of our unspoken language. The Kabbalah has long emphasized this point. In the mid-1920s, Rabbi Abraham Isaac Kook, the chief Rabbi of Palestine, cogently observed:

> One can recognize the anxiety that comes through in marks on the face, in gestures, in the voice, in behavior, in the handwriting, in the manner of communication, in speech, and especially in the style of writing, in the way one develops thoughts and arranges them . . . [The] imprint will be discernible to those who look with clear eyes.[6]

It is intriguing that this traditional feature of the Jewish visionary system has now become fully validated by the modern behavioral sciences. Known as *kinesics*, the study of nonverbal communication has attracted serious interest today in such fields as psychology, sociology, anthropology, and medicine. Common to these disciplines is a growing awareness that what we convey with our bodies contains the utmost significance. In fact, research evidence has steadily shown that people who manifest certain specific illnesses, like heart disease, high blood pressure, and perhaps even cancer, have definite styles of body language. In an earlier book which I coauthored, *The Man Who Dreamed of Tomorrow* (Tarcher: 1980) Professor W. Edward Mann of York University and I summarized much of this exciting inquiry. By way of simply one example, investigators have found that persons who are at high risk for heart attacks typically speak too fast, interrupt others, and frequently lose their temper when forced to wait; they also exhibit a pervasive sense of time-pressure.

Based on this holistic perspective, the Kabbalah has therefore taught that the best way to heal ourselves is through confronting our underlying emotional tensions. We must learn to acknowledge our feelings but not let ourselves be ruled by them. Adepts have emphasized that on an ongoing, daily basis, it is important to observe how we make ourselves stressful in various ways. In this manner, we can next begin to systematically eliminate our undesirable personality traits, like impatience or restlessness. One means to do this is through meditation, to be discussed in the next chapter. But equally important is the cultivation of an unforced detachment from what we are doing, an ability to momentarily stand aside at various times during the day, and simply gain a little perspective on our whirl of thoughts and activities. The Baal Shem Tov advised his followers that the development of this inner quality is the surest path to emotional and physical health. Later, his disciples similarly preached this notion to their own minions. For instance, Rabbi Bunam declared, "We should not go about in haste to do a [deed], but we should first consider and observe the proper way and the proper spirit for its performance."[7]. Likewise, Rabbi Mose Leib of Sassover admonished, "Be deliberate and thou wilt have no regrets."[8]

It is particularly fascinating to see that Jewish mystics

have long identified certain specific emotional states as related
to potential physical disturbances. Predicting by centuries
the discoveries of contemporary health scientists, Kabbalists
have focused on the presence of suppressed frustration and
anger, as well as severe depression, as signs that suggest
oncoming bodily disorders. In general, adepts of this tradition
have highlighted the importance of honest expression of feelings as a deterrent to health impairment. For as one Hasidic
founder commented, "He who is careful not to utter lies will
not be compelled to lie in bed by reason of illness."[9] In
several major professional publications, such as the *Journal of
Psychosomatic Research*, the *Journal of Chronic Disease*, and
Psychosomatic Medicine, the connection between our inner well-
being and our physical vitality is becoming more and more
clear.

Interestingly, the Hasidic leaders of the eighteenth century
especially stressed melancholia or severe depression as a major
precursor to debilitating health difficulties. Rabbi Nachman
of Bratslav declared that, "Melancholy oftentimes presages
illness,"[10] and, "He who is sad brings upon himself many
afflictions."[11] The repeated vehemence with which the early
Hasidic masters related severe depression to the triggering of
disease suggests that this mental disorder may actually have
been far from rare among East European Jews of the time.
Given their extreme poverty and ruthless political oppression, this fact hardly seems surprising. In any case, the Hasidic *rebbes* of this era not only antedated current concern for
the physical effects of depression, but even pinpointed one of
its major diagnostic signs: namely, the inability to shed tears.
Moreover, they carefully distinguished this condition from
normal sadness or grief and accurately related it to pent-up
anger.

Jewish visionaries have consequently deemed it essential
that we express these suppressed feelings, whether in emotional prayer or in conversation with people around us. In
fact, some contemporary observers trace the modern structure of psychotherapy—with its one-to-one encounter between
therapist and patient—directly to the relationship between

the Hasidic *rebbe* and his congregant. Once more, it seems no act of historical chance that Freud and most of his disciples were of Jewish background, some from Hasidic ancestry. In an elucidating article, "The Dynamics of the Yehidut Transaction," in the Fall 1978 issue of the *Journal of Psychology and Judaism*, Rabbi Zalman Schachter drew many parallels between the two approaches to human healing. He stated, "The *rebbe* . . . functions as a conjunctive person; he responds to the *hasid*'s problems by answering, scolding, and even by giving the needed pat on the back . . . the *rebbe* must integrate the various factors of the hasid's makeup: divine, animal, and rational souls, temperament and constitution."[12]

Yet, it is important to realize that by emphasizing the emotional factors in many of our physical ailments, the Kabbalah has never ruled out more exogenous (originating from outside the body) causes of illness. It is truly astonishing that the *Book of Splendor*—as far back as the 1200s—again and again marked the link between our contact with "unclean" items and susceptibility to sickness. Over half a millenium before the scientific discoveries of Robert Koch, Louis Pasteur, and other modern "microbe hunters" convinced a sceptical world that proper hygiene is essential for human well-being, the *Zohar* had precisely identified such influences as decaying flesh, fecal matter, and stagnant water as dangerous sources of disease.

Though it alludes to the "spirits" (what are, after all, invisible bacteria) that linger about these sites, the *Book of Splendor* clearly specifies the hygienic connection. For example, in one passage, we are told, "It is forbidden, after one has been in a privy, to pronounce a blessing or to read even one word of the *Torah* . . . without washing the hands."[13] And, in another section, "Nor is it permissible to put . . . polluted water to any use, or even to let it stay overnight in the house, but it must be emptied in a spot where people do not pass."[14] And, even more tersely, "Whoever does not wash his hands as required . . . endangers his health."[15] Such admonitions date all the way back to the Talmud, which is replete with advice on daily hygiene.

Thus, the Kabbalah has for centuries incorporated bodily oriented methods of healing in combination with the psychological. It has particularly recommended the use of medicinal herbs and works such as the *Zohar* contain many references to the specific curative properties of various plants. It should be remembered too that before his emergence as a leader of the rapidly expanding Hasidic movement, the Baal Shem Tov was known throughout many villages of Eastern Europe as a "wonder-worker," who excelled in the use of herbal remedies to heal the sick and dying. Even after his accession to fame and widespread influence, he is said to have personally carried out healing rituals for those brought before him. The Kabbalistic way has always viewed our health as a totality and sought to integrate all aspects of our being.

Exalting the Sensual

Consistent with its emphasis on the importance of physical well-being as a prerequisite for inner development, the Kabbalah has repeatedly stressed respect for our sensual needs. Though of course ascetics have been involved with this ancient tradition from time to time, Kabbalistic leaders have almost unanimously condemned the ascetic way of life. They have repeatedly rejected the philosophy that our bodies are inherently evil or perverted. Even those Kabbalists like Rabbi Schneur Zalman of Liady—the founder of the Lubavitcher Hasidic sect—who have favored a rather intellectual path to the divine have acknowledged the sacred nature of our physical makeup. In fact, it is somewhat remarkable that a spiritual system that, after all, has as its goal the transcendence of the mundane world has long been on such good terms with the realm of the body.

As mentioned earlier, the Jewish visionary way postulates that three broad and interwoven aspects comprise our being— the *nefesh*, *ruach*, and *neshamah*. The *nefesh* is associated with our lowest, most instinctive attributes, said to encompass drives such as for food and water. Obviously critical to our sheer survival, we could not even exist without them. Hence, the Kabbalah has never condemned them. For example, Rabbi Moses Chaim Luzzatto commented, "Because of its physical nature, man's very constitution forces him to engage in worldly pursuits. It is impossible for him to live without eating, drinking, and other essential bodily functions."[16]

However, for the Kabbalists, the mere fact that we possess a *nefesh* or bundle of instincts does not imply that we should automatically surrender to our most primitive impulses. The chief leaders of this tradition have certainly never embraced a libertine or hedonistic viewpoint of "do whatever feels good." Instead, they have consistently preached that our objective should be to refine and exalt our bodily feelings. By applying our higher willpower or *kavvanah*, we can actually transform the senses into tools of enlightenment. To do this, though, we must first face and accept our innate urges, not pretend we function without them.

The Kabbalah has therefore stressed that to simply deny or repress our physical side is at best a mere subterfuge, a temporary measure. It will not work. In fact, the great sages have indicated, this practice may even result in greater emotional turmoil. The Jewish esoteric system has thus anticipated by centuries the fundamental principles of modern psychotherapy, that likewise emphasize the importance of honest acknowledgement of our impulses we wish to change. Nearly two hundred years ago, Rabbi Nachman of Bratslav succinctly observed, "You should not seek unnecessarily harsh disciplines, for these can lead to depression."[17] Interestingly, this brilliant Hasidic thinker was not speaking here only in abstractions. As a young man, he was much given to self-mortification but later repudiated it after discovering it was worse than useless for his own inner development.

For this sort of reason, Jewish mysticism has decisively repudiated the kind of extreme self-denial favored by some other spiritual traditions around the globe. Kabbalists have felt that the harm that may result from such efforts, however well-intentioned, can far outweigh the potential benefit that may be gained. One notable exception to this viewpoint, though, was the twelfth-century German Hasidic movement, which did seem to preach self-mortification as a path toward higher consciousness. Nevertheless, although their writings recommended methods like smearing oneself with honey in the summer and then exposing oneself to bees, there is little evidence that these techniques were really carried out very extensively. Furthermore, even this circle of Kabbalists drew the line of asceticism at sexuality, for they maintained normal marital relations. Later in this chapter, the vital role of the erotic in the Kabbalah's system will be highlighted in some detail.

Moreover, it is crucial to note that Jewish visionaries have never been impressed with tales of those who severely burden themselves physically to escape the confines of day-to-day living. Such figures have rarely been admired but rather severely criticized for their dissatisfaction with the tangible delights of the world around us. In fact, some of the major Kabbalists have not hesitated to brand such behavior as totally misguided and incorrect. For instance, Rabbi Luzzatto flatly condemned those persons who foolishly "abstain not only from that which is not essential to them, but also from that which is, punishing their bodies with strange forms of affliction."[18a]

Indeed, this influential Italian mystic explicitly rejected the notion that to deprive ourselves of all sensual enjoyments is in the least bit helpful to achieving a harmonious, happy life. Ironically, today we are surrounded by various authoritarian religious cults that, in the name of the sacred or divine, seek to destroy every vestige of normal pleasure for their young followers. Referring to the "pseudo-saints" of his own era in the 1730s, Rabbi Luzzatto observed that they erroneously confuse the way of the spiritual life with nonsensical methods of behavior—such as lengthy confessions and esoteric self-mortification. "Saintliness," he commented, "is not founded upon them at all."[18b]

Several decades later, the early Hasidic masters emphasized this same approach to our bodies. In fact, the Baal Shem Tov fervently believed that a key means to transcend our daily cares is to wholeheartedly savor our physical pleasures. He insisted that our sensual needs must not be denigrated, but prized and hallowed. The Besht declared that asceticism should be practiced only when we are beginning the quest for personal growth, such as trying to break bothersome habits. Later, when we have learned to control these annoying behaviors, like overeating, we should conduct ourselves "in a normal way and be in communion with [our] comrades."[19]

In one classic tale that has come down to us, the Baal Shem Tov received the renowned Rabbi Dov Baer of Mezritch, the "Great Maggid," who wished to join the growing Hasidic movement. The Besht was honored to be greeted by the famous scholar. Nonetheless, after silently inspecting the gaunt intellectual for a moment, he advised his future colleague to stop pursuing such a self-denying way of life and begin to enjoy physical pleasures more fully. Later, when his mentor had passed away, the Maggid told his own many followers, "When one makes a tiny hole in the body, one makes a big hole in the soul."[20]

The Hasidic leaders of this period not only denounced activities like idle fasting as self-destructive; they actually extolled the virtues of food and beverage. These substances are meant to be savored as divine gifts of everyday existence, they taught. With the proper sense of inner devotion, we can enjoy them as a sacred experience. After all, did not the Baal Shem Tov insist that we must not view as wasted the time we spend for eating?

Some *rebbes* apparently practiced this philosophy with such ardor—reveling with their disciples at festive Sabbath and holiday banquets—that their colleagues accused them of gross overindulgence. Indeed, the erstwhile Hasidic opponents, the *Mitnaggedim*—uneasily viewing the flowing plates and glasses—often leveled precisely this criticism against them, arguing that truly spiritual persons could not possibly relish their meals so intensely. Doubtless, a few Hasidic leaders did seem to get carried away with the viewpoint that, "If we are deserving, we will learn to find [the divine] in all our enjoyments, even in eating."[21]

Yet, they certainly did not advocate gluttony for their followers and were quite aware of its physical dangers—as well as its roots in the unquiet mind. For instance, Rabbi Nachman of Bratslav explicitly observed that overeating is the cause of many illnesses. Anticipating modern behavioral medicine's viewpoint, he astutely linked our over-dependence on food to specific emotional conflicts, especially the suppression of anger. For he and his colleagues of this period, it was not at all the sheer quantity of food and drink that shows our respect for our bodies, but the attitude with which we sit at the dinner table.

Here again, the key idea is that we must make use of our higher intentionality or *kavvanah* to exalt what is ordinarily a very mundane, even trivial activity. We are urged to eat slowly, tasting each morsel. Nor should we gulp what we drink. The meal itself should be surrounded in a calm and reverent atmosphere, and even prepared with loving attention. In this manner, by riveting our awareness fully on each facet of our senses, we can experience greater inner peace and physical health.

The Mysteries of Sex

One of the most fascinating and no doubt controversial aspects of the Kabbalah is its strong sexual undercurrent. It flows openly through nearly all of the major works and especially surges through the *Zohar*, the most important body of Jewish esoteric thought. This heady stream has imbued Judaism's visionary tradition with much of its evocative power. For it regards sexuality as a fundamental force in human life, the cosmos, and even the deity.

Such thematic material has excited the imagination of Jews and non-Jews alike for centuries. Yet, this exotic allure has also contributed directly to the orthodoxy's historic unease with the Kabbalistic way. Even after rabbinical leaders throughout the world ambivalently embraced it in the sixteenth century, they considered its outlook to be too inflammatory for ordinary, unlearned Jews and therefore taboo to all but a chosen few. And, it must be acknowledged, this wariness on the part of the rabbinate has not been altogether mistaken. On several occasions, the passions that the Kabbalah has helped arouse led to disastrous messianic movements tinged with the brush of eroticism.

For the Kabbalists, sexuality has always been viewed as a basic quality in the universe, no trivial matter at all. As briefly mentioned in Chapter 2, adepts have argued for the existence of two primary influences that are seen together to underlie every aspect of creation. These twin forces, opposite but complementary, appear in the tiniest blade of grass to the furthest galaxies of space. The better able we are to penetrate the nature of this mysterious union—in all its diverse manifestations—the more we will grasp about the highest realms that surround us and consequently our innermost makeup as well.

The most exalted reflection of the erotic is revealed to us in the essence of the divine, Jewish visionaries have asserted. Since the inception of this tradition, its teachers have stressed that the stern, patriarchal "God-the-Father" (*Yahweh*) of the Bible has its own female counterpart, just as we are divided into two complementary sexes. "The King without the Matrona is no king," the *Book of Splendor* tersely declares, "nor He great nor highly praised."[22] Hence, only when the two are united—depicted in explicit sexual terms—does harmony truly govern the universe.

This startling Jewish idea, that a heavenly Mother—the *Shekinah*—rules beside the male-stereotyped deity has long been central to the Kabbalah. Often regarded with the utmost misgiving by non-Kabbalist rabbinical authorities, they constantly sought to dilute its powerful hold on large numbers of Jews. One way to accomplish this task was to render the doctrine as meek and inoffensive as possible, or else to even brand it as sacrilegious. After no mild struggle, by the rise of the Industrial Age, almost all traces of this immensely appealing notion were obliterated from prayers and rituals. Few persons are thus at all aware of this doctrine any longer.

For this reason, some Kabbalists today insist that a major cause of the decline of impassioned Jewish religious belief and worship is precisely due to this elimination of feminine images and symbols from day-to-day practices—leaving a more barren, masculine repository of values. Strikingly, in recent years a variety of books in a related vein have argued that the modern, mainstream Judeo-Christian systems have indeed cut themselves off from an androgynous or sexually balanced approach to the transcendent. Works such as Merlin Stone's *When God Was A Woman* (Dial: 1976) and Mary Daly's *Beyond God the Father* (Beacon: 1973) make this point in a quite compelling manner. Most currently, Dr. Elaine Pagels, in her highly popular *The Gnostic Gospels* (Random House: 1979), has shown that ancient Christianity—heavily influenced by Jewish mystics of the time—seems to have espoused a more female-embracing and nurturant theology than that under official Roman sponsorship. In the light of such analyses, it may prove interesting to trace the evolution and nature of the Kabbalah's alternative conception of the divine.

The term *Shekinah* (from the Hebrew root-word "the act of dwelling"—female gender) does not appear in the Bible itself. Yet, the Scriptures seem to contain the implicit notion of the deity's "dwelling" amidst humanity in the holy sanctuary of the Jews. In the late Biblical period, spiritual teachers made increasing reference to various personified entities, said to be instrumental in carrying out the Holy One's purpose on earth. For instance, the Book of Job, believed written about one thousand to eight hundred B.C.E., depicts Wisdom as a feminine-gender personage whose way and place is understood only by God himself. Several centuries later, the Book of Proverbs more explicitly describes Wisdom as a female entity who has been the deity's "partner" and "delight" ever since the origin of the cosmos.

With the terrible destruction of the Second Temple of Jerusalem and the concomitant dissolution of Judaism as a state religion, a new orientation to the nature of the divinity made its beginnings among pious Jews. The *Shekinah*'s first appearance, it seems—at least in written records that have survived to the present—is in the Aramaic translation-paraphrase of the Bible, the so-called *Targum Onkelos*. Composed between the first and fourth centuries C.E., it overlapped to some extent with the intriguing *Merkabah* or "Chariot" school of hidden knowledge. In this age-old document, whenever the original Hebrew Biblical text speaks of a manifestation of the Holy One through a particular attribute as perceived by people, the *Targum Onkelos* substitutes the term *Shekinah*. But the purpose was mainly to avoid attributing a too human-like quality to the divine; the fact that the *Shekinah* had the feminine (*"ah"*) gender was apparently without larger significance at the time.

In the Talmudic era, though, an alternative notion to a wholly male personified deity began to emerge more clearly. Interestingly, the rabbis who compiled the Talmud did not seem to agree consistently on this ostensibly crucial concept to Judaism. That is, some thinkers flatly continued to view the *Shekinah* in the old way, as simply another name for God. For example, "Rabbi Yose said: 'Never did the *Shekinah* descend to earth, nor Moses nor Elijah ascend to heaven. . . . It is correct that the *Shekinah* never descended to earth? It is not written, 'And Yahweh came down upon Mount Sinai?' "[23] At the same time, however, some Talmudists—perhaps secret mystics of the "Chariot" way—endowed the *Shekinah* with a more transcendent reality as well as a physical one.

It is intriguing to speculate whether advocates for this more eroticized version of Judaism gained their beliefs through their own esoteric practices. It is known that among such circles at the time, menstruating women were regarded as embodying sacred and volatile powers. Though little is recorded about the lives of these often anonymous figures, they distinguished—as did later Kabbalists—between the most immaterial reaches of the divine and its more tangible, personally relevant appearance as the wondrous *Shekinah*.

During this period, too, Jewish mystics linked the female counterpart of the deity to the creation of the universe through the divine "contractions." For example, attempting to resolve the dilemma as to how a Power beyond all space and time could "dwell" within the wooden Tabernacle of the Israelites, a Rabbi Yohanan bar Nappaha offered the following explanation. When Moses heard God say, "Let them make Me a Sanctuary," the Hebrew prophet became alarmed by what he imagined to be an impossible task. For how could the Creator be housed in a mere tent? But, the Talmudic visionary relates, God reassured Moses—in a rather sexualized image, it seems—that a small Tabernacle would indeed be sufficient. "I shall descend and contract my Shekinah between [the planks of the Tabernacle] down below."[24]

Yet another mystic of that period explicitly observed that the *Shekinah* draws near this realm whenever sexual intercourse occurs. This evocative notion was to become a key feature of the Kabbalah.

Indeed, with the emergence of its first key texts, such as the *Sefer Bahir* in twelfth-century France, the Kabbalistic tradition has ascribed great significance to human sexuality as a mirror of the divine structure, and vice versa. Thus, the *Book of Brilliance* is replete with allusions to the splendor of the feminine counterpart of the Holy One. In one illustrative passage, its anonymous author comments:

> What is "God's glory?". . . . A king had a matron in his chamber, and all his troops delighted in her. She had sons, and each day they came to see the king and to bless him. They asked him, "Where is our mother?" He replied, "You cannot see her now. They said, "Let us be blessed wherever she is."[25]

This same often enigmatic work contains several references to male and female genital organs. Rather than condemning our sexual parts as unclean or unspiritual, the *Bahir* affirms that they indicate to the wise the higher potencies of the universe. For instance, the penis and vagina are explicitly mentioned as earthly counterparts to loftier forces around us. "The seed of the date has a split like a woman," the *Book of Brilliance* informs us. "Paralleling it is the power of the moon."[26] And, "The spinal cord originates in man's brain and extends to the [sexual] organ, where the seed is. It is therefore written (Isaiah 43:5), 'From the east I will bring you seed.' "[27]

However, it is the multifaceted *Book of Splendor* that has truly infused the Kabbalah with its vivid eroticism. Permeating this volume are repeated portrayals of how the celestial "King" and "Queen" unite in sexual ecstasy to sustain the cosmos each day. Often taking as its starting point a passage from the beautiful Song of Songs of the Bible, this dazzling work emphasizes in the most detailed language imaginable that whenever marital partners engage in lovemaking with intense concentration, they help to harmonize all the realms of the universe. That is, just as the full sexual embrace—if performed with the proper attitude and desire—is seen to bring the human couple together on many levels of their being, so too does this act cause peace and love to reign more thoroughly everywhere. "As above, so below."

While the "bible" of Jewish visionary thought is clearly referring to sex only within the context of marriage, it has the highest praise for the transcendent powers of this fundamental life experience. Kabbalists have therefore regarded lovemaking as one of the most powerful spiritual practices we can engage in, possessing an almost incredible capacity to shatter our daily ego and mundane concerns. "The *Shekinah* is always present when marital intercourse is performed as a religious duty," the *Zohar* warns, "and whoever obstructs such a performance causes the *Shekinah* to depart from the world."[28]

More specifically, Jewish mysticism even stipulates that married persons carry out lovemaking at least once a week. In keeping with their notion that the Sabbath is a particular time for joy and inner sustenance, adepts have preached that this day is especially appropriate for conjugal union. Thus, the *Zohar* stresses that other than when the woman is in that phase of her monthly cycle when she is not to be "touched," husband and wife are to enact sexual intercourse every Friday night. Each one is to focus as totally as possible on the experience, so that it actually becomes a sacred form of meditation. Rather than regarding lovemaking as something unclean or unsavory, the *Book of Splendor* assures us, even the greatest sages of old carried out this special practice with their loved ones. A remarkably lucid passage explains:

> And when is a man called "one"? When he is male with female and is sanctified with a high holiness and is bent upon sanctification; then alone is he called one without blemish. Therefore a man should rejoice with his wife at that hour to bind her in affection to him, and they should both have the same intent. When they are thus united, they form one soul and one body.[29]

Another, perhaps even more fascinating element of the Kabbalah, is that it has always recognized sexual desires in women and not just in men. In this respect, this ancient offshoot of Judaism has anticipated by centuries virtually every branch of Western science and philosophy. Even Freud— whose first publications at the turn of the century led him to be viciously attacked as a "pornographer" by his medical colleagues—had little to say about this subject. This fact is a bit surprising, since the great psychoanalyst was fairly familiar with Kabbalistic concepts. At any rate, despite the bold writings of a handful of iconoclasts like Wilhelm Reich and D. H. Lawrence, it was not until well into the mid-twentieth century that the medical profession would concede that women too have natural sexual feelings as intense as men's. It has taken surveys like the immensely popular *Hite Report* (Dell: 1976) to make this point clear. And yet, since at least as far back as the thirteenth century, the Kabbalah has over and over emphasized the concept of womanly sexuality.

Thus, the *Book of Splendor* flatly states that pregnancy is usually the result of an "equal and reciprocal desire" between marital partners. Similarly, the *Zohar* even compares the creation of the universe to what seems, from all appearances, to be a precise description of mutual sexual orgasm between man and woman:

> When the upper world was filled and became pregnant, it brought forth two children together, a male and a female, these being heaven and earth after the supernal pattern. The earth is fed from the waters of the heaven which are poured into it.

These upper waters, however, are male, whereas the lower are
female. . . . [they] call to the upper, like a female that re-
ceives the male, and pour out water to meet the water of the
male to produce seed.[30]

Even to the rather jaded sensibilities of our age, it is hard
to imagine an intimacy with sexuality much more explicit
than this. Of course, there is the Eastern approach, namely
tantric yoga, that seems to likewise elevate lovemaking to a
divine act with cosmic significance. In a fascinating parallel
to Kabbalistic notions, this age-old variant of yoga postulates
too that the universe is ultimately a vast dance between two
opposite but complementary forces. Known as *yin* and *yang*
(receptive and thrusting respectively), they are said to be in
constant interflow. Tantric masters teach that during the sex
act we may experience this eternal balance directly—and
hence go beyond our normal state of ceaseless distraction and
confusion. Therefore, they emphasize that the realm of the
body and the erotic is a key inner gateway, leading us into
higher worlds of awareness.

But, like their Jewish counterparts, tantric adepts have
repeatedly highlighted the importance of our attitude and
one-pointed attention in this sacred dialogue between man
and woman. *How* we approach lovemaking is thus of the
utmost significance—and here, these two outwardly very different spiritual systems are in exact agreement. For the
Kabbalists, the chief mood is one of reverence bound with joy.
"The esoteric doctrine is that men of true faith should concentrate their whole thought and purpose"[31] on the divine in
this act. Likewise, for tantric practitioners, we are to engage
in sex with full attention. When it becomes a mechanical
routine, it can no longer take us on the path of oneness.

Paradoxically, then, the Kabbalah stresses that for both
men and women, we can transcend the physical world through
the exalted path of our own bodies. We must never take its
functions for granted, for as the *Zohar* gently reminds us, we
were formed "after the supernal pattern, each limb corresponding to something in the scheme of Wisdom."[32] It is necessary to deliberately cultivate an awareness of our sensual

needs, for our society gives us little preparation to do so. "In every action, a man must regard his body as the Holy of Holies," declared an early Hasidic master, "a part of the supreme power on earth."[33]

Passover *Haggadah* illustrating the upper Sefirot of the Tree of Life (Netherlands, 17th century).

CHAPTER FOUR

TECHNIQUES OF INNER PEACE

"The days pass and are gone, and one finds that he never once had time to really think. . . . One who does not meditate cannot have wisdom."

"In truth, the one thing man is afraid of is within himself, and the one thing he craves is within himself"

—Rabbi Nachman of Bratslav

IT HAS BECOME ALMOST A TRUISM to say that we live in a tense and hurried society. After all, this has been popularly called the "Age of Anxiety," the seemingly inevitable accompaniment to our urban, technological civilization. Millions of people in the West suffer daily from afflictions like hypertension and cardiovascular disease, illnesses that appear to relate very much to our characteristic way of life. To try to cope with our modern-day strains, many persons turn to medication, either prescribed or illicit. Others seek refuge in alcohol or the monotony of evening after evening in front of the television set. None of these means, of course, deals directly with the underlying cause of our inner discontents.

Beginning in the 1960s, though, the exciting influx of Eastern spiritual teachings brought to public awareness for the first time an alternative approach to our emotional well-being. This method is meditation, the conscious effort to transform our mind and body through specific techniques. Not long ago, for the most part, this ancient practice was mainly associated with images of skinny Hindu ascetics wearing loinclothes and turbans. The term itself usually connoted the arcane religious dogmas of a vanished time; meditation seemed to hold little utility for our own sophisticated era.

Moreover, the claims made by adherents loomed as extravagent, almost ludicrous. Even the most patient individuals, science assured us, could not possibly learn to control their heartbeat or respiration simply by staring at their navel or a colorful symbol. It appeared clearly nonsensical that we might be able to regulate our autonomic nervous system or totally direct our fleeting thoughts. Outside of a few zealous devotees, there was meagre interest in the West in this long favored orientation to the human personality.

Yet, in just a few years, the entire situation has radically changed. All over the globe, people in every walk of life now regularly perform one or another of the meditative systems, such as Transcendental Meditation, sponsored by mass organizations with international headquarters and large staffs. Books elucidating this stimulating subject have been repeated best-sellers. In biofeedback laboratories in this country and elsewhere, researchers have clearly demonstrated that each of us is indeed capable of subtly influencing the most minute aspects of our mental and physical being. Thus, even the health care establishment itself has begun to promote meditation—frequently under the guise of "relaxation training," "guided imagery," or similar euphemisms—as a powerful tool of self-healing. Innovative professionals are now actively using these techniques to more effectively treat a host of contemporary ailments, from chronic anxiety to heart disease and cancer.

Nevertheless, to many the topic of meditation has remained virtually synonymous with the exotic countryside and mores of India. No doubt, this erroneous perception derives from the very real impact that Hindu philosophers and yogins have exerted on the current Western world. The ease with which some of these figures have absorbed the latest methods of mass marketing has certainly been another factor. However, nearly every culture in recorded history seems to have been familiar with formal methods for enhancing our normal flow of consciousness.

In the Far East, Chinese Taoists carried out exercises incorporating altered forms of breathing to modify their mental states in special ways. In the vast Siberian wastes, shamans relied on the psychedelic properties of sacred plants as well as extremes of bodily self-punishment to propel themselves into heightened realms of awareness. On our own continent, Native American tribal leaders and medicine men have made use of fasting and arduous treks alone in the wilderness to provoke dramatic changes in their experience of the cosmos.

Through systematic inquiry into such disciplines, farsighted explorers of the human potential have gained a variety of valuable insights. Psychologists and others have started to discover astonishingly cogent views about how our mind ordinarily functions and, perhaps more significantly, provocative notions as to how we can greatly improve our mental capacity by diligent training. Nearly universal to these approaches is an emphasis on meditation, structured and unstructured, to accomplish this goal. It is becoming very clear that these age-old systems of knowledge, long dismissed as superstitious relics from another age, possess a relevance undimmed by the mere passage of time.

One of the most venerable and comprehensive of these traditions of inner development is the Kabbalah. For hundreds of years, the Jewish visionary way has been avidly interested in meditation and what it can offer us in our daily lives. To be sure, Judaism's chief concern historically has been the larger community and the individual's ethical relation to it. Yet, its Kabbalistic side has for centuries focused intensively on the nature of our habitual thought-stream and its elevation through systematic personal endeavors. To those who view the study of higher consciousness as lying solely within the province of Hindu gurus or Tibetan lamas, it may come as quite a revelation to learn of the Kabbalah's major involvement with this fascinating topic. Furthermore, Kabbalistic thinkers have provided a model of our growth within, which not only parallels strikingly that of several other spiritual disciplines, but even anticipates some of the most up-to-date investigations occurring in the social and behavioral sciences today.

To Still the Raging Mind

We are often convinced that our own historical period is the only one to have burdened men and women with worries and tensions. Those in other times, we commonly tend to believe, led serene lives, glowing with clarity and purpose. We feel certain that the whirl of distractions that appears to surround us continually is a recent phenomenon. In fact, since the Romantic Era of the nineteenth century, a dominant theme in both literature and philosophy has been that the industrial world has cast humanity into a state of exile from the innocence of nature. Nearly all of us, therefore, at one time or another, have longed for the carefree and idyllic existence said to have been our lot before the advent of the machine. With the undeniably frenzied tempo of so much of contemporary life, it is tempting to envy our forebears for their supposed inner tranquility and contentment.

From its inception, however, the Kabbalah has insisted that our normal mental state is by its very essence filled with conflicting thoughts and desires. For over half a millenium, its leading thinkers have stressed that the average person is ceaselessly at odds inside himself or herself. "Within [each human] are all the warring nations," Rabbi Nachman of Bratslav, an extremely insightful observer of the mind, poetically stated. "His personality is that of the victorious nation. Each time, a different nation is victorious [and] he must change completely. . . . This can drive him insane."[1] Similarly, in the early eighteenth century, Rabbi Moses Chaim Luzzatto succinctly commented, "The Highest Wisdom decreed that man should consist of two opposites ... in a constant state of battle."[2]

The Kabbalists have always regarded this inner unease as basic to the human condition. Indeed, it is deemed an essential part of our earthly purpose as both individuals and members of a species. That is, as already mentioned in Chapter 3, the Jewish esoteric system argues that we each have been created with several separate but interrelated levels of consciousness or "souls." Our lowest desires, originating in the *nefesh* and *ruach*, urge us to fulfill our instinctual needs and little else. These innate animalistic drives are by necessity very powerful, since they ensure our physical maturation and survival. But, the Kabbalah adds, we are also born with a *neshamah*—a transcendent Self that yearns to rise above our petty, material wants. Moreover, according to some Kabbalists, we also comprise even more exalted cognitive aspects. These are said to lie almost wholly dormant during our day-to-day existence, so tenuous is their connection to the body. Yet, we cannot help but sense the presence within us of vast, unused potentialities. Thus, throughout our lifetime, we experience an ever-present struggle among the different parts of our personality.

In the eyes of the Kabbalists, though, this state of affairs is hardly insoluble. By exerting our conscious willpower, we can learn to overcome the emotional bonds that keep us fettered to trivialities. Though few of us can realistically aspire to complete power over our negative feelings like anger and depression, we have far more ability than we often think. "Every man can have absolute control over his thoughts and direct them as he wishes,"[3] Rabbi Nachman of Bratslav emphatically declared. His Hasidic contemporary, Rabbi Schneur Zalman of Liady, likewise observed in the *Tanya* that any of us can become at least a *benoni*, an intermediary in mental status between the lowly "normal" and the true *zaddik*—one who experiences each moment as filled with splendor. Describing the *benoni*, the Lubavitcher founder explained, "That is to say, the three 'garments' of the animal soul, namely, thought, speech, and act, originating in the *kelipah* [realm of impurity] do not prevail within him over the divine soul."[4]

But the attainment of even this "intermediary" goal can still seem very elusive, the Kabbalists have long been aware. Intimately familiar with the workings of the human mind, they have acutely understood the chasm that divides our daily mental condition from more lofty perceptions. Thus, in language strikingly reminiscent of twentieth-century thought, an anonymous disciple of Abraham Abulafia metaphorically lamented, "It is not seemly that a rational being held captive in prison should not search out every means, a hole or a small fissure, of escape."[5] As seen earlier in this book, Einstein himself expressed this same longing.

In the Jewish visionary tradition, though, there *is* a way out of the isolated cell of our anxious mind. That path lies directly through meditation. The Hebrew term used to describe it for centuries has been *devekuth*, referring to the state of cleaving to the divine. Its meaning goes far beyond that of simple relaxation or freedom from tension, though certainly it encompasses those qualities too. Rather, *devekuth* implies an inner realm in which everyday worries recede from all importance, so ecstatic and complete is this form of higher consciousness. The crucial notion is that through calming the whirl of thoughts that is our ordinary mind, we open a door that leads to an exalted awareness of the wonder of the entire cosmos. "If one sanctifies himself. . . ," observed Rabbi Luzzatto, "even his physical actions come to partake of Holiness."[6] Everything around us is therein transformed.

The major thinkers of the Jewish meditative system have consequently emphasized that specific mental techniques can enable us to transcend the conflicts we feel inside us. In fact, one of the key distinguishing features of the Kabbalah is this stress upon our own efforts to uplift our mundane awareness— an approach that has generally differed from mainstream Judaism's greater focus on communal prayer and activity. From the *Merkabah* or "Chariot" practitioners of ancient Palestine to the Hasidim of eighteenth-century Eastern Europe, initiates on this path have accorded the highest respect to private meditation as a direct gateway to the sacred.

The Kabbalists have typically utilized a wide variety of methods to accomplish this objective. The precise means have varied considerably according to time and locale—and even the personality of the teacher. Some spiritual masters like Rabbi Nachman of Bratslav have borrowed freely from several Jewish meditative systems, to best serve the needs of their congregants. Thus, his colleague and chief scribe, Rabbi Nathan of Nemirov, informs us that his mentor would look at the "root" of each person's soul and prescribe the specific practice necessary to correct his or her flaws. We are further told that there were practices that Rabbi Nachman prescribed for a man's whole lifetime, whereas in other instances, the *rebbe* "prescribed a certain practice for a given period of time, and then substituted another routine."[7]

This flexibility with respect to technique has reflected the Kabbalistic dictum that the particular method of self-develop ment is much less significant than our actual attitude and commitment to growth within. Although Jewish visionaries have felt tremendous reverence for the meditative tools passed down from one generation to the next, they have never elevated these devices above our personal makeup. Indeed, works like the *Zohar* are quite clear on this point. If we are emotionally unequipped to handle the rigors of rather powerful mental disciplines, then we will reap little benefit at all. In fact, we may even come to substantial harm, however sincere our motivation. Referring to advanced methods of altering our consciousness, Rabbi Luzzatto commented, "It is obvious. . . . that it is not appropriate for a commoner to make use of the King's scepter. Regarding this, our sages teach us, 'He who makes use of the Crown will pass away.' "[8] What ultimately counts is our willingness to be diligent and patient, without expecting any immediate, dramatic rewards.

In the Kabbalistic tradition, therefore, a key issue is the necessity for adequate training before beginning meditation. We must be ready to undertake what can be quite taxing efforts; otherwise, subsequent attempts will be doomed to failure. Moreover, our goals must be clear in advance. Many people today have briefly flirted with Eastern exercises of the mind and body, anticipating quick results. But for the Kabbalists, the first step—and even planning for the first step—are as crucial as all later developments of inward exploration.

Preparing for the Inner Journey

Before initiating any of the Kabbalah's meditative techniques, it is necessary that we are as physically healthy as possible. The *Book of Splendor*, the "bible" of Jewish mysticism, flatly states that the pursuit of loftier awareness "must be approached with proper preparation, not only of the mind but also of the body."[9] Even those with some familiarity with this tradition often forget that most of its greatest adepts were in superb physical condition. Rabbi Akiva was a woodcutter for much of his adult life before venturing forth into the secrets of higher consciousness. The Baal Shem Tov was likewise an outdoor laborer for many years prior to his most popular spiritual influence. He is supposed to have been quite virile, with a healthy respect for our bodily nature.

In many ways, though, the importance of physical well-being as a prerequisite for mental expansion rarely had to be made an explicit precept for most Kabbalists. Until very recently, few persons anywhere could even dream of the kind of physically effortless, sedentary way of life that we take for granted today. One searches in vain among the Jewish eso-teric texts for any sort of disdain for bodily courage or stami-na. Indeed, the tales that surround the lives of the early Hasidic leaders are replete with references to their remark-able physical vitality.

For those currently interested in meditation, it is thus worth stressing this Kabbalistic principle that corporal health is essential before we begin experimenting with altered states of awareness. Confirming the warnings of the Kabbalists, there have been reports that some Westerners have suffered unhappy or even adverse reactions while attempting arduous yogic positions or meditative breathing techniques without having had skillful preparation or guidance. In his fascinating book, *Stalking the Wild Pendulum* (Dutton: 1977), the late Israeli thinker Itzhak Bentov addressed this issue in some detail. He observed that, "The incidence of.[physical] disturbances having a spiritual origin is rapidly increasing nowadays, in step with the growing number of people who . . . are groping their way towards a fuller life."[10]

In the lucid words of the anonymous disciple of Abraham Abulafia, therefore, "the Kabbalistic way of method consists, first of all, in the cleansing of the body itself, for the bodily is symbolic of the spiritual."[11] Typically, adepts have recommended fasting as a helpful means to purify the body. However, they have always hastened to add that to deprive ourselves of food and water is not a matter to be undertaken lightly. As discussed in Chapter 3, the Kabbalah has never viewed asceticism as a virtue in itself, but only as a path toward a greater goal. Hence, even fasting should be done as cautiously and slowly as possible, as the Hasidic founders often advised their disciples.

Another approach to physical training favored by some initiates has been to expose their bodies to extremes of temperature—for example, bathing in very cold waters during inclement periods of the year. The German Hasidim of the thirteenth century (not to be confused with their namesakes in Eastern Europe several hundred years later) very much advocated this method. The principle behind this apparently self-destructive practice is that we thereby learn to exert our mental power to shape our ordinarily involuntary physical processes. Interestingly, Tibetan Buddhists have similarly long incorporated this technique to attain the very same objective; they too speak of a "fire" that arises from one's body to generate intense heat.

Of course, our frame of mind constitutes the major element in preparing for meditation. The Kabbalistic term to describe the ideal mental state is *kavvanah*, not dissimilar to the Eastern notion of one-pointedness of attention. We are to be as completely focused as possible on the present moment, making a deliberate effort to marshall all of our willpower to concentrate. Even seemingly pressing concerns are to be postponed during the time of the mental exercise. Our consciousness is to be fully riveted on whatever symbolic image, sound, or inward activity the particular method calls for.

Wisely recognizing, too, our mind's tendency to become distracted by external stimuli, the Kabbalah repeatedly indicates the importance of privacy for our exploration within. "The forms [inside us] are extremely subtle," Abulafia's proselyte explains. "On this account, seclusion in a separate house is prescribed, and if this be a house in which no [outside] noises can be heard, the better."[12] Similarly, more than a half-millenium later, Rabbi Nachman of Bratslav remarked that it is useful to have a special room set aside for meditation, "even if you sit there and do nothing else."[13]

Not only does this specific arrangement help to screen out distractions that might disturb us, but it also ensures that we can better relax. Psychologists have consistently found that our immediate environment very much affects our capacity to perform a given task, whether it involves analytic or intuitive functions. For instance, laboratory research on dreams has been relatively unable to investigate nightmares, so rare are they in the clinic. For some as yet unknown reason, people simply do not allow themselves to experience truly frightening dreams while under the watchful eye of scientific instruments. Indeed, a whole line of current psychological inquiry has arisen to study precisely how we are subtly conditioned, mentally as well as physically, by the laboratory setting. Therefore, if we practice meditation in a specially designated room— or even part of a room—we should definitely enter into a deeper state of calmness.

An additional way to facilitate our mental development is through performing the technique at the same specified hour each day. Jewish visionaries have almost unanimously advocated this feature in their approach toward higher consciousness. Our meditative sessions should be carried out on a daily basis, regardless of how we may feel at the particular moment. We should not wait to be "inspired," because our ego is tricky enough to hinder that sensation from coming into being. Rather, once the schedule has been set, we must follow it with an iron will. As Rabbi Nachman of Bratslav aptly stated, sometimes we may be devoid of enthusiasm. In such moments, we must force our emotions and make ourselves committed to continue. "The enthusiasm may be forced at first," he commented, "but it will eventually become real."[14]

From my own experience while teaching meditation, this precept is an extremely important one. Many people initially rush into whatever form of "sensory relaxation" or "guided imagery" they are adopting, anticipating to be swept along by their eagerness. Not unexpectedly, their early euphoria soon fades, especially when such persons discover that no instant breakthroughs have occurred. In what usually amount to no more than clever rationalizations, they persuade themselves they will resume practice when less hurried, at a "better time." All too often, that time never arrives and their fledgling efforts toward inner peace are aborted.

Our ego or social self typically manages to find an almost infinite number of excuses to delay real self-examination. By their very nature, the Kabbalah declares, our lower urges are unconcerned with the development of our most transcendent qualities. Simply look at how often we postpone performing tasks that we know are absolutely necessary and are clearly unavoidable. The only solution, the Kabbalists stress, is to establish a daily regimen, and to stick with it. By doing this, we also reap the added benefit of strengthening our *kavvanah*. Thus, Rabbi Nachman of Bratslav gently commented that we must make sure to set aside a specific time each day for self-review. "Consider what you are doing," he declared, "and ponder whether it is worthy that you devote your life to it."[15]

Though adepts have definitely acknowledged that any convenient time for meditation is acceptable, they have singled out two particular periods of the day that are most conducive. These are early in the morning, immediately after rising, and at midnight, subsequent to a short period of sleep. Chapter 6 will explore in some detail the intriguing nature of this late-night "vigil." Suffice it to say here, however, that originating at least as far back as the appearance of the *Zohar*, Kabbalists have recommended that our waking day be punctuated by several brief, complete rests. In this manner, the boundaries that ordinarily separate our analytic and intuitive selves are blurred, leading to a closer integration of both aspects. In both of these periods, we have just returned from our unconscious mental state and consequently are most in tune with our latent, creative abilities.

In all cases, though, the Kabbalah admonishes us not to begin meditating right after eating or drinking; nor are we to attempt our practice while we have the need to evacuate our bowels. To explicitly mention this subject may seem a bit trivial. Yet, the seriousness with which the Kabbalists have approached it indicates that our body must be totally refreshed and prepared for the inner discipline to follow.

TECHNIQUES OF DEVELOPMENT

The Way of Concentration

Over its many centuries, the Kabbalistic system has encompassed a host of meditative techniques. Some fell into disuse hundreds of years ago; others are still practiced today. In the confines of this chapter, it will not be possible to review in detail even a partial listing of all of them. However, following the conceptual format of Claudio Naranjo and Robert Ornstein in their relevant book, *On The Psychology of Meditation* (Viking: 1971), these methods can be loosely grouped into three main categories: 1) Directed or Concentrative Exercises; 2) Annihilation of the Ego; and 3) Spontaneous Means of Expression.

The first refer to mental exercises which have a special focus, such as a visual symbol or a liturgical chant. The goal is to bring our attention to bear so intensively that everything else recedes into insignificance. The second include means to deliberately erase our socially imposed personality traits, so that we may more easily experience the divine Source inside us. The last involve efforts to release our pent-up anxieties and to thereby experience the sacred moments that come only when our restless mind is stilled. Of course, these orientations overlap. They have never been regarded as mutually exclusive, and indeed, some Kabbalists have taught a combination of techniques to their followers.

Perhaps the most ancient, directed meditative technique in Judaism is that of the *Merkabah* or "Chariot" school of pre-Kabbalistic times. This method, which seems to have disappeared with the spread of world Jewry into Iberia and Western Europe, had the vision of Ezekial as its central target. The ultimate goal for each initiate was to personally experience the awesome realm of the celestial Chariot. After depicting four angelic-like beings who appeared out of a great cloud flashing fire, Ezekial declares:

> Now as I looked at the living creatures, I saw a wheel upon the earth beside the living creatures, one for each of the four of them. . . . The four wheels had rims and they had spokes, and their rims were full of eyes round about. . . . And above the firmament over their heads there was the likeness of a throne . . . and seated above the likeness of a throne was a likeness as it were of a human form. And upward from what had the appearance of fire enclosed round about; and downward from what had the appearance of his loins I saw as it were the appearance of fire and there was brightness round about him. . . . Such was the appearance of the glory of the LORD.[16]

This remarkable passage has been the subject of immense controversy for millenia. Modern biblical scholars have differed over its interpretation and the origin of what they regard as the specific symbols in Ezekial's vision. Most recently, some science-minded observers have speculated that the Hebrew prophet was actually describing a "close encounter" with an extraterrestrial spaceship. In any event, Jewish visionaries have viewed this image as the end point of an extremely exciting and potentially dangerous voyage within. Through detailed, systematic writings—only a handful of which have survived to the present—its practitioners depicted in precise terms the signposts along the way. In this manner, initiates could safely traverse the difficult inner terrain.

In this highly structured meditative system, nothing was to be left to chance. Seven separate heavens or *heikhalot* were carefully described. For each dimension of inward awareness, the disciple had to memorize an entire array of repetitive prayers, rhythmic chants, and sacred "passwords" of entry. Some of these intriguing auditory devices—in some ways, resembling Hindu or Buddhist *mantras*—will be explored in Chapter 6. Special breathing techniques and body postures were also utilized. It is important to note though that this approach to higher consciousness was a supremely concentrative one. If your attention wavered for an instant, you were lost. For, practitioners were warned, they could easily become overwhelmed by the demons—what today we might call deep-seated inner fears—said to abound at every level.

Thus, in the archetypal tale of the "four sages who entered the garden," we are told that "Ben Zoma beheld the splendor of the marble plates [of the sixth heavenly palace] and he took them for water . . . and he went out of his mind."[17] It was absolutely critical that the adept know every step of the way and retain full consciousness while experiencing even the most breathtaking and exotic visions of the divine; otherwise, the disciple might never emerge out of the trance to return to earthly reality.

Hieroglyphics of the Mind

Another venerable, directed form of Jewish meditation is that of centering our mind on the letters of the Hebrew alphabet. The origins of this classic Kabbalistic technique date at least as far back as the appearance of the *Sefer Yetzirah* ("Book of Formation") between the third and sixth centuries C.E. In this ancient text, the twenty-two Hebrew letters and ten primary numbers are said to represent the thirty-two cosmic energy routes that underlie all of the universe. That is, each Hebrew letter corresponds to a particular manifestation of the awesome force that propelled Creation into being and keeps it generating.

For instance, *Aleph*, the first letter, stands for the power of thrusting, outwardly directed energy; the *Beth*, the second letter, is an insignia for the passive, receptive aspects present in any given situation, and so forth. In fact, Kabbalists insist that the pictorial image of each letter specifically conveys a deeper meaning. For example, a *Beth* is supposed to signify a house; a *Lamed* is a glyph of a man with his arm raised. To add to the complexity of this approach, the precise meaning attached to each Hebrew letter has varied according to the particular Kabbalistic system employed.

The notion that the letters of the Hebrew alphabet possess a wider, symbolic character may seem strange, even to those well-versed in mainstream Judaism. However, it is fascinating to observe that in Chinese mysticism, each of the sixty-four hexagrams of the *I Ching* ("Book of Changes") likewise communicates in visual form the meaning of the cosmic situation described in words. We might think of both metaphysical systems as based on a structure with much the same purpose as the modern-day Periodic Table of the Elements—in which each element is represented by a special alphabetic and numerical code. For with these forces depicted by the ancient Hebrew letters, the *Book of Formation* explains, "He created [the] twelve constellations in the universe, twelve months in the year, and twelve chief organs in the male and female person."[18]

For Jewish visionaries, therefore, the Hebrew alphabet carries with it a sacred connotation. Every sentence and even every word of Scripture conveys a secret meaning. Related to this belief, several different meditational approaches have been advanced through the centuries. *Gematriyah* is the system in which words with dissimilar meanings but equal numerical values—as each Hebrew letter also has a number associated with it—are probed for their hidden correspondences. In *Notarikon*, words are broken down into sentences composed of initial letters. Thus, the first word of the Ten Commandments, *ANoKhY* ("I Am"), alludes to the sentence *Ano Nafshoy Katovit Yahovit* ("I have written and given myself to you in this book"). In his appealing work, *Fragments of a Future Scroll* (Leaves of Grass Press: 1975), Rabbi Zalman Schachter provides these and other examples of this special system, which obviously requires extensive familiarity with the Hebrew language.

A related form of meditation, likewise based on written Hebrew, has similarly flourished for hundreds of years. Most closely associated with Abraham Abulafia, it involves the permutation and rearrangement of letters, especially those comprising the names of God. Its practitioners' objective is to attain an altered state of consciousness, in which their ordinary frame of mind is radically transformed. In *The Book of Eternal Life*, Abulafia explains:

> You will whirl the letters front and back and create many melodies. One should begin comfortably, and then, hurrying, train himself so that he becomes very accomplished in the art, familiar with all the changes and combinations.[19]

While some historians have interpreted Abulafia's method as a magically oriented system, this does not appear to actually be the case. To be sure, Abulafia declared that "if he [the initiate] is lucky, there will pass over him the spirit of the living God, bringing wisdom, understanding, good counsel [and] knowledge. . . ."[20] Yet, Abulafia's goal was not supernatural prowess but a deeper awareness of the divine. Unquestionably, some Kabbalists—Jews as well as non-Jews—have sought to gain psychic abilities through this approach. But a careful reading of the Kabbalah's long history shows that such motives generally came much later, when the Jewish esoteric tradition had penetrated into Christian circles. In fact, Abulafia's anonymous disciple explicitly stated that, "even granting the possibility of such a form of [magical] experience, I for my part want none of it, for it is an inferior one, especially when measured by the perfection which the soul can attain spiritually."[21]

Abulafia's system has been an influential one in the Kabbalah. In the sixteenth century, Isaac Luria, Chaim Vital, and other Safed luminaries practiced variations of it, such as *yechudim*, involving a binding of Hebrew letters to fashion new words. This technique is an extremely directive one, which demands powerful concentration. Through practice, it seems, we become detached from our whirl of typical thoughts and transported to a realm of dazzling peace and beauty. While the Baal Shem Tov was apparently well-acquainted with this means to exalted awareness—and performed it himself—he did not advocate it as a mass method toward higher knowledge. In turn, his own disciples downplayed this inner device even further, preferring more spontaneous ways of harmonizing the mind. For example, the chief scribe of Rabbi Nachman of Bratslav relates that his mentor advised his followers not to attempt *yechudim* and similar efforts, but to focus instead on simple acts of devotion—carried out with deep concentration.

Though these methods with the Hebrew letters do require a rather intimate familiarity with the language, in a modified format they may be of practical worth to many of us today. All that you need is a set of art paper and drawing utensils like pen and ink. Using a model depicting each of the Hebrew letters, you can informally copy the various figures. Eventually you can try to combine letters into various arrangements.

If you devote adequate concentration to this exercise, you may soon start to discover that each letter indeed evokes a certain set of mental associations—just as the Kabbalists have claimed for centuries. If you keep at the activity, you may find your mind beginning to form new ideas and insights related to your daily life. There do not seem to be any adverse effects; though similar to other forms of meditation, this one is best carried out when you are reasonably alert and physically refreshed. It is also best to terminate the session immediately upon feeling tired or restless.

In the stimulating Kabbalistic journal *Tree*, the poet and artist Jack Hirschman describes his own experiences in performing this technique. After depicting his style of "splatter-ing" the black ink against the Hebrew letters, he cogently writes:

> At first glance it may seem that I use these letters as a painter does, that is, with no other intention than in the form of them, their non-objective spatter; at best, the visualized music of so-called "modern art." But, in fact, I do not think of them in that way. . . . My pages are thus not simply exercises in one's ability to "free" oneself in the act of making art. They repre-sent a sort of deep continuity between my present concerns and the concerns of . . . the miraculous history we call this processing and ever transformative river of life.[22]

The Tree of Life

Besides focusing our awareness on the letters of the He-brew alphabet, the Kabbalah has encompassed another di-rected means of meditation. Its chief symbol is the Tree of Life, the divine structure said to underlie every animate and inanimate form in the universe. Chapter 2 has reviewed in broad outline the nature of this energy matrix in Jewish esoteric theory. For practitioners of this discipline, though, the Tree of Life has also been a primary image for raising our ordinary frame of mind to higher perceptions. Over the cen-turies, several meditative techniques have derived from this evocative approach.

One of the oldest and simplest has been to gently dwell on the poetic majesty of this powerful symbol. Thus, the *Zohar* is filled with vivid descriptions of this heavenly entity and entices our imagination. In this way, our mundane concerns fade from awareness and we enter a sphere where every aspect has rich meaning and beauty. The *Book of Splendor* declares:

> [In the beginning] the House of the world was made. This House forms the center of the universe, and it has many doors and vestibules on all sides, sacred and exalted abodes where the celestial birds build their nests, each according to its kind. From the midst of it rises a large tree, with mighty branches

and abundance of fruit providing food for all, which rears itself to the clouds of heaven and is lost to view between three rocks, from which it again emerges, so that it is both above and below them. From this tree the house is watered. In this house are stored many precious and undiscovered treasures. That tree is visible in the daytime but hidden at night. . . .[23]

In the modern era, the Swiss psychoanalyst Carl Jung devoted considerable attention to the subject of symbols and their importance for humanity. In his book, *Man and His Symbols* (Doubleday: 1964), he observed that the meaning of our most ancient symbols can never be totally connoted in words. The truly symbolic—such as the Kabbalah's long entrancement with the Tree of Life—has a wider, "unconscious" quality that can never be exactly defined or fully explained. "As the mind explores the symbol," Jung wrote, "it is led to ideas that lie beyond the grasp of reason."[24]

Perhaps intuitively sensing this potent effect of the symbolic, Kabbalistic adepts have also performed a specific method of meditation—one which today might be called "guided imagery"—related to the celestial Tree. With this technique, you sit comfortably and prepare yourself in the manner outlined earlier in this chapter. The room should be dark and quiet. Then, visualize a white light surrounding you with warmth and tranquility. Next, picture this light as circulating upward from the *Sefirot* corresponding to the systems of your body (see Chapter 2 for the appropriate diagram)—until the light merges into the brilliant sea of the *Ein Sof* ("Infinite"). Briefly dwell on the image of this endless, dazzling light around you.

Thereupon, visualize this light as traveling downward, through each of the *Sefirot*, until it descends into the most earthbound aspects of your being—transforming with radiance your cares and worries. Feel the intensity of the light dissolving them. Chaim Vital, the sixteenth-century Safed thinker, explains:

Think and intend to receive light from the ten spheres from that point tangential to your soul. There you intend to raise

the ten spheres up to the Infinite so that from There [beyond
the *Sefirot*] an illumination will be drawn to them—to the
lowest level [of your mind and body].[25]

A third meditative system to evolve from the Tree of Life
symbol encompasses the Hebrew prayerbook. Isaac Luria devised this special set of liturgy to carry out exercises known
as *kavvanoth*. When reciting the prayers, the initiate has in
mind the various combinations of divine Names that relate to
the realms of the ten *Sefirot*. In an extremely complex manner, each word therefore connotes a multiplicity of meanings.
Like the arduous visualizations required by the *Merkabah* and
yechudim approaches, the *kavvanoth* proved very difficult for
many Jews interested in the quest for inner peace and transcendence; even the early Hasidic masters recognized its lack
of usefulness for most of their followers. Thus, beginning
with the Great Maggid, the Baal Shem Tov's chief associate,
the term *kavvanoth* became generalized to include any intense, passionate binding of our concentration to the divine.
Because the "metaphorical map of the Sephiroth had become
blurred," it could no longer "serve as an object of religious
meditation during prayer."[26]

Ego Annihilation and the Way of Surrender

In this respect, a quite different Kabbalistic orientation to
harmonizing the mind has also been practiced for centuries.
This approach encompasses both deliberate means to "annihilate the ego" (*bittul hayesh*) and inward devices to release our
suppressed feelings. The Hasidic founders especially promulgated such methods, as they are indeed much less intellectually
demanding than the highly structured activities discussed
earlier. In fact, by the late eighteenth century, some of the
major Hasidic thinkers advised their disciples to dispense
altogether with the classic techniques associated with the
Hebrew alphabet and the *Sefirotic* system.

Rather, they taught that we can also meditate by focusing
our mind on the higher worlds that lie beyond our normal

veils of perception. During each session, with as much will and enthusiasm as we can muster, we should concentrate as fully as possible on the splendors of the sacred universe. In this manner, we will gradually learn to transcend our mundane desires. In the *Tanya*, Rabbi Schneur Zalman tersely observed:

> The essential thing, however, is the [mental] training to habituate one's mind and thought continuously, that it ever remain fixed in his heart and mind, that everything one sees with one's eyes—the heavens and earth and all that is therein—constitutes the outer garments of . . . the Holy One.[27]

The Lubavitcher founder went on to stress that even with this easier technique, practice is absolutely necessary. He insightfully compared the effort to develop inner strength to that of a "craftsman who trains his hands."[28]

In this regard, the Kabbalists have viewed our ordinary personality as a direct barrier to the awakening of our hidden potentialities. To truly attain peace within, they have taught, we must strip our mind of its artificial wants. One way to accomplish this is to meditate on one emotional trait at a time—say, our tendencies to anger or fear—and then ruthlessly confront the emotion, through self-examination, until it no longer holds sway over us. When this task is completed, we will have totally mastered our lower aspects.

Rabbi Nachman of Bratslav favored this method, insisting that the main thing is to work on nullifying each one of our habitual personality characteristics. We should begin with one trait and then move on to others, thereby allowing the transcendent to flow into us. "When you are bound to an emotion or desire," he declared, "it obstructs [the] glory and casts a shadow." But as we eliminate these restless desires, we "remove this shadow. And as the shadow departs, the light . . . is revealed."[29]

In each meditative session, we should strive to minimize our emotional preoccupation with worldly matters by a process of intentional detachment. For instance, if someone insulted you earlier in the day, you review the episode as it happened but now erase the anger that you felt. If you were lonely at a social gathering, then later, while meditating, deliberately nullify that feeling of loneliness. Over time, you will discover an increasing ability to lift yourself out of the immediate tensions of a situation, and remain untouched by the negativity of others.

The Kabbalists indicate that to achieve this objective, we should sit as quietly as possible in a darkened room. Closing our eyes and shutting out all sounds, we must rivet our attention on the individual trait we wish to obliterate. All distractions are to be ignored. We may discover that a particular melody helps to relax or guide us into a conducive frame of mind; in that case, we should hum it softly until we have reached the proper calmness for the mental exercise.

A final meditative technique for our purposes here involves the spontaneous discharge of suppressed feelings like anger or frustration. In general, the Kabbalah has offered few such methods compared to its emphasis on directed means to elevate the mind. In this respect, the Jewish esoteric tradition differs from Eastern disciplines like tantric yoga that prefer unstructured devices. Perhaps this fact reflects the strong preference of Kabbalists for relying on the intellect rather than emotions as a tool of self-liberation. In any event, Rabbi Nachman of Bratslav disseminated this highly interesting method of the "silent scream."

To perform this exercise, you must imagine the sound of your own scream. Keep this up until the scream occupies your entire consciousness—let it express all of your pent-up rage, longing, and disappointments. The trick is to not form words, but to simply give free reign to the feelings welled up inside. A chief advantage of this technique is that it can even be practiced in public. You can scream in a crowded area in this manner, Rabbi Nachman observed, without anyone even noticing.

It is striking to see the similarity between this approach to inner peace and the contemporary system known as Primal Therapy. Developed by Dr. Arthur Janov several years ago, its central premise is that since birth each of us holds in a veritable ocean of unexpressed pain. The only way we can truly liberate ourselves from the experiences of our past, Janov has insisted, is to ventilate our feelings through utterly spontaneous screaming. Though it is unlikely that the Kabbalah directly influenced this popular form of psychotherapy, the prescience of Judaism's visionary tradition seems startling. Perhaps, as Ecclesiastes stated millenia ago, there is indeed little new under the sun.

Challenges Along the Way

One of the most common problems that beginners often encounter while attempting to still their jumble of thoughts is how to maintain their concentration. Our daily mind constantly flits from one idea or image to another without cease. To convince yourself of this fact, simply try to stare for one whole minute at the moving second hand of a watch: do not permit your attention to wander for even an instant. The task is surprisingly difficult. If you can accomplish it easily, you may be well on your way to reaching the higher states of awareness highlighted later in this book.

Yet, the Kabbalah has always been sensitive to this basic feature of our ordinary mental state. In fact, the subject of how we can best enhance our attention has long been a prime topic in Kabbalistic lore. For instance, the early Hasidic leaders devoted much discussion to this issue, presumably because of the meditative difficulties experienced by their followers. Interestingly, the Hasidic minions of the eighteenth century appear to have been most distracted by thoughts relating to either sexual desires or finances—certainly not very different from our daydreams today.

The Kabbalists have advocated several separate ways to improve our concentration. By far, the most complex—and also perhaps the most ancient—method has been to deliberately "elevate" what the rabbis have called "strange thoughts." With this challenging technique, an intrusive image is deconcretized and translated metaphorically into its position in the

Sefirotic scheme, such as the Tree of Life. For example, suppose while meditating you are suddenly reminded of an attractive person you saw earlier in the day. Your task is then to place the inner essence of the likeness where it appropriately belongs in the divine realm.

Thus, in this light, Rabbi Jacob Joseph of Pulnoye, a chief disciple of the Baal Shem Tov, reports: "As I have heard from my master ... if it is thoughts of women, he [the initiate] should intend to elevate them by attaching them to their root in *Hesed* ["Loving-kindness"]. ... And thoughts of idolatry produce a flaw in the *Tiferet* ["Beauty"] of Israel. Enough has been said."[30] The reference here is to the *Sefirot* of Hesed and Tiferet; by focusing on their brilliant attributes, the disciple succeeds in returning his or her wavering attention to loftier aspects of the cosmos. Our inner powers are even strengthened in the process, we are told. "If there comes to man lustful thoughts about women," Rabbi Jacob continues, "He should understand that if he has this desire, merely because of the single holy spark that is there, how much greater will be his delight if he attaches himself to the Source of this delight."[31]

Because of the intellectual rigor demanded by this method, some Kabbalists have preferred another means to handle intrusive thoughts. Indeed, recognizing the powerful concentration needed to perform the appropriate symbolic transformation of the literal to the symbolic in the *Sefirotic* scheme, later generations of Hasidim have limited its use to only the most learned. With this second technique, we must deliberately shut out the "strange thought," by using as much willpower as possible. An early Hasidic thinker describes this method in detail:

> How can [you] know which thought to reject and which to bring near and elevate? A man should consider. ... If no sooner than the strange thought arrives there immediately comes ... the meaning of putting it right and elevating it, then ... bring it near and elevate it. But if the thought of how to put it right does not come ... [you are] then permitted to reject that thought, for if one comes to slay you be first to slay him.[32]

Again, the Jewish mystical system shows an uncanny pre-science for the insights of modern psychology. Contemporary psychotherapists have recently begun to use a technique known as "thought stopping," to treat people with troubling repetitive thoughts or phobic fantasies. Whenever the person senses the onset of the upsetting idea—for example, "I will make a fool of myself at work today," or "I will never be loved by anyone"—he or she must totally eradicate the notion, then immediately substitute a positive, competing idea. These might include such self-statements as, "I will be successful at work today," or "I will be in a love relationship in the near future." Results so far have been quite encouraging with this behavioral approach, just as the Kabbalists have long argued.

A third orientation favored by some initiates has been to merely not pay any attention to the interfering thought. You do not bother to struggle against the troubling idea, but rather, let it go away of its own accord. "Do what you must," stated Rabbi Nachman of Bratslav, "and disregard these thoughts completely."[33] That is, the more mental energy we expend in fighting or denying the extraneous stimulus, the worse our concentration becomes. But if we withdraw the spotlight of our attention from the offending thought, it quickly loses the power that our conscious mind extends it.

This intriguing viewpoint closely parallels that of several other spiritual systems such as Sufism and tantric yoga. They likewise urge that in meditation—as well as other altered mental states like dreaming sleep—we should view intrusive thoughts as part of ourselves and not as something to be bitterly contested. In this way, we can best achieve an inner harmony—after all, that is what meditation is ultimately all about.

The other chief difficulty that many people experience in initiating the inner voyage seems to be a more puzzling one. Nearly every formal means of mental enhancement currently declares that if we practice their particular exercise as prescribed, we will inevitably feel calmer and more at peace within. Typically, no qualifying or cautionary statements are given. As a result, when some persons start to feel greater waking tensions or sleep disturbances soon after taking up meditation, they blame themselves and drop the whole matter. A growing number of health care professionals have observed this perplexing phenomenon while teaching "relaxation training" or similar methods. Paradoxically, it seems, some people actually become *more* restless and apprehensive as a direct result of their performance.

In this vein, at the 1980 Annual Convention of the Association for Advancement of Behavior Therapy, Frederick J. Heide and Thomas D. Borkovec of Pennsylvania State University reported that some anxious clients clearly increase their anxiety levels as a consequence of practicing relaxation. This effect has been noted anecdotally, they observed, "with a range of techniques, including EMG biofeedback, mantra meditation, and progressive relaxation."[34] In a carefully designed research study, they found that a surprisingly high proportion— ranging from nearly one-third to over one-half—of participants described themselves as more tense following their meditative session. The investigators concluded that one cause for these findings might relate to the fear of losing control during deep relaxation.

Strikingly, the Kabbalah has anticipated by centuries this latest experimental area. Thus, in a marvelously lucid analogy, Rabbi Nachman of Bratslav compared meditation to boiling a pot of water. The heat generated will soon reveal all of the imperfections; obviously, these were present all the while, but were simply undiscernible under ordinary conditions. In a like manner, he explained, our normal thought-current is filled with a variety of useless effluvia—conflicts, worries, resentments—yet we characteristically suppress them from our day-to-day consciousness. The tremendous gift of meditation, therefore, is that it makes visible our inner flaws to us, the very first step before we can confront and transform our tensions. In other words, the apparent calm of our mind's surface is really an illusion. "When these impurities are removed," Rabbi Nachman of Bratslav explained, "the water is truly pure and clear."[35]

In my own therapeutic work, I have consistently found that

people who are anxious or withdrawn typically feel more tense than others during their initial attempts at "relaxation training." But if they resolve to see this difficult time through, they can soon make rapid growth in attaining their goal of calmness and serenity. As Rabbi Nachman once more advised, we must be patient with our progress, for gains are most long lasting when they occur little by little, in gradual amounts. "You think that everything comes at once," he observed. "This is far from the truth. You must work . . . before you can achieve any good quality."[36]

For the Kabbalists, when that matter is accomplished— and they certainly deem it no overnight event—our greatest potentialities become awakened. We are far more receptive to higher states of awareness—and may even experience the ecstasy described by the sages of old. This provocative subject will be explored next.

Opening page of the Hebrew Bible: the word Bereshit ("In the beginning") and a pictorial summary of the biblical narrative (Germany, ca. 1300).

CHAPTER FIVE

AWAKENING ECSTASY

"As the hand before the eye conceals the greatest mountain, so the little earthly life hides . . . the enormous lights and mysteries of which the world is full."
—Rabbi Nachman of Bratslav

"O, ye terrestrial beings who are sunk deep in slumber, awake!"
—the *Zohar*

ONE OF THE MOST EXCITING DEVELOPMENTS of psychology today is its growing exploration into the highest reaches of human existence. Over the last ten to fifteen years, there has been a massive awakening of interest, both among professionals and the general public, in those fateful moments during our lives when we feel most joyful, creative, and even inspired with a pervasive sense of wonder. Since the immensely influential work of Abraham Maslow in the late 1960s, few of us have remained indifferent to popular inquiry into the origin of these "peak experiences," as he poetically called them. The quest for transcending our day-to-day perceptions of ourselves and the world has come to occupy a paramount position in such arenas as sexuality and social relations, psychotherapy, and even the workplace. Almost all of us now search for the right mixture of environment and people that will help ignite these dramatic episodes of tremendous happiness. Whether we can consciously "trigger" them, or rather must wait passively for them to happen, is currently the subject of much controversy.

Yet, this fascinating field of investigation is scarcely new. Even within the halls of orthodox science, for nearly a hundred years researchers have sought to understand the peak or visionary experience. About the turn of the twentieth century, Professor William James of Harvard University, among the most brilliant thinkers of his time, concluded that the average individual was using only a tiny bit of his or her full potential. Dr. James considered this finding to be extremely important and commented, "Compared to what we ought to be, we are only half awake. Our fires are dampened, our drafts are checked, we are making use of only a small part of our mental and physical resources."[1] In works such as *The Varieties of Religious Experience*, he delved into those mental phenomena typically regarded as "mystical" and argued forcefully that we must take these experiences seriously, if only to comprehend what they really are. He insisted that however unusual the person's inner event, scientists should not unthinkingly dismiss it.

Unfortunately, Professor James's farsighted viewpoint held little attraction for his more conservative colleagues. They generally explained the feelings of great oneness and serenity described by mystics and ordinary folk as reflecting some type of temporary or even permanent insanity. Both laboratory experimenters and psychiatric practitioners were far more interested in studying the mentally ill, the "average" individual, or animals. Outside of the achievements of a handful of iconoclasts like Carl Jung, very little was thus done until recently to unravel the mysteries of our highest capacities and how to develop them. In the 1960s, Dr. Herbert Otto, a social psychologist who pioneered in this realm, observed, ". . . the topic of human potentialities has . . . been almost totally ignored as a focus of research activity by workers in the social and behavioral sciences."[2]

At present, though, this whole situation has radically changed. With an impetus borne from many sources, more and more people in the West are gathering information about the transcendent dimensions of human experience—in which we seem to pass beyond our daily perceptions of life. As psychologists have turned to the East in the last few years, they have discovered the remarkable truth that some of the most longstanding spiritual traditions possess a startling intimacy with states of consciousness that still appear enigmatic to us. Once we are able to penetrate the initially unfamiliar terminology and symbolism of these ancient disciplines, they offer us a vast territory of knowledge about the highest capabilities of our species.

The Kabbalah is an especially useful and powerful tool in helping us to grasp the nature of peak experiences. From its very beginnings, lost in the legends of antiquity, the Kabbalistic system has been deeply concerned with the human potential. For many centuries, its chief thinkers have provided both theoretical and applied writings dealing with this intriguing topic. In a systematic and detailed manner, they have addressed such puzzling questions as: What are visionary experiences? How do they occur? And, why are they so rare or elusive in everyday living? Moreover, the major works of the Kabbalah incorporate a specific model of *ordinary* consciousness— presenting a perspective that strikingly anticipates the most up-to-date notions of how our mind normally functions. Without the benefit of our modern array of technological instruments and computer-age statistics, the Kabbalists have somehow managed to antedate the very latest laboratory insights concerning our brain and central nervous system.

Higher States of Consciousness

It is a fundamental principle of the Jewish esoteric way that in daily life we are attuned to only one state of awareness among many. The Kabbalah emphasizes repeatedly that we characteristically move through mundane, waking activities as though surrounded by veils, which hide other possible spheres of perception from conscious sensation. "Man, whilst in this world," observes the *Zohar* in one passage, "considers not and reflects not what he is standing on, and each day as it passes he regards [it] as though it has vanished into nothingness."[3] These other states of consciousness exist, the Kabbalah informs us, even though, virtually from birth onward, we tend to become oblivious to them.

In fact, the Kabbalists teach us that when we are born, our minds are focused almost exclusively on sheer physical survival. Eating, drinking, and sleeping are our main concerns; as we grow, the companionship of family members and friends begins to become important to us. And, somewhat later during early life, moral and spiritual vistas start to open. Though children are sometimes more in touch with the immediate delights of the world than are adults, the Jewish meditational system stresses that the ability to enter into higher mental realms must be acquired through normal development. "When an individual is born," comments Rabbi Moses Chaim Luzzatto, "he is almost completely physical, with the mind having only a very small influence. As he matures, his mind continues to gain influence, depending on the individual's nature."[4]

In order to ensure our physical adaptation on earth, we are told, we exist with a full range of bodily needs and desires. Though we are admonished not to condemn or punish our corporal selves, our goal is clearly to strengthen the higher aspects of our being. "Because of his body ... man is therefore embedded in the physical," Rabbi Luzzatto adds. "As long as he is impelled to pursue the material, both great effort and a powerful struggle will be required if he is to elevate himself to a more enlightened state."[5] Thus, stemming from our animalistic component, our minds are forced to devote considerable attention to the necessities of physical endurance. This innate part of our emotional makeup, though, if not sufficiently overcome through conscious exertion, can definitely blind us to higher realities.

The Jewish esoteric tradition portrays the universe as manifesting an incredible richness and dazzling radiance. Employing a wide variety of similes and metaphors, it indicates over and over again that at every moment, we are encircled by an awe-inspiring cosmos. Indeed, the Hebrew word *Zohar* means "splendor" or "brilliance," as we have seen. Passages in this eloquent work abound that describe the "tens of thousands of worlds" and their multitude of wonders, "for there is door within door, grade behind grade, through which the glory . . . is made known."[6]

The marvels of creation that dance around us are there continually, the Kabbalists tell us. There is a never-ending stream of celestial music and light that bathes this world and all of the unseen ones. These strains of song, as we shall see in the next chapter, are said to be so extraordinarily beautiful that they can shatter the unprepared mind. Likewise, these invisible colors—what today we might term "unperceived vibrational frequencies"—are depicted as giving off a brilliance that far surpasses what we ordinarily see in the rainbow. Once more, it is our normal consciousness that typically shuts these out. "There are colors disclosed and undisclosed," the *Book of Splendor* declares, "but men neither know nor reflect on these matters."[7] It goes on to explain that the visible colors represent reflections of higher ones, of which the spiritually advanced, such as the prophets, were not wholly ignorant.

In the late eighteenth century, the Hasidic masters gave strong emphasis to this interesting idea. The Baal Shem Tov repeatedly described our ordinary consciousness as engulfed in a state of almost tragic exile from the divine Source. There are worlds upon worlds of wonder around us, but we typically remain attentive only to our most fleeting physical wishes, he taught. Our greatest misfortune on earth is to sink into complete forgetfulness of the potential realms of ecstasy that lie latent within. Through joy, the most exalted gates of perception open to us. Sadness and depression, in contrast, close them up.

Thus, in the Besht's cogent view, we are most likely to

undergo visionary or peak experiences when we are already in a serene, receptive frame of mind. And, the Hasidic founder advised, any event can awaken our higher faculties, for the transcendent can be found "in everything and everywhere." We must learn to see beyond the seemingly trivial, inconsequential happenings of everyday life, he stressed. The better able we are to do this, the greater the probability of attaining lofty states of awareness. A beautiful parable that is ascribed to the Baal Shem Tov relates:

> A king had built a glorious palace full of corridors and partitions, but he himself lived in the innermost room. When the palace was completed and his servants came to pay him homage, they found that they could not approach the king because of the devious maze. While they stood and wondered, the king's son came and showed them that those were not real partitions, but only magical illusions, and that the king, in truth, was easily accessible. Push forward bravely and you shall find no obstacle.[8]

With this notion, the Besht poetically portrays our day-to-day consciousness as filled with deception; what we think is absolutely solid and real is actually not so at all—and what we regard as an insurmountable chasm between us and the experience of the divine is really no chasm at all.

The Great Maggid, the Besht's chief disciple, offered an even more explicit model of the creative, inspirational, or revelatory moments studied by Maslow and other modern-day psychologists. The Maggid insightfully observed that our ego—the habit-oriented, social self—tends to prevent such episodes from happening more often. We are afraid to "let go," afraid to surrender our calculating mind to the nonrational and spontaneous. Only when our minds are totally emptied of all daily, mundane effluvia can we reasonably expect to enter into a radically different state of consciousness, he preached. Commenting that, "every Heavenly Gate requires the proper key to open it,"[9] he prescribed specific meditational techniques to help "annihilate' the ego. Once this difficult task is accomplished, he explained—in a remarkable parallel to various Eastern spiritual descriptions—

our small conscious mind unfolds into a much larger, wiser Self.

The Maggid's brilliant student, Rabbi Schneur Zalman of Liady, formally developed this interesting idea in the *chabad* system that is still practiced today. In a quite sophisticated approach to human personality—one which antedates William James's and Freud's by a century—the founder of the Lubavitcher sect explicitly compared our ordinary state of attention to that of a sleepwalker. He insisted that the average person is almost wholly oblivious to the myriad celestial mysteries which lie before us at our every step; the central task of each of us is to "wake up" from our inner slumber. In keeping with traditional Kabbalistic theory, he emphasized that our willpower is crucial to this process. "Through a powerful fixation of the mind and an intense concentration touching the depth of the heart," he informs us in the *Tanya*, "a person must strain . . . to apprehend 'eternal love.' "[10]

At about the same time, in the beginning of the nineteenth century, Rabbi Nachman of Bratslav vividly promulgated this same message. From the available reports of his life, we know that even as a young child he was convinced of the realities of other dimensions of human consciousness beyond the mundane. Like his contemporary William Blake, the English poet and artist, Rabbi Nachman as a boy underwent mystical experiences that shaped his view of the cosmos. Through solitary wandering in the forests and meadows of the East European countryside, he directly felt the presence of divine being in every living thing. Each blade of grass is aflame with its own song of ecstasy, he later told his followers; but only one person in ten thousand or more ever becomes aware of such true perceptions.

For this fascinating spiritual thinker, peak experiences are so rare because we so seldom venture inward. He condemned philosophizing as a hopeless attempt to understand the universe, because it does not operate by human logic in the first place. Like Blake, he blamed idle intellectualism as a false road to knowledge. Nor did Rabbi Nachman encourage people to merely practice the traditional Kabbalistic techniques of meditation to awaken higher faculties. For these activities too, he believed, could become sterile exercises of the mind if not carried out with real spontaneity and fervor.

For him, the way of the heart was the surest path to exalted states of consciousness. "Always be joyful, no matter what you are," he taught. "With happiness, you can give a person life."[11] Every day, he further stressed, we must deliberately induce in ourselves a buoyant, exuberant attitude toward life; in this manner, we will gradually become receptive to the subtle mysteries around us. And, if no inspired moments seem to come, we should act as though we have them anyway, he advised. "If you have no enthusiasm, put on a front. Act enthusiastic, and the feeling will become genuine."[12] Thus, the single most important determinant of visionary experiences is our mental "set" beforehand, Rabbi Nachman declared. Moments of wonderful happiness and peace do not simply arrive by accident or random chance, but rather very much relate to our characteristic emotional makeup—our day-to-day feelings and desires.

Interestingly, this basic Kabbalistic belief has been confirmed by recent scientific investigation. In his ground-breaking research, Maslow found that highly gifted, creative people—those he termed "self actualizers"—reported more frequent peak episodes than the rest of the adult population. In a follow-up study by the noted sociologist Andrew M. Greeley, reported in his *The Sociology of the Paranormal* (Sage Publications: 1976), people who had undergone mystical experiences measured quite superior on the scale of psychological well-being. Somehow, these extremely successful persons had prepared themselves to be in a frame of mind conducive to such ecstatic occurrences.

In short, the Kabbalah tells us that by wallowing in sadness, self-pity, or depression, we can inadvertently shut out of our lives exactly those kinds of joyful "highs" that we all wish for in our relations with others. We are *not* passive recipients of our experiences, but create them each day, the Jewish esoteric indicates. We must intentionally seek these events of great inner beauty, by maintaining a self-confident, optimistic outlook. The more we can accomplish this—and we should expect no instant, miraculous changes—the more often such episodes will occur, at an ever-quickening pace. As Rabbi Moses Chaim Luzzatto astutely observed, "Each individual's ultimate level is therefore the result of his own choice and attainment."[13]

The Protective Blinders of the Mind

The Kabbalistic system has always argued that our inner blinders possess an important adaptive function. Despite the way in which they are said to limit our highest perceptions of the cosmos, they insure our physical survival on earth—by keeping us focused on our bodily needs for growth and development. Of course, as we have already seen, the major thinkers of the Kabbalah almost universally agree that we typically become too immersed in the desires of the material world. Yet, they have insisted repeatedly that we must not attempt to remove these shutters too suddenly, lest we suffer serious emotional and even physical repercussions. We cannot hope to storm the celestial gates within by force, and if we try, we are risking a great deal that we ordinarily take for granted. In fact, the Kabbalistic tradition is filled with tales of would-be spiritual masters who sought to break open the doors of divine awareness, and died or went mad with the onrush of knowledge they were not yet mentally prepared to receive.

Perhaps the most famous legend that illustrates this point is that of the "four sages who entered the garden." This story, which deals with very real historical figures, recounts how Ben Azai, Ben Zoma, Ben Abuyah, and Rabbi Akiva—each renowned as a scholar during the time of the second destruction of the Temple in Jerusalem—pursued the most lofty visions of the universe. None but Rabbi Akiva survived with mind and body intact. The rest never recovered from their inner voyage. And these men, it must be remembered, were among the most celebrated sages of their epoch in Jewish history. They were hardly idle thrill seekers, looking for a "high." The message of Jewish mysticism is clearly that our ordinary consciousness is a very delicate and even potentially fragile thing. We must not tamper with it recklessly, however praiseworthy our goal.

This viewpoint continued down the centuries as a key element in Kabbalistic teaching. The *Bahir*, which first appeared in writing in twelfth-century France, stresses that in order for us to exist in a physical form, some of the heavenly light that permeates the cosmos must be hidden from our sight: otherwise, we would not be able to bear it. The more spiritually advanced we are, though, the better able we become to perceive—and withstand—the splendors of this illumination. "The light [of Creation] was very intense," the *Bahir* explains, "so that no created thing could gaze upon it. God thereupon stored it away for the righteous in the Ultimate Future."[14]

Similarly, the *Zohar* contains many references to the same intriguing concept. It views the human brain as "contained in a shell which will not be broken" until the end of days; only then "will the shell be broken and the light [shine] out into the world from the brain, without any covering on it."[15] In both symbolic and perhaps even literal expression, the *Zohar* is definitely suggesting that our inner blinders are a physiological necessity. For the greatest Biblical leaders, such as Abraham and Moses, were not able to completely penetrate the barriers which surround our ordinary perceptions of the world. They attained glimpses of the higher realms, the *Book of Splendor* comments, but that was all even they could absorb without losing their sanity or life. The gates within must be opened gradually, we are told, in a beautifully poetic and lucid description:

> At that time, He will first open for them a tiny aperture of light, then another somewhat larger, and so on until He will throw open for them the supernal gates which face on all the four quarters of the world. . . .
> . . . For we know that when a man has been long shut up in darkness it is necessary, on bringing him into the light, first to make for him an opening as small as the eye of a needle, and

then one a little larger, and so on gradually until he can endure the full light. . . . So, too, a sick man who is recovering cannot be given a full diet all at once, but only gradually.[16]

The Hasidic masters a half-millenia later very much maintained this central Kabbalistic belief about our emotional makeup. Rabbi Schneur Zalman, the Lubavitcher founder, devoted considerable attention to the nature of our mental shutters. In his *Tanya*, he systematically taught that every animate being in the universe must be shielded from the awesome, incomprehensible grandeur of the divine light. Without such a shield—which is built into our physical structure from before birth—we would dissolve into nothingness, like a wax figure placed too close to a burning fire. Yet, he observed, each of us feels an ever-present longing, nevertheless, to merge into that celestial warmth. Intuitively sensing our highest reaches, we crave to escape the daily, prosaic aspects of our lives. The human essence is "always to scintillate upwards," he wrote, "for the flame of the fire intrinsically seeks to be parted from the wick in order to unite with its source above . . . although [we] would thereby be extinguished."[17]

In a quite similar vein, Rabbi Nachman of Bratslav identified this same feature of our mental capabilities. He taught that despite our most exalted yearnings for going beyond the normal confines of space and time, we must recognize the importance of our ordinary perceptions as an inner starting point. Though Rabbi Nachman was himself a tremendous visionary, seized with the power of his dazzling experiences of the sacred, he warned his followers to be patient and not to look for peak episodes too impetuously. People do not consider the capacity to focus on the mundane a benefit, he insisted with his usual sense of irony. But without this quality, the great *rebbe* observed, we might be driven insane by the prosaic aspects of our lives. "Imagine that you would constantly [experience] all that we know about the [higher] world. . . . If you could, it would be impossible for you to endure life."[18]

To summarize here, we can see that the Kabbalah offers us

an imaginative and yet coherent model of how our mind typically works. But how relevant actually is this viewpoint? Is it still viable?

Modern Validation for the Kabbalah

It is fascinating to discover that contemporary psychology is converging on this precise notion of Kabbalistic speculation. In recent years, there has amassed a growing scientific literature dealing with the character of our ordinary consciousness, as well as unusual divergences from it. From fields as seemingly disparate as the psychobiology of perception, severe mental illness, and even the effects of certain drugs on the mind, it is becoming clear that the Kabbalah has anticipated by hundreds of years our most up-to-date research conclusions.

In the late 1950s, psychologist William Broadbent first advanced the revolutionary concept that our central nervous system contains within it a "filtering" mechanism that screens out those stimuli that are unimportant to our particular task at hand. Thus, for example, in a noisy party, we are usually able to focus on our own conversation despite the din around us—unless, of course, we've had too many drinks, thereupon temporarily impairing this "filter." But it is virtually impossible to fully concentrate on more than one conversation at the same time; our minds do not seem to work that way. In fact, this phenomenon has by now been studied so thoroughly that it has been dubbed the "cocktail party syndrome." Over many laboratory experiments spanning nearly two decades, investigators have become convinced of the basic truth in Dr. Broadbent's now-classic work, *Perception and Communication* (Pergamon Press: 1958). All of us appear to possess a powerful capacity to narrow our attention on whatever is most relevant at the moment, whether it is driving, reading, or playing a game of tennis.

For instance, as you're silently reading this page, there are undoubtedly a host of subtle sounds around you. A plane may be roaring its engines in the far distance, a car may be starting across the street, perhaps a child is calling to its mother. Even your own body is constantly producing a range of sounds. But ordinarily none of these random, scattered noises will interfere with your concentration. You may briefly look up, then resume your reading, still immersed in your train of thought.

This filtering mechanism, most psychologists currently argue, is built into us before birth. With the natural unfolding of normal maturation, children gradually develop this inborn capacity to focus their attention. Thus, a ten-year-old in a classroom rarely reacts with the same intensity as his or her four-year-old sibling when the same truck backfires in the street outside. This filtering structure also presumably enables us to rivet our attention to a particular thought or emotion. Researchers speculate that at some level in this process, if the outside stimuli is sufficiently urgent—say, the odor of smoke or a voice crying help—our rational self will suddenly shift its awareness. Otherwise, we effectively screen out of consciousness most of the countless sensations that impinge upon us in daily life.

Aptly summarizing years of scientific investigation of this fact, Dr. John Zublin commented at the American College of Neuropharmacology in 1970, "Since our receptors are bombarded continuously by a wide spectrum of both internal and external stimuli, we must have some way of separating the relevant stimuli [from] . . . those we cannot ignore. . . . This is selective attention."[19] The inner mechanism involved is characteristically so efficient, in fact, that we take it for granted. We are ordinarily not even conscious that it is working.

Unfortunately, in some respects, our ability to make use of selective attention behaves only *too* well. Research evidence has convincingly shown that most of us are remarkably oblivious to much of what is occurring in our sensory environment. In a very real sense, as the Kabbalah informs us, we go about our daily routines as though half asleep, never fully waking up to the realities around us.

For example, in one revealing set of experiments carried out by psychologist Jerome Bruner and his colleagues, research participants were asked to play a game of cards with a preselected laboratory deck. Few persons were at all aware that certain cards had been deliberately disfigured, so accustomed were individuals to see things in timeworn ways. Other investigators have likewise highlighted our striking "talent" for ignoring what our nervous systems are registering, so involved are we in our own mental activities—especially repetitive thoughts and anxieties. Our inner shutters are indeed closed a great deal of the time; we must make a conscious effort, it seems, to open our senses wide so that new experiences— and potentially peak ones in particular—may transform our day-to-day mental orientation.

Corroboration for this perspective in current psychology has surprisingly come too from scientific inquiry into the nature of severe mental illness, especially schizophrenia and psychotic states. In this condition, people typically have trouble differentiating reality from their own fantasies or fears: the disorder has been identified in virtually every human culture in recorded history. For many decades—dating back to the very formation of modern psychiatry—professionals in the field have been aware that patients often spoke of their inability to focus their attention, to concentrate. For the most part, though, such complaints were regarded simply as another manifestation of the absurd delusions of such persons.

Then, beginning in the early 1960s, investigators began to take these comments more seriously. In a landmark study in the *Journal of Mental Science*, Drs. J. Chapman and A. McGhie actually gathered a collection of statements from schizophrenics about what the disease really feels like from the "inside." Over and over again, the interviewees reported a tremendous problem in differentiating the various stimuli impinging upon them. As one articulate individual commented, "Everything seems to grip my attention although I am not particularly interested in anything. I am speaking to you just now but I can hear noises going on next door and in the corridor. I find it difficult to shut them out."[20] In my own work with severely emotionally disturbed people, this description is a common one. Patients relate that at certain times sounds, lights, and even their own thoughts become hopelessly jumbled together. I have learned to counsel schizophrenic men and women that what they are experiencing is not due to their imagination, but reflects a very real impairment that they will have to face and try to overcome.

Thus, at present, the rapidly emerging model to explain extreme mental illness is that it involves a breakdown of our normal sensory filter. For some reason, as yet unknown, a biochemical or neurological deficit occurs—throwing the person's usual central nervous system into disarray. As Keith Nuechterlein summarized in the 1977 issue of *Schizophrenia*, published by the National Institute of Mental Health, "The tendency of the schizophrenic to respond to irrelevant stimuli has played a key role in many formulations of attentional dysfunction. It is the clinical phenomenon that most strikingly suggests that deviant attention may be the fundamental [mental] disorder in schizophrenia."[7] In others words, just as the Kabbalah declares, madness may very well befall us if we push too suddenly to discard our inner blinders. Without them, few of us can withstand the sweeping gulf of sensory stimuli that surges around us at every moment.

The third line of fascinating confirmation for Kabbalistic notions about our characteristic awareness derives from research on the effects of various mind-altering drugs. Though widespread interest in the West in mood-affecting chemical substances really awakened in the 1960s, it is clear that around the globe many so-called primitive tribes have long been knowledgeable about this dimension of human experience. For centuries, American Indian tribes have utilized such natural materials as mescaline, peyote, and psilocybin, under carefully controlled rites, to evoke exalted states of consciousness. In conjunction with the deeply spiritual mood that would pervade these ceremonies, participants have reported dramatic episodes of wondrous kinship with the cosmos. Ordinary perceptions of separateness from the universe dissolve into an ecstatic oneness.

In our own culture, one of the foremost explorers of the human potential, writer Aldous Huxley, experimented with mescaline in the early 1950s. In his brilliant essay, *The Doors of Perception*, he described his experience while under the chemical's influence. It is extraordinary that not only did he antedate the prevailing theory of human consciousness, but he also offered a precise synopsis of the Kabbalistic view as well. Few modern analyses of the peak or visionary episode are portrayed as poetically as his:

> I spent several minutes—or was it centuries?—not merely gazing at those bamboo legs, but actually *being* them.... Each person is at each moment capable of remembering all that has ever happened to him and of perceiving everything that is happening everywhere in the universe. The function of the brain and nervous system is to protect us from being overwhelmed and confused by this mass of largely useless and irrelevant knowledge, by shutting out most of what we should otherwise perceive.... To make biological survival possible, Mind at Large has to be funneled through the reducing valve of the brain and nervous system. What comes out at the other end is a measly trickle of the kind of consciousness which will help us to stay alive on the surface of this particular planet.[22]

Of course, such drug-induced psychological insights are not without their negative counterparts. Many people have reported disorienting, even terrifying moments during the psychedelic, mind-altering experience that Aldous Huxley found so joyous. The brilliant writer acknowledged this fact in his discussion, explicitly observing that schizophrenics seem to undergo many of the same bizarre sensations that he noticed in his visionary session under mescaline's effects. In my own therapeutic work with former heavy drug users, I have repeatedly found that their sense of personal identity is very impaired. Either they feel completely isolated and insignificant, or else they have immense, grandiose delusions about daily communing with celestial beings who share with them the innermost secrets of the universe; in either case, such people are sometimes barely even able to bathe or dress themselves anymore. In some very real way, as yet not well understood by scientists, their minds were not able to withstand the impact of all the gates of awareness opening at once.

As the Kabbalah itself has suggested for centuries, the trick in triggering peak experiences is not at all to merely batter apart our inner blinders. To accomplish that is not especially difficult, as research on psychedelic substances has shown. There seems to be convincing evidence that within our nervous system are specific chemicals that manage to help us maintain an even keel of attention during waking consciousness. Drugs such as LSD or mescaline appear to knock out these chemicals, so that we become flooded with stimuli, both internal and external, and everything appears extremely meaningful. How each of us will then respond to this situation depends on many factors, but a key one is our own mental stability and attitude toward life. Huxley cogently speculated, "If you started in the wrong way . . . [all] that happened would be a proof of the conspiracy against you. It would all be self-validating . . . I couldn't control it. If one began with fear and hate as the major premise, one would have to go on to the conclusion."[23]

Thus, we return full circle to the original teachings of the Kabbalists. We are indeed limited in our perceptions of the universe because of the shutters within. Yet, we must learn to gently remove them, in a careful step-by-step manner. At the same time, we must immerse ourselves with positive, confident images about our individual makeup and the human enterprise as a whole. As Rabbi Nachman advised, "When a house burns down, people often rescue the most worthless items. You can do the same in your confusion. Do not be hurried."[24]

The Transcendent Experience

Here we come to that realm of human existence that seems by its very nature to elude or defy verbal description. It is difficult enough for us to provide abstract labels to depict even our ordinary feelings; to attempt a similar effort regarding those experiences that go far beyond our normal perceptions appears virtually impossible. How would we go about portraying a sunset to a person who has been blind since birth? Or explaining the unique power of music to someone who has always been deaf? At best, our words might carry a barest hint of what the sensation is actually like. For this reason, the Kabbalistic tradition, like many of the great spiritual systems of the world, has not said a great deal about what the transcendent reality actually encompasses. A classic Zen Buddhist adage states that, "The finger pointing to the moon is not the moon." Another one comments equally succinctly, "The raft across the river is not the other shore." The major writings of these spiritual disciplines all appear to emphasize that whatever descriptions they offer us are thus *not* to be taken literally; they are merely the most general guideposts.

This same belief pervades the Kabbalah. Perhaps the single most important quality of the visionary experience for the Kabbalists is its ineffableness. Isaac Luria, the dazzling sixteenth-century thinker of Safed, Palestine, is said to have told his disciples, "I can hardly open my mouth to speak without feeling as though the sea burst its dams and overflowed. How then shall I express what my soul has received, and how can I put it down in a book?"[25] Luria's influence on Jewish esoteric thought was unparalleled and his reluctance to concretize the ecstatic reality is illustrative of the entire history of this exotic approach to knowledge. Like those both before and after him, Luria did share some of his experiences with a handful of intimate colleagues and students. Yet, one searches in vain among the writings of his circle or others for detailed portraits of the specific content of higher perceptions— such as given us by the Swedish scientist and theologian Emmanual Swedenborg; in volume after volume, this fascinating figure of the eighteenth century recorded precise descriptions of his inner excursions into realms of heaven and hell.

Interestingly, Rabbi Nachman of Bratslav explicitly commented upon the inherent incommunicability of the divine reaches within. "You may have a vision," he declared, "but even with yourself you cannot share it. Today you may be inspired and see a new light. But tomorrow, you will no longer be able to communicate it, even to yourself. For the vision cannot be brought back."[26] His own teachings stress the methods by which we can attain these episodes, but do not therefore specify what genuinely occurs.

Nevertheless, accounts do exist in the various Kabbalistic sources. Particularly in the *Zohar* do we find mention—if only tantalizing clues—of the aspects involved in these experiences of incredible rapture. As we shall see, such descriptions bear some startling parallels to those of other ancient traditions, as well as to the reports of men and women today.

A key element characteristically present in this type of episode is the pervasive feeling that we can see our life in absolute perspective. It is as though we are gazing down from a tremendous height, with an awesome calmness and love, at everything that we have done, both the seemingly good and bad. Even the most minute, insignificant moments of our days fall into place and cohere with meaning. The sensation stands in almost complete opposition to the far more typical sense of inner confusion and uncertainty with which we are all too familiar. Our intuition of personal direction is unmistakably clear.

In an inspiring and poetic portrayal of this experience, Rabbi Luzzatto compared our everyday existence to that of a person lost in a garden maze. He noted that the individual between the paths has no way of discerning whether he or she is on the true path. The walker who holds a "commanding position in the portico, however, sees all of the paths before him."[27] Intriguingly, Maslow and others have discovered that this sensation of suddenly being elevated above the mundane is a central one in what he in fact came to call "peak" experiences.

Another major feature of these moments is an intense outpouring of emotion. The Kabbalists inform us that the feelings involved go far beyond our ordinary ones and can therefore only be suggested, not defined. As we have seen briefly in

Chapter 3, the *Zohar* compares the highest reaches of spiritual awareness to the throes of bliss that are hinted at during sexual intercourse with love. It is in no way referring to lust or physical desire, but rather the orgasmic sense of transcending our daily ego into a union with the oneness of all. Thus, in one representative passage, the *Book of Splendor* comments, "No other love is like unto the ecstasy of the moment when spirit cleaves to spirit and become one—one love."[28] In the tantric yoga tradition, the sexual embrace—with all of its delights—is likewise depicted as a foretaste of the most exalted dimensions of our consciousness.

Though differences do exist among the Kabbalistic writings as to the specific emotionality of this experience, there are however sharp agreements that bind them. The *Merkabah* or "Chariot" approach that predates the Kabbalah itself conveys a mood of solemn awe and wonder; the initiate is always aware of the chasm that still separates physical form from the divine. Much later, the Hasidic masters generally described a far more personal encounter with the ineffable and particularly stressed the utter joy that the devout feel in this state. Yet, basic to all Kabbalistic portrayal of this experience is an emphasis on the magnificent harmony and unity of the cosmos. Everything is suddenly glimpsed as beautiful and full of meaning. It is striking that despite the vast boundaries of history and geography that distinguish the various Kabbalistic works, nowhere do we hear of such daily emotions as disgust, anger, outrage, disappointment, or embarrassment. Indeed, the feelings that seem to predominate—and which are ordinarily rarely in our own vocabulary—are those such as reverence and splendor. The same observation, of course, can be made about the great visionary experiences recounted in many other spiritual approaches.

Furthermore, our sense of self-identity radically changes. Practitioners of the Jewish esoteric system have characteristically commented that their normal mental perspective was annihilated, and yet, they felt uplifted into a much greater consciousness of their true worth. One of Abraham Abulafia's disciples in the thirteenth century observed that in this realm of awareness, "you pass beyond the control of your natural mind ... beyond the control of your thinking."[29] Our real nature no longer appears to be limited by the confines of our corporal form; "one sees that his innermost being is something outside of himself."[30]

Our bodily receptors are also overwhelmed in this experience. Over and over again, the key sensation described is that of Light permeating every animate and inanimate object in the universe. This Light is depicted as possessing a brilliance and a translucent quality that far exceeds anything we can imagine. As the *Zohar* tersely comments, "The primal point is the innermost light of a translucency, tenuity, and purity passing comprehension."[31] "Up to this point only," the *Zohar* goes on to say, "it is permissible to contemplate the Godhead, but not beyond it, for it is wholly recondite."[32] Interestingly, in describing his ecstatic view of the universe after he had ingested mescaline, Aldous Huxley wrote, "I was in a world where everything shone with the Inner Light, and was infinite in its significance."[33]

The highest levels of divine perception are depicted as encompassing a realm of infinite, dazzling light. Termed the *Ein Sof* by the Kabbalists, no other attribute can be reported about it. In the Kabbalah, it is regarded as the region from which all elements of creation flow, both good and evil and other apparently polar opposites. In Tibetan Buddhism, this state of awareness is also considered a most exalted one. Initiates in this spiritual discipline term it "luminosity-emptiness," the experience of which simply surpasses any attempts at description. As Lama Govinda declared in *The Way of the White Clouds*, "[emptiness] is not the negation merely of our limited personality, but ... includes, embraces, and nourishes ... the womb of space in which the light moves eternally without ever being lost."[34] It is most intriguing that in contemporary scientific investigation into death and dying, to be discussed in Chapter 8, researchers have found that many people at the "gates of death" have reported the feeling of being surrounded in the glow of a "being of light," infinitely understanding and loving. In his recent and exciting book, *Life at Death* (Coward, McCann & Geoghegan: 1980), Dr. Kenneth Ring discusses in detail this "core" aspect of dying and suggests that it may be present in other states of awareness as well. The Kabbalists would most certainly agree.

One of the most powerful constituents of the visionary experience, as the Kabbalah portrays it for us, is the overturning of our most tightly-held concepts of time and space. Our normal, day-to-day sensations seem to vanish altogether, or else cease to matter anymore. In the *Zohar*, we are told that this occurrence was true for Rabbi Simeon bar Yochai and his son. "Thus, they continued for a space of two days, neither eating nor drinking, nor noticing day nor night. When they came forth, they found that they had not tasted anything for two days."[35] In the many inner transformations depicted symbolically by the *Book of Splendor*, the stars become as near to us as the trees on the ground, long-departed sages speak, and the future unfolds with clarity. Indeed, psychic powers are said to be awakened during such peak episodes, though such abilities are not at all essential in the eyes of the Kabbalists. The crucial aspect is once again the complete certitude of the interconnectedness of all facets of the universe.

It is this central viewpoint that defines the Jewish mystical approach to both ordinary and exalted states of consciousness. Not surprisingly, this same perspective seems to be inherent in many spiritual traditions around the globe, throughout history. As William Blake aptly observed, "If the doors of perception were cleansed every thing would appear to man as it is, infinite."[36]

CHAPTER SIX

RETURNING TO THE SOURCE: DREAMS AND MUSIC

"When prophets were no more, their place was taken by the Sages, who, in a sense, even excelled the prophets; and, in the absence of Sages, things to come are revealed in dreams."

—the *Zohar*

"Every science, every religion, every philosophy, has its particular song. The loftier the religion or the science, the more exalted is its music."

—Rabbi Nachman of Bratslav

IT HAS BECOME ALMOST A TRUISM to say that we typically walk through life using only a fraction of our potential. In the modern era, many brilliant thinkers have turned their attention to this elusive subject. The French philosopher Jean Jacques Rousseau blamed civilization itself for our inner enslavements; several generations later, Karl Marx indicted the Western economic system of capitalism for the mass alienation and unhappiness he saw around him. In the late nineteenth century, the allied disciplines of sociology and psychology arose and pointed to many causes for our estrangements from one another and our deepest selves. Beginning with Freud, contemporary psychotherapies have attempted to alleviate our feelings of emotional unrest. However, some observers argue that the sense of displacement within is basic to the human condition and part of our very makeup as biological creatures.

But this entire issue is not quite as recent as we might tend to think. For centuries, the Kabbalah has emphasized the notion that we ordinarily make use of very little of our abilities and that only in rare moments do we typically come alive with our full range of talents. Works such as the *Zohar* teach us that though we usually exist in a state of time-worn habit resembling sleep, there are definite pathways for recovering a full awareness of who we are as unique persons and what our purpose is on earth. Rather than bemoaning the obvious failings of humanity, the Kabbalists have preferred to accent the virtually unlimited strengths that each individual possesses. Yet, they insist, means of action are necessary to bring out the latencies that lie dormant inside us. Furthermore, not all methods are helpful or even advisable for everyone. But two of the most direct—and universal—are through the worlds of dreams and music.

Kabbalistic ideas on dreams anticipate by hundreds of years current conceptions and in some ways are yet ahead of mainstream science. Though investigators in the scientific community are only just beginning to understand how sound intimately affects us, the Jewish visionary tradition has focused extensively on this subject. Through these approaches, the Kabbalah tells us, we can enhance our personal well-being and return to the Source that fires our creative sparks.

Dreams: Across the Inner Terrain

Dreams have fascinated nearly every culture in recorded history. The ancients regarded dreams with respect and even awe, considering them to herald important messages for our lives. During their golden age, the Greeks built more than three hundred temples in homage to their god Asclepius; supplicants would travel long distances to these temples and participate in sacred rituals designed to elicit a useful dream. In the Orient, dream incubation temples were similarly erected in serene and peaceful settings. On our own continent, Native American tribes valued dreams as a wellspring of godlike inspiration. Their shamans would journey deep into the wilderness; depriving themselves of food, water, and companionship, they would induce a dream of power or knowledge that they could take back to their people.

With the rise of the Industrial Age, however, such intuitive wisdom fell on hard times. When Freud began to research the medical literature of his day for information on dreams, he found that almost nothing had been written on the topic. Most of his colleagues viewed the whole matter as one of superstition, unworthy of serious attention. Indeed, when in 1899 he published his landmark *The Interpretation of Dreams*, he was greeted with ridicule and derision. For several years, his cogent probings of the hidden meaning of our dreams were dismissed as the ravings of a madman or a pornographer.

Eventually, of course, the psychoanalytic movement that he headed gained momentum. Freud's bold ideas on the nature of our dreams seemed to possess an uncanny accuracy. Though the source of his penetrating insights remained unknown, his emphasis on dream interpretation as a powerful tool of self-understanding became part of the therapeutic mainstream. In fact, as happens so often with the ideas of great thinkers, his dicta acquired the status of dogma among many of his followers. Not until the last decade or so have orthodox investigators started to study dreams from new perspectives. Without disparaging the significance of Freud's bold contributions, current experimenters are uncovering more and more information about this still enigmatic human activity.

Though much of this exciting work is happening in laboratories around the globe, interested persons today are also turning to the ancient spiritual systems. It has become increasingly clear that these disciplines have often incorporated a highly subtle and sophisticated body of knowledge about the human mind and body. Innovative psychologists have already begun to mine such sources as Yoga, Tibetan Buddhism, Taoism, and other age-old approaches for their provocative teachings on dreams. As yet, however, there has been little recognition of the richness and complexity of the Kabbalah's views on this subject.

This fact is ironic. For over a half-millenium, the Jewish esoteric system has considered dreams to hold a central importance in our everyday life. There is convincing evidence that writings such as the *Zohar*—which dates back to about the year 1290—may have strongly influenced Freud's seemingly unprecedented discoveries on how our dreams function. Moreover, not only has the Kabbalistic perspective antedated in many respects our modern-day orientation to dreams; in some ways, this ancient visionary approach offers a *more* thorough, inclusive viewpoint than that typically put forth by contemporary researchers.

The Kabbalists have always believed sleep and dreams to play a vital role in our lives. They have never condemned sleep as a waste of time, but rather have regarded it as directly contributing to our emotional and physical health. In keeping with their image of the human body as something beautiful and divine, Kabbalistic thinkers have also prized sleep—alongside such other physical activities as eating and drinking—as having a crucial spiritual purpose. Through sleep, we replenish our bodily stamina and also open ourselves to higher influences, declares the Kabbalah. We are therefore admonished not to deny ourselves adequate rest—for whatever reason—just as we are advised not to attempt needless fasting or other forms of bodily self-punishment.

The Hasidic masters in particular stressed this idea. Many of their fervent followers sought to keep themselves going during all hours of the day and night, to better attain lofty knowledge. Consequently, their mentors gently but firmly preached that we must maintain satisfactory rest to lead a truly harmonious way of life. No matter how strongly we may feel impelled to busy ourselves in activity, time is needed for respite. Without it, we will quickly begin to lose our inner powers. Thus, the famous Hasid, Rabbi Sussya, commented, "Even sleep has its purpose. The man who wishes to progress . . . must first put aside his life-work in order to receive a new spirit, whereby a new revelation may come upon him. And therein lies the secret of sleep."[1]

Interestingly, the early Hasidim even judged the mental well-being of their followers according to the quality of their sleep. In a well-known anecdote, one prominent Hasid was asked in later life what he had most learned from his own teacher. His answer was, "How to sleep properly." It is painfully obvious that our society has not yet learned this lesson, as evidenced by the millions of adults who require one or more sedatives each night in order to fall asleep. From the Kabbalistic perspective, this is a clear sign of the imbalance that exists within many of us.

One intriguing and longstanding practice of the Kabbalah in this respect is the midnight prayer or study vigil. Originating at least as far back as the Middle Ages, this method has been much favored by adepts in the Jewish esoteric tradition. At precisely the hour of midnight, the initiate awakens from several hours of sleep. He or she then meditates, sings the various holy chants and hymns, and delves into the mysteries of the sacred books. The Kabbalah points out that we are especially receptive to the wisdom of our inner Source at this time and can confidently expect most rapid self-development. For instance, the *Zohar* comments that King David knew this because his kingship depended on it, and therefore he was accustomed to rise at this hour. Characteristically, practitioners continue with their exotic pursuits until the break of dawn. In this manner, the *Book of Splendor* goes on to say, the

Mystical Hebrew calligraphy from the *Book of Raziel* (Netherlands, 17th century).

initiate "is encircled with a thread of grace; he looks into the firmament, and a light of holy knowledge rests upon him."[2]

This technique may indeed have particular benefits for us today. Besides the apparent advantages of greater quiet at this hour of the night, we may also gain physically from the increased availability of negative ions in the air. Scientists have become aware that we are acutely affected by the presence of electrically charged particles in the atmosphere. As Fred Soyka reports in his interesting book, *The Ion Effect* (Bantam: 1978), it is now clear that ions exert a helpful influence upon us and that they typically exist in higher concentrations after the sun goes down. Furthermore, this cycle of alternating short periods of sleep with waking activity may in itself be of value; from a wide variety of research studies, there is increasing evidence that our creativity is most enhanced when we adopt a daily rhythm involving frequent brief naps. Perhaps intuitively, in modern times such brilliant inventors as Thomas Edison have made use of precisely this daily tempo. He would likewise sleep briefly at night, then arise to concentrate on his work until the early hours of the morning.

Here again, though, the Hasidic leaders issued cautionary advice for us. For example, the Lekhivitzer *rebbe* criticized the tendency of some of his disciples to stay up long hours after dark in pursuit of the higher mysteries of the spiritual world. While he lauded the praiseworthy motives behind such practices, he commented that, "Many pious folk . . . eat the food of the spirit in sadness [for] their brain is bemused for lack of sleep. This is the wrong way . . . [with] sufficient sleep . . . we may gain a clear head for sacred studies."[3] Similarly, the *Zohar* itself declares that without proper attention of mind and piety of heart the midnight vigil is useless, even self-destructive. In other words, if we are tired and lack the capacity for really exerting ourselves mentally, we might better obtain a good night's rest.

For the Kabbalists, though, dreams are clearly the most important aspect of sleep. Again and again, the major visionary writings of Judaism insist that dreams offer us a key avenue for self-exploration, as well as a path to greater wisdom concerning the universe. In fact, even within the normative Jewish tradition, dreams are prized for their potential aid in our day-to-day living. For instance, the Talmud—compiled between the second and fifth centuries C.E.—contains several cogent discussions as to the meaning of dreams. In his well-documented article, "Anticipations of Dream Psychology in the Talmud," published in the scholarly *Journal of the History of the Behavioral Sciences*, Moshe Halevi declares, "The Talmudic psychology of dreams . . . includes a detailed picture, albeit scattered among the opinions of many . . . of the nature and mechanics of dreams which anticipates much of the modern experimental observations."[4]

With their masterful insights into our inner makeup, the Kabbalistic thinkers focused intensely on our dreams. Far from simply seeing them as ethereal, inexplicable experiences, they regarded most dreams as reflections of our daily frame of mind. That is, whatever we most usually think about as we go about our daily activities—*that* is what will typically occupy our dreams as well. A lucid description of this process can be found in the thirteenth-century *Book of Splendor*. It states, "David was all his life engaged in making war, in shedding blood, and hence all of his dreams were of misfortune, of destruction and ruin, of blood and shedding blood, and not of peace."[5]

For the Kabbalists, dreams are meant to be taken seriously. Because they reveal our ordinary emotions, they can provide us with definite pathways into our own hidden depths. "A dream uninterpreted is like a letter undeciphered,"[6] the *Zohar* succinctly says. We are to confront our dreams honestly, rather than ignore them or dismiss them as irrelevant to our waking life. Even more emphatically, the *Zohar* stresses that, "A dream that is not remembered might as well have not been dreamt, and therefore a dream forgotten and gone from mind is never fulfilled."[7] Throughout the Kabbalah, this teaching echoes; we are to heed the messages of our dreams most closely.

To accomplish this task requires a decided technique in the

eyes of the Kabbalists. Consistent with their peculiarly powerful mixture of rationality and poetic exuberance, they have
always insisted that dreams must be interpreted according to
certain well-defined rules. These dicta are viewed as invio-
late and do not vary from person to person. That is, every
human being's dreams—regardless of his or her station in
life—can typically be decoded in the same specific manner.
Thus, while the Jewish visionary system views dreams as
often enigmatic, perplexing, or even inspired by higher powers within us, it does not consider them to be inherently
unfathomable. "All dreams follow their interpretation," we
are told. "Because [Joseph] penetrated to the root of the
matter, he gave to each dream the fitting interpretation so
that everything should fall into place."[8]

The key element in dream interpretation is to understand
each separate aspect of our dream. In an approach that remarkably antedates classic Freudian theory, the Kabbalah
indicates that our minds work during sleep by means of
symbols. While texts such as the *Zohar* do not adhere to
Freud's overriding emphasis on sexuality as the main symbolic force in our dreams, they do tell us that many features
of dreams actually represent abstract thoughts and hidden
feelings. Thus, we are informed, "According to the lore of
dreams, a river seen in a dream is a presage of peace"[9] and
"every dream which contains the term *tob* [good] presages
peace . . . provided the letters are seen in proper order."[10]
Likewise, the *Book of Splendor* observes that all colors seen in
a dream are of good omen, "except blue."[11]

Here, once more, the Jewish esoteric tradition strikingly
predates modern psychology; for contemporary research has
demonstrated that colors are indeed linked to our deepest
emotions. People who typically "dream in color," that is *remember* such dreams (for our dreams seem to be characteristically in this form) are generally more in touch with their
inner world. Furthermore, as the *Zohar* astutely reports, dark
colors are associated with feelings of personal unhappiness.
In our popular English usage, we are well acquainted with
"blue Mondays" and "singing the blues."

The Kabbalah further explains that once every element in the dream is correctly unraveled, its meaning will become clear. A dream is considered to be determined by its interpretation, and once comprehended, it may then serve as the springboard for our response. But the Kabbalists caution us closely about whom to share our dreams with. In keeping with their view that dreams are hardly trivial matters, they have always stressed that we ought not to discuss our dreams with just anyone. Strangers or casual companions are likely to distort or misconstrue the significance of our dreams; they may even deliberately downplay an important message conveyed. For instance, someone may dream of being very happy after resettling in another locale—while an acquaintance, opposed to the potential move, might persuade the person to disregard the "obviously meaningless" dream. Thus, the *Zohar* flatly states that a person should not reveal his dream except to a friend, for the listener may pervert the importance of the dream. But, this insightful book is equally emphatic that we should not keep our dreams buried within us. "When a man has had a dream, he should unburden himself of it before . . . his friends."[12] Of course, few of us ever share such deeply private feelings with even our intimates; and yet, such behavior might help to bring us closer to one another and avoid future misunderstandings.

The Kabbalistic belief in the importance of dreams as a key inner path is mirrored in the practice known as the "dream-fast." Dating back to Talmudic times, this ancient custom calls for fasting and self-examination after a foreboding dream. We are explicitly instructed to do so on the same day as the dream happened. Rabbinical leaders advised that this intriguing custom be observed even on the Sabbath, the traditional Jewish day of feasting and rejoicing. They explained that a portentous dream represents a warning and not an irrevocable decree from on high. Thus, by immediately initiating action to face the causes of the disturbing dream, we may be able to rectify the imbalance within that produced the anxious dream in the first place. And, fasting and meditating are quite likely to help us become more in tune with feelings below our mind's surface. Typically, this interesting custom also involves a group ritual at the end of the dreamer's fast day. Three close friends are assembled round the dreamer; in their comforting presence, he or she then recites several encouraging phrases from the Scriptures—perhaps therein implanting positive self-images in the dreamer's consciousness.

In the sixteenth century, the prominent Kabbalist Joseph Karo dealt specifically with this fascinating spiritual prescription. In codifying past rabbinical dicta on the kinds of dreams permissible to fast after, on the Sabbath, he identified these three: a Torah scroll being burned, the conclusion of the Day of Atonement prayers, and the beams of one's house or one's teeth falling out. During a mediumistic trance state, Karo was told by his *maggid*, "You have correctly ruled that one should not fast on the Sabbath, except for these."[13] Parenthetically, it is striking that more than three hundred years later, Freud named the dream of our teeth falling out as reflecting fears of losing physical vitality, especially our sexual potency! Nearly a century since Freud's own formulation, this type of dream remains in psychoanalytic circles a classic example of castration anxiety. As for the other sorts of dreams Karo mentioned, their interpretation is similarly not difficult to make—in Judaism, the Day of Atonement is one in which persons ask forgiveness for their misdeeds as well as for unexpressed actions that should have been carried out. To dream of this religious holiday probably indicates deep guilt feelings about something, the Kabbalists undoubtedly reasoned. And, dreams of one's possessions being destroyed—material or spiritual in the form of the Torah—likewise suggest inner emotional conflicts that need to be resolved.

The Kabbalah therefore admonishes us to take dreams of sickness, death, or destruction, quite seriously. "Observe, too, that a man is not warned in a dream without [cause]," the *Book of Splendor* declares. "Woe to him who has no warning dreams."[14] It is compelling to note that contemporary health researchers are beginning to find a very literal meaning to this Kabbalistic insight. Some investigators have found that our dreams may actually signal our inner *physical* well-being—

and the lack of it—months or even years before a disease becomes clinically manifest. As Dr. Patricia Garfield reports in *Pathway to Ecstasy* (Holt, Rinehart, and Winston: 1979), Soviet scientists have been able to predict forthcoming illness with great accuracy based upon their patients' dreams. At the Leningrad Institute, they have found that dreams of, say, a stomach wound might indicate a liver or kidney ailment before the person is consciously aware of pain or difficulty in that part of the body. In the United States, researchers are similarly discovering that cancer patients frequently have had "warning" dreams about their impending illness, sometimes significantly prior to the actual diagnosis of the dread disease. Such examples readily point out the validity of the Kabbalistic view that we should take seriously all of our dreams—and if we do so, the healthier we are likely to be.

Another evocative practice related to dreams that the Kabbalah teaches is that of actively soliciting guidance from them for our daily lives. Several steps in this consciousness-altering technique are involved. Perhaps you have been feeling ill lately, and want to get in better health. Or possibly, you have been feeling doubts about whether to remain at your present job. Before going to bed at night, you then write down your personal question, framing it as specifically and tersely as possible. Then, you meditate for several minutes and help focus the mind with some means such as chanting, performing certain rituals, or permutatigi letters of the Hebrew alphabet. Characteristically, these methods are also recommended by the Kabbalists in conjunction with this approach.

You thereupon address your dream source for an answer to your dilemma. One formula that has come down to us from the twelfth century goes as follows:

> I adjure you with the great, mighty, and awesome Name of God that you visit me this night and answer my question and request, whether by dream, by vision, by indicating a verse from Scripture, by [automatic] speech . . . or writing.[15]

This interesting method is prized by several diverse spiritual disciplines. Known as "dream incubation," the practice of going to sleep to receive a dream of inspiration has been valued by the ancient Greeks as well as Native American tribes. In his stimulating article, "Dream Incubation," in the Fall 1976 issue of the *Journal of Humanistic Psychology*, Dr. Henry Reed argues that this technique can be a very potent tool of psychotherapy. He also reports that shared dream incubation rituals, involving several persons, seem to trigger paranormal dreams such as telepathy. Today, this exercise has apparently been recreated independently by various psychologists as yet unaware of the Kabbalah's longstanding familiarity with it. Like others who have practiced this self-healing device, I have found it to be most effective when I am at least somewhat lucid before going to sleep, rather than groggy with fatigue: within a few days, I usually experience a dream that is directly relevant to the question posed.

Perhaps the most intriguing aspect of Kabbalistic thought about dreams is its belief that they may communicate extrasensory information to us. Such dreams, the Kabbalists insist, are rather rare and not to be expected on a regular basis. They caution us, in fact, that the overwhelming majority of dreams can easily be attributed to mundane thoughts and feelings. For instance, the *Zohar* repeatedly explains that, "There is not a dream that has not intermingled with it some spurious matter, so that it is a mixture of truth and falsehood."[16] In the eighteenth century, Rabbi Moses Chaim Luzzatto similarly observed that it is impossible to have a dream that does not include irrelevant information. The crucial factor that determines the visionary power of dreams is, then, our daily frame of mind in waking life. The more inwardly serene we are—and the less our sleep is troubled with idle fantasies and restless anxieties— the better able we are to attain "higher" dreams of knowledge. In those lofty states, psychic abilities become manifest, we are told.

For the Kabbalists, dreams are the most pervasive source of paranormal wisdom. The *Book of Splendor* succinctly states, "A dream is more precise than a vision and may explain what is obscure in a vision."[17] Rabbi Luzzatto, again echoing earlier Jewish mystics, declared that dreams are pathways to prophecy. During sleep, the Kabbalah informs us, our minds are far more receptive to our inner wellsprings of creativity; our conscious flow of thoughts is shut off, thus allowing divine inspiration to enter—if we are open enough to receive it, rather than preoccupied with day-to-day worries and desires. Indeed, about the year 1800, Elijah Gaon of Vilna advised his disciples that sleep exists for the sole purpose of conveying the mysteries of the cosmos through the vehicle of dreams.

In our own era, innovative explorers of the mind are now beginning to corroborate even this more exotic aspect of Kabbalistic notions about dreams. Freud himself was quite fascinated by cases of apparent extrasensory perception in our dreams and in the 1930s speculated that "telepathy could be the original archaic means by which individuals understood each other."[18] More recently, several psychoanalysts have similarly reported evidence for such communication in the dreams of patients undergoing psychotherapy; their research shows that psychic dreams between patients and their therapists are far from unusual. In fact, Carl Jung was even more intrigued by this phenomenon than his mentor Freud and wrote at length on dreams involving telepathy, precognition, and clairvoyance.

In the 1970s, the Maimonides Dream Laboratory of the Maimonides Medical Center in New York was the site of intensive investigation into the possible paranormal qualities of our dreams. Over a series of many experiments, carried out over several years, convincing data was obtained on this issue. In his article, "Dreams and Other Altered Conscious States," in the Winter 1975 *Journal of Communication*, Dr. Stanley Krippner reviewed the findings of twelve separate studies and concluded that, "Telepathy and dreams can be demonstrated in a laboratory setting."[19] His colleague at the Maimonides Dream Laboratory, Dr. Montague Ullman concluded in the same publication that our dreams sometimes appear able to attract and incorporate information regarding events occurring "at a spatial distance from us, about which we would have no way of knowing."[20] Even more striking, he noted, "they appear to gather information distant in time, as in the

case of events which have not yet occurred."[21] As yet, however-
er, such farsighted researchers are not able to predict *who*
will manifest these unusual abilities, for not all of us seem to
possess them in equal measure.

Here again, though, the Kabbalah may be of direct relevance to our modern-day inquiries. The Jewish esoteric tradition connects extrasensory perception in dreams to our
emotional makeup—especially the presence of inner contentment, a calm and lucid mind, and compassion for others.
Whether focusing on the most prophetic dreams or the most
ordinary, the Kabbalists have always regarded this realm of
experience as a potent fountain of understanding. As the
Zohar aptly tells us, "At night, all things return to their
original root and source."[22]

In the next section, we will examine another key Kabbalistic
path to self-growth, namely, the gateway of music. Similar to
dreams, this entrance way within requires only our willing
receptivity and openness to experience.

On Wings of Song

We live in an ocean of sound. For the most part, though, our
upbringing and education in modern society has led us to
ignore its impact upon us. We take for granted or simply
block out many of the sounds in our environment. Yet, psychologists and other investigators have become increasingly
aware of just how powerfully we are all affected by the
sonances around us. Recent research evidence shows that
even before our first day of life outside the womb, we react
with exquisite sensitivity to noises; in countless ways, for
better or worse, our personalities and moods are shaped by
sound. Indeed, whole industries have arisen to provide a
bland, superficially soothing musical cocoon in our supermar-
kets and banks, airports and elevators, office buildings and
restaurants.

But the growing scientific interest in acoustics is hardly a
new development. The ancients were acutely attentive to the

often subtle manner in which sound shapes our behavior. Nearly every culture in the distant past had at least some belief in the efficacy of music as a means of altering our daily frame of mind. The American Indians seemed to have regularly practiced healing rites involving music. Among the Greeks, both Aristotle and Plato ascribed curative strengths to certain types of melodies; in Greek mythology, Apollo was the god of both medicine and of music. Confucius, the great Chinese philosopher, argued that only the superior person who is intimately familiar with the world of song is equipped to govern.

For the Kabbalists and their Jewish precursors, though, sound has been regarded as an unbelievably potent spiritual force. For many centuries, these thinkers have offered fascinating views on the exotic mysteries of music. Sonances, if correctly comprehended and applied, the Kabbalah tells us, can shatter mountains or even the stars, or transport us to the highest reaches of ecstasy.

Almost since its inception four thousand years ago, Judaism has attributed to melody the ability to transform our ordinary perceptions of the universe. During the era of the biblical Prophets, harp players would perform special pieces of music to provoke a mental state in which extrasensory powers were thought to be activated. Thus, for example, the Bible relates, " 'But now bring me a minstrel,' " said Elisha. And it came to pass, 'when the minstrel played, the power of the Lord came upon him.' "[23] In the story of David and Saul, we also see the importance of music as a healing influence. When Saul became the first king of Israel, he apparently suffered from bouts of recurring depression mixed with paranoia. His attendants were quite alarmed and urged him to "seek out a man who is skillful in playing the lyre; and . . . he will play it and you will be well."[24] And so young David was brought to play before King Saul, who subsequently felt much better.

During the long centuries in which the *Merkabah* or "Chariot" approach was favored by Jewish visionaries, sound was accorded a tremendously crucial place in their meditational system. Adepts taught that every sonance has a specific effect on our bodies; consequently, they combined their complex visualization exercises with various hymns and chants. Usually, practitioners also carried out specific bodily postures, such as bowing their heads between their knees to improve concentration. They recited highly repetitive hymns to help loosen their concern with trivial day-to-day thoughts or feelings. These chants, typically intoned in privacy and solitude, were designed to convey a solemn mood and a trance-like state of consciousness. A representative formula from the *Heikhalot* ("Heavenly Halls") literature went as follows:

> Wonderful loftiness and strange dominion
> Loftiness of exaltation and dominion of majesty
> Which come to pass before the throne of glory
> Three times each day in the height
> From the time the world was created and until
>   now for praise[25]

These Hebrew hymns expressed the conviction—central to the later evolution of the Kabbalah—that the entire cosmos is alive with celestial song. The proselyte was also required to voice this next hymn, which was symbolically described as sung by the very angels before the throne of the deity. Like other poetic paeans from this period, it possesses greater power if we recite it aloud:

From the praise and song of each day
From the jubilation and exultation of each hour
And from the utterances which emanate from the mouth[s] of the
    holy ones
And from the melody which wells from the mouth[s] of the servants
Mountains of fire and hills of flame
Are [amassed] and hidden and poured out each day[26]

Interestingly, those on the Jewish esoteric path of this era also insisted that sound has potentially dangerous and even devastating properties. The heavenly songs that permeate the material world are better left unheard for most of us, the *Merkabah* masters explained. For should we become exposed to the awesome harmonies that vibrate through the universe, we would not be able to bear it and would be destroyed instantly. Thus, one fifth-century rabbi commented on the Biblical passage in which the soldiers of Sennacherib's army unsuccessfully tried to beseige Jerusalem (II Kings 19:35), that God "opened their ears and they heard the song of the divine Beasts and died."

The *Sefer Bahir* ("Book of Brilliance") which appeared around 1175 in Provence contains numerous references to sound as a vital force of creation. The anonymous author of this intriguing work declares that the mysteries of the universe were revealed to the knowledgeable through seven "voices." Each of these sonances is described as conveying an almost overpowering sense of the vast and hidden symmetries of the cosmos. In metaphorical terms, the *Bahir* explains, "A King stands before his servants wrapped in white robes. Even though he is far away, they can still hear his voice. This is true even though they cannot see his throat when he speaks."[27] Though the innermost secrets of nature remain elusive, the *Book of Brilliance* indicates, if we understand the meaning of these ordinarily inaudible sounds, we can penetrate veil after veil of mystery.

During the Jewish "Golden Age" in the Iberian world— then under Islamic influence—Kabbalistic and Sufi paths frequently crossed. The Sufis themselves had long studied the effects of music on our bodies, such as by chanting the same tone for a half hour or more and then monitoring closely their internal reactions. Thus, in the thirteenth century, Abraham Abulafia devised special techniques, resembling those of Islamic and Hindu disciplines, for using sound to catapult us into paranormal mental states. Abulafia focused mainly on how to utilize the Hebrew alphabet as a consciousness-altering tool, but he was nevertheless keenly aware of the power of sound over us. In his work, *Closed Garden,* he observed:

> Know thou that the combination of letters can be compared to the listening of music. . . . The proof can be found in the [music] . . . formed by the *kinnor* and *nevel* [Biblical lyres] . . . [which] bring through their vibration sweet sensation to the ear. . . . It is impossible to produce such delights except through . . . music, and the same is true of . . . letters.[28]

For him, musical harmony induces a definite response upon our minds. Not only did he speculate on the meaning of music and its products, but he also laid down specific rules for intoning particular notes and vowel pitches. Typically, his students would voice these sounds while engaged in certain kinds of physical postures resembling hatha yoga. Their goal was to achieve actual psychic abilities, especially the gift of prophecy. One of the chief keys to accomplish this, Abulafia taught, is the correct and repetitive pronunciation of one of the sacred names of the divine. "Never utter the names without concentration," Abulafia advised his disciples, "but sanctify them, know them, and reflect."[29]

With the appearance of the *Zohar* at roughly the same time as Abulafia's treatises, esoteric Jewish thought on music was firmly set into place. The *Book of Splendor,* which soon became the authoritative work of the Kabbalah, is replete with references to sound and its major importance in the cosmos. Among the *Zohar*'s many themes on this subject is that in a very real sense the universe is aflame with the song of every aspect of creation. Not only do the higher celestial creatures sing, we are told; the stars, planets, trees, and animals all voice their melodies before the supreme presence. Few of us are ever gifted enough to discern even the barest echos of this vast harmony, the *Book of Splendor* emphasizes; but with inner devotion, meditation, and the performance of good deeds, we may be sufficiently fortunate to catch at least a fleeting strain sometime in our lives.

No one on earth, the *Zohar* explains, has been fully able to hear this music except for Moses and Joshua. As to the latter, it is alleged that he heard whilst in the midst of fierce battle the melody of the sun and became seriously disturbed—which is why he said, "Sun stand thou still at Gibeon. . . ." meaning "stop singing." In the Israelites' fight against the city of Jericho, the Bible, of course, relates how Joshua used the power of sound as a weapon. He instructs the Israelite army to surround the walled town, make a sevenfold march around it, "while the trumpets blew continually." At that moment, "as soon as the people heard the sound of the great trumpet, they raised a great shout, and the wall fell down flat."[30] Interestingly, scientists today are exploring the capacity of highly focused sound to shatter material forms, and medical researchers are beginning to employ sound as an unbelievably sensitive "cutting" instrument. Perhaps we are not as advanced as many scientists would have us think.

Another prominent idea in the *Zohar* is that song may be capable of expressing profound mysteries of the universe, whereas purely verbal descriptions may fail. Much of creation, the Kabbalah tells us, is absolutely beyond the limits of human vocabulary to express. Despite the Kabbalistic belief in the awesome power of the word, its thinkers have been well aware of its inherent limitations. Thus, in speaking of the higher songs of esoteric knowledge that resound through the cosmos, the *Book of Splendor* states, "Blessed is he who is worthy to perceive such singing, for, as we know and have been taught, he who is deemed worthy to comprehend this song becomes adept in doctrine and obtains wit to discern what has been and what will be."[31]

The *Zohar* goes on to say that David was well aware of this hidden song and was therefore able to compose many inspiring hymns in which he hinted at future events. Solomon, however, was "gifted with a still greater knowledge of that song," and consequently, was able to penetrate into even further spheres of understanding. His *Song of Songs*, we are informed, "contains all the mysteries . . . of wisdom, the song where is power."[32] Indeed, in the Kabbalistic tradition, the *Song of Songs*, seemingly but a beautiful love poem, is actually one of the most potent sources of visionary insight ever put into writing. Diligence and patience are held to be necessary to interpret this work; similar to earlier Jewish esoteric books, the *Zohar* stresses that we should open ourselves up to the celestial melodies only gradually, lest we be shattered.

In the fifteenth century, the Kabbalist Isaac Arama in his treatise, *The Binding of Isaac*, focused specifically on our human relationship to the cosmic balance of sound. He argued that each one of us, through our daily actions, intimately affects the harmony of the whole. Our seemingly most minor acts or even thoughts contribute to either symmetry or discord in the worlds around us. When we are properly "tuned," both mentally and physically, we become perfectly aligned with all the chords of existence, he explained. This alluring viewpoint is found in other spiritual systems, such as Tibetan Buddhism.

During the time up through the early sixteenth century, Kabbalistic beliefs about music remained sheltered from normative Judaism. Practitioners of the esoteric tradition carried out their meditative exercises and hymns in isolation, usually in small groups. They exerted little impact, for the most part, on their fellow Jews, many of whom barely knew that the Kabbalah even existed. But as the Jewish visionary offshoot flowered in the decades after the expulsion from Spain in 1492, Kabbalistic concepts about sound gained increasing influence. Issac Luria, the brilliant spiritual thinker of sixteenth-century Palestine, regarded music as one of the most powerful means of bringing us to higher realms of awareness. Moreover, he insisted that through correct musical intensity, the Jewish people could actively restore their own status in the world and simultaneously end the divine Exile of the *Shekinah* (the female aspect of the deity). Not only did he encourage his disciples to express their dreams and yearnings through music, but he also composed various songs as well.

Every Sabbath eve, Luria and his proselytes would form a procession and dressed in long, flowing white robes, conduct their sacred rituals under the open sky. They sang psalms and played musical instruments, concluding each ceremony with the song *Lekha Dodi* ("Come, My Beloved"); this piece was sung to greet the supposed presence of the *Shekinah* and is still in liturgical existence today. Written by Solomon Alkabez, it was favored by Luria because of both its exalted mood and its poetic rendering of his mentor's bold ideas. Luria's own songs were written in Aramaic and are likewise extant.

One of the most significant composers of the Safed group was Israel Moses Najara (1542–1619). Living in Palestine and Syria, he published his *Songs of Israel* in 1587, perhaps the first such work to appear in print in the Orient. In setting his texts, he either invented his own melodies or freely adapted tunes of Arab, Turkish, Greek, or Spanish origin. Typically, he would rework the melodies to fit the Hebrew text and the traditional Jewish style of singing. This open-minded approach to song, which was well accepted by the Kabbalists of the day, might be compared at present to the borrowing of various pop tunes—rock, jazz, folk or otherwise—and incorporating them for meditational or healing purposes.

Invitation to the Dance

Before long, Najara's exotic compositions and those of his colleagues in Safed were carried throughout the Jewish world. Their songs quickly became integrated into use in the synagogue and provided the Jewish people with renewed fervor. Unquestionably, though, it was the Hasidim nearly two hundred years later who truly raised singing and dancing to a primary spiritual status in the eyes of large numbers of Jews. As true with many other aspects of the classic Kabbalah, the Hasidic founders helped to popularize and make accessible for the masses this compelling feature of the Kabbalistic system. Indeed, the Baal Shem Tov himself, the originator of Hasidism, is said to have viewed music as among the most direct ways that we can all experience the splendors of the universe, regardless of our station in life or degree of formal education. From the very beginning of their mission, the Besht and his disciples had the highest regard for the emotional potency of music.

For the Hasidic masters, every person on earth has his or her own special song that provides a gateway to higher states of consciousness. "Each soul can only ascend to the root of the Source whence she was hewn by means of song,"[33] wrote Rabbi Dov Baer of Lubavitch in his intriguing *Tract on Ecstasy*. Written about 1815 by the grandson of the Lubavitcher sect founder, this work contains specific mention of melody as a force upon our minds and bodies. In it, Rabbi Dov Baer explains that of all the Biblical leaders, Moses alone knew the hidden song to awaken each soul to its full potential; the true spiritual master or *zaddik* is therefore acutely familiar with music and its effects. Furthermore, the Lubavitcher leader comments, each one of us actually comprises a certain "song" of existence—the one by which our innermost Self was created and is defined. Here again, the spiritual adept is able to hear these tunes and thereby help his followers mature to their full capacity.

The early Hasidic teachers particularly valued the unpremeditated quality of music. They recognized its unique power to transform us emotionally; a well-played melody, they observed, can quickly alter a mood of boredom, lethargy, or depression. The most uplifting kinds of music can even transport us beyond our ordinary perceptions of the world, they said. Most importantly, in such instances, we are recalled back to our true awareness of our meaning on earth. Rabbi Dov Baer tells us, "First, it is necessary to understand the nature of ecstasy produced by melody. This is in the category of spontaneous ecstasy . . . without any choice or intellectual will whatsoever."[34] Marveling about our ability to be so thoroughly moved by song, he adds, "There is a total lack of self-awareness,"[35] and therefore, a release from our daily, petty concerns.

In keeping with their conviction that we cannot attain peace and wholeness through our reason alone, the Hasidic masters regarded singing and dancing as key pathways to knowledge of the divine. They rejected the notion that solely through study can we gain comprehension of the universe; in certain aspects of our lives, they insisted, perhaps we can achieve inner completeness through *only* nonverbal means.

Thus, in a characteristic Hasidic parable, one of the great Hasidic teachers noticed that among his listeners was an old man who obviously did not grasp the meaning of the discourse. He summoned the elder to his side and said, "I can see that my words are unclear to you. Listen to this melody. It will lead you to what I have been saying." Thereupon, the Hasidic master began to sing a melody without words. Captivated, the old man slowly replied, "Now I understand what you wish to teach. I feel an intense longing for God." In this instance, the teacher was the renowned Rabbi Schneur Zalman of Liady, founder of the Lubavitcher sect. After this incident, he incorporated the tune in every lecture he gave, though the song contained no words at all.

In another Hasidic tale, a certain teacher was passing through a neighboring town. Having heard of his great wisdom, the elders of the city came to greet him and placed their many personal problems before him. The Hasidic leader listened attentively but said nothing. The elders then decided to assemble in the synagogue and invite him to speak there. Perhaps, they hoped, he might be more responsive in that holy atmosphere. The pious man accepted their invitation, came to the synagogue, and mounted the steps to the podium. He said, "Rather than preach to you and discuss your problems, I will sing you a melody." All became silent. As the *zaddik* sang his tune, each person is said to have suddenly found the strength to solve his own problems.

Indeed, virtually all of the Hasidic founders avidly practiced what they preached concerning the power of music as a healing force in our lives. Many of them were musically talented and composed songs for their congregations. These figures include Rabbi Schneur Zalman of Liady, Rabbi Nachman of Bratslav, and Rabbi Levi Isaac of Beritchev. Each of their songs has a wholly unique style that expresses nonverbally the particular metaphysical outlook of its author. For instance, Rabbi Nachman's work is more emotional and sentimental; Rabbi Schneur Zalman's more serenely meditational. Those leaders unable to compose their own pieces relied upon the services of musicians who interpreted the moods of the *rebbe* precisely.

Central to the entire Hasidic flowering, though, was a firm belief that wordless melodies are the most far-reaching ones. Known as *niggunin*—and numbering today in the several hundreds—they embody the early Hasidic emphasis on songs without texts as the highest form of musical eloquence. The Lubavitcher founder taught, for example, that a melody with words is limited and finite. The tune must end with the conclusion of the text. But a song without words, he declared, can be repeated endlessly—and in that manner, raise us into heights of spiritual ecstasy. "Music has the power to elevate one to prophetic inspiration,"[36] observed one Hasidic teacher. "With song, one can open the gates of heaven."[37]

Like the Kabbalists of the sixteenth century, the Hasidic founders were quite willing to borrow from the songs they heard around them. Many of the most dazzling tunes come from peasant folk songs, military marches, and even romantic love ballads of the time. In one anecdote that sums up well this eclectic attitude, two Hasidic masters were walking along the road and chanced to overhear a shepherd singing on a pasture. The melody was entrancing. "God would not want that to go to waste," one of the Hasidim said, and shaped it for later use by his congregation. Usually, then, these rough folk tunes were recast into a form more relevant to the specific ceremonies of the Hasidic way of life. On nearly all festive occasions and weekly at the Sabbath afternoon meal, singing and dancing were especially prized.

Recent investigators, by analyzing these pieces as still sung by Hasidim today, have begun to identify some of the distinguishing features of the *niggunin*. They have been found to possess a definite musical structure. In their article, "The Hasidic Dance-*Niggun*," published in 1974 in the Israeli musical journal *Yuval*, Yaacov Mazor and André Hadju of Jerusalem comment, "The musically sensitive Hasid is aware of the concept of organic unity in a *niggun*, and apprehends both with his senses and with his reasoning faculty."[38] Each part of the overall song, moreover, corresponds to a special method of approach to the divine and also expresses a certain mood.

It is intriguing how the Hasidic emphasis on the wordless melody and its uncanny power upon our minds has striking parallels in other spiritual traditions. The ancient Hindus apparently subscribed to this same viewpoint. The modern-day Hindu poet Tagore thus reports that, "In the classic style of Hindustan the words are of no account, and leave the melody to make its appeal in its own way."[39]

For the early Hasidic leaders, vigorous bodily movement was also prized as a means to step outside the confines of our ordinary frame of mind into reaches of joy. The Baal Shem Tov is said to have prayed with such vitality that every part of his body shook in all directions simultaneously. Several of his original disciples actually encouraged their own minions to turn somersaults while praying. It is extraordinary that at the same time the religious sect known as the "Shakers" emerged in England and later flourished in the United States; the Shakers practiced a peculiar rolling exercise which consisted of doubling the head and feet together, and rolling like a hoop. They echoed the Hasidic teaching that such bodily activities bring us closer to a unity with the divine. The Besht himself is attributed as saying, "Just as no child can be born except through joy and desire, so it is with study and prayer. When performed with joy and delight, then do they give birth."[40] Eventually, though, the intense rhythmic swaying during Hasidic prayer and meditation was downplayed, to appease their caustic opponents among the rabbinate, the *Mitnaggedim.*

However, the original emphasis of the Hasidic founders on the transformative strength of dancing remains part of the tradition today. During celebrations, singing and dancing are still practiced with great exuberance. In an interesting article entitled, "Music, My Hasidic Adventure," which appeared in the October 1974 issue of *East West Journal*, Joseph Haleri describes his powerful experience while observing a holiday festivity at the Lubavitcher sect's main meeting hall in New York City. He writes:

> He [the rebbe] smiled and then began to sing. . . . He began slowly—a melody with no words—a melody that didn't need words as they'd only detract from the emotional intensity. . . . Little by little both the song and his swaying body began to pick up speed. Minutely at first, but then faster and faster, the audience matching him exactly all the while. Before I knew it, the same song with the same melody became a shout of such joy and ecstasy that I found myself jumping and swaying with everyone else . . . The *Rebbe*'s face was transformed; it was all aglow with vitality. He was invoking all the ecstasy in the

universe. I felt like Ulysses listening to the song of the Sirens. . . .

Who cared about studying or earning a living, or death or anything at that point. The song was important—the ecstasy was all.[41]

Today, the healing professions are increasingly recognizing this unique power of music upon us. In the last twenty-five years or so, the field of music therapy has grown to impressive stature. The ability of sound to heal both our minds and bodies is becoming more and more apparent. Especially with severely impaired children, such as those with neurological conditions like autism, music is proving to be a highly effective tool for learning and rehabilitation. Some children will respond to music though not to spoken or written communication; something in the sonances they hear somehow evokes in them a desire for human warmth and relationship. As one therapist put it, "Children are willing to listen to music while they may be impervious to words."[42]

The capacity of music to affect our daily consciousness is likewise being corroborated by contemporary investigators. Around the globe, musicians and therapists are utilizing sound as a powerful means of combating depression and altering our very perceptions of ourselves and the cosmos. In their interesting article in the Summer 1972 issue of the *Journal of Music Therapy*, Helen L. Bonny and Walter Pahnke relate in "The Use of Music in Psychedelic (LSD) Psychotherapy" how sonances have been incorporated into medical programs for patients with alcoholism, drug addiction, and terminal cancer. For such persons, music has been found to help release pent-up feelings of frustration and self-pity, and even sometimes trigger what Abraham Maslow calls "peak experiences." Combining recordings of specific pieces of music with mood-changing substances in a highly controlled setting, therapists find that their patients often report dramatic and beneficial shifts in their self-image—and their attitudes about life as a whole. As one patient commented, "I had a feeling that everything in the Universe fit together and there was some sort of higher order to everything."[43]

In a follow-up article entitled, "Music and Consciousness," published in the same Journal in 1975, Ms. Bonny dealt more extensively with the power of sound to effect such self-transformative changes. In a technique that bears amazing resemblance to classic Kabbalistic methods, she describes how we may unite visual imagery in meditation with music to produce enhanced emotional well-being and induce new directions for our own development within. In his book, *Tuning the Human Instrument* (Spectrum Research Institute: 1979), Dr. Steven Halpern likewise focused at length on the specific ways in which music may stimulate our highest creative impulses. He has composed and recorded works designed to this end. Many other persons are now active in this fascinating endeavor.

Echoing sentiments that pervade the Jewish mystical tradition, the statesman and artist Jean Paderewski observed, "Wherever Life is, Music is also; she lives in the earth's seismic heavings, in the mighty motion of the planets, in the hidden conflict of inflexible atoms; she is in all the lights, in all the colors that dazzle or soothe our eyes; she is in the blood of our arteries, in every pain, every passion of ecstasy that shakes our hearts."[44]

CHAPTER SEVEN

THE DIMENSION BEYOND

"Each individual is bound to everyone else, and no man is counted separately."
—Rabbi Moses Chaim Luzzatto

"There is a rising series of the intimations by which deeper knowledge is conveyed to men—dreams forming one grade, vision another, and prophecy a third . . . in a rising series."
—the Zohar

THE JEWISH TRADITION is widely regarded today as one which has spawned some of the greatest minds of Western civilization in such fields as mathematics, physics, and astronomy. Yet, its Kabbalistic side has always maintained a lively interest in the paranormal. To those who equate Judaism solely with its rationalistic emphasis, it may come as quite a revelation to discover that for centuries it has also embraced such intriguing phenomena as clairvoyance, telepathy, trance mediumship, spiritual healing, and prophecy.

Persons currently interested in these and related issues can find in the Kabbalah a long and venerated history of serious inquiry on such matters. Not only has Judaism been avidly concerned with this fascinating realm, but some of its intellectual giants have devoted considerable attention to it. In fact, foremost scholars of their time, men like Joseph Karo and Elijah Gaon of Vilna, were themselves said to possess striking talents in this area. They regarded their own extrasensory experiences as linked, from one generation to the next, back to the very founders of the Jewish people.

Thus, the Kabbalists have typically credited the major Biblical figures with psychic abilities. Works such as the *Zohar* portray them as having attained the special knowledge necessary to awaken the unusual powers latent in us all. This learning the Kabbalah has generally viewed as deliberately concealed, passed down from one age's spiritual masters to the next. Hence, we are metaphorically told, "God did indeed send down a book to Adam, from which he became acquainted with the supernal wisdom. It came later into the hands of the 'sons of God,' the wise of their generation, and whoever was privileged to peruse it could learn supernal wisdom."[1] Later, the *Book of Splendor* informs us that in the midst of this book was a secret writing which explained the hundreds of keys to "higher mysteries."

Besides mentioning Adam, the *Zohar* explicitly names such biblical characters as Enoch, Noah, Abraham, Joseph, Moses, Joshua, King David and King Solomon, and the Prophets, as having gained access to this body of advanced knowledge. Once uncovered and then correctly understood—by no means a simple matter, the Kabbalah stresses—it would enable the practitioner to wield a myriad of powers that normally lie dormant within us. Moreover, the higher the person's spiritual attainment, the greater his or her ability to develop the talents to their full potential.

Consequently, as the founder of the Jewish people, Abraham has characteristically been depicted as a brilliant psychic by the various Kabbalistic writings. His prophetic dreams and visions are said to have flowed directly from his heightened awareness of the divine in everyday life. He was able to assess all the upper powers that guide the world "in all realms of the inhabited section," the *Zohar* states. Furthermore, "he eventually penetrated into the Divine Wisdom and united himself with his Divine Master after he had duly prepared himself by a life of pious deeds."[2] As a direct result of his many years of piety, Abraham is thus said to have achieved extrasensory states of knowledge.

Similarly, the Jewish esoteric tradition describes prophetic figures such as Daniel and Ezekial as having attained clairvoyance and precognition through their long·spiritual practice and devotion. That is, the Kabbalah regards their inspiring messages to our still conflicted world as genuine paranormal visions and not simply as poetic commentaries on the human condition. When individually they evolved to a certain level of awareness, the Kabbalah indicates, the biblical Prophets achieved their powers—even if they were not conscious of the process as it was occurring before the full-blown psychic state was manifested.

In keeping with this view, the Kabbalists have considered the prophetic realm of consciousness as one which any of us may aspire to and possibly reach. It is *not* restricted to the ancient times. However—and on this the Kabbalah has been very emphatic—very definite efforts are necessary beforehand. In addition, this phenomenon has been seen to encompass specific mental and even physical changes within the practitioner. It is far from a matter of simply sitting down and pondering about the future, we are told. Succinctly explaining this notion, the eighteenth-century Italian poet and mystic Moses Chaim Luzzatto observed, "When a revelation comes, his [the initiate's] senses cease to function and he loses all consciousness."[3] While one is in such a trance, certain visions then become apparent, Rabbi Luzzatto continued. Through such inspiration, we can then become aware of things that lie outside the realm of human rationality. "These include hidden [mysteries] as well as future events."[4] Interestingly, Rabbi Luzzatto here was not merely speaking in abstract terms. He was a trance medium himself since early manhood.

Typically, then, the Kabbalists have regarded the prophetic state—their name for a variety of parapsychological experiences—as one radically different from our ordinary frame of mind. Indeed, this altered state of awareness is virtually incompatible with our daily, limited perception of the world, the Kabbalah insists. The goal is to hold back or suspend our day-to-day, mundane concerns—such as worrying about work or bills—to allow our higher Self to take over. When this event occurs, the Kabbalists explain, our normal sensory channels are temporarily turned off and our extrasensory faculties become awakened.

Furthermore, we are advised that this is no impossible objective for us to achieve. Rather, the unfolding of this process is deemed a basic human potential. In fact, the *Zohar* gently relates that in the days of Enoch, even young children were knowledgeable about these mysterious arts. However, we must be patient and willing to progress one step at a time. "Before they [people] can reach this [state], they need much guidance, each one according to his degree of preparation."[5]

In the Jewish mystical tradition, the individual who most fully realized his innate potential was Moses. More than any other biblical leader or prophet, he was able to tune in fully to extrasensory forms of knowledge, we are told. The *Book of Splendor* and other key texts praise him repeatedly as a kind of superman in humanity's efforts to evolve beyond our normal mental constraints. For several reasons, the Kabbalists differentiate Moses from all the other biblical figures; in so doing, these sources also shed light on esoteric Jewish beliefs about paranormal experiences in general.

Thus, for instance, Rabbi Luzzatto comments that not only was Moses able to experience prophecy while wide awake and in a normal state of consciousness, but he could also "voluntarily initiate a prophetic vision . . . at will."[6] The other prophets, the Italian Kabbalist indicates, were neither wholly aware during their experiences nor always capable of directing them. The *Zohar* stated this same view centuries earlier, with its usual bold and striking imagery:

> Moses was separated by many degrees from all the other prophets, who bore the same relation to him as an ape to a human being. Other prophets beheld visions in a glass that did not illumine, and even so they did not venture to lift up their eyes

and gaze above . . . nor was their message given to them in clear terms. Moses raised his head without fear and gazed at the brightness of the supernal glory without losing his senses like the other prophets.[7]

Elsewhere, the *Book of Splendor* poetically relates that Moses gazed with lucidity into the mirror of prophecy, whereas all the other prophets looked into a cloudy surface. In short, both in the clarity and depth of his vision, he was unsurpassed in the eyes of the Kabbalists.

In contemporary psychological language, they regarded Moses' psychic states as occurring without any interference from his own daily ego. In contrast, the paranormal experiences of the others were affected or even distorted by their own desires or wishes for the future. "Because of the nature of Moses' vision," Rabbi Luzzatto comments, "the information that he received was both clear and voluminous. In this respect also, Moses exceeded all other[s]."[8]

Interestingly, psychologists today have discovered that even the simplest and most unemotional scenes we remember are colored by our own thoughts and feelings. The more complex events that we witness firsthand become clouded even more by our prior expectations or beliefs. For instance, as mentioned in Chapter 5, when playing cards with slight errors built into them are shown experimentally, most people do not even notice the alterations. Turning to less measurable parapsychological experiences, researchers similarly believe that the information received becomes shaped by our unconscious wishes. Thus the Kabbalah's description of Moses seems to make sense. For of all the biblical leaders—and despite his flaws and errors of judgment—only the prophet of Mt. Sinai was egoless enough to allow his visions to flow in complete wholeness, we are informed. Therefore, he did not have to be deprived of his senses or lose ordinary consciousness in order to experience prophecy.

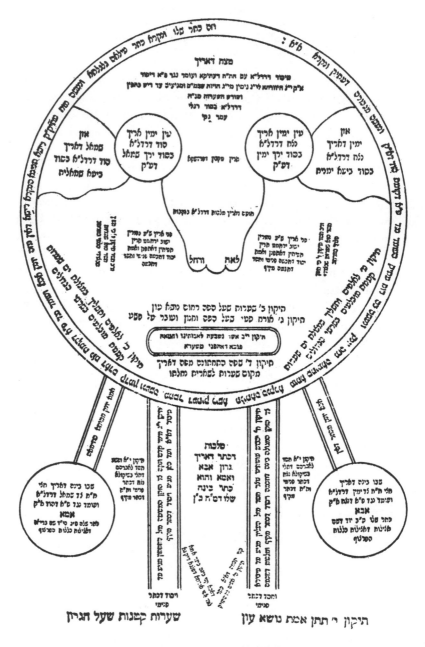

Detail from the Lurianic system (Poland, 19th century).

Psychic Explorers in the Modern Jewish Era

Consistent with their belief in the accessibility of paranormal phenomena, in more-recorded times many Jewish visionaries have been described as psychic by their peers, or have deliberately tried to cultivate extrasensory powers. For the most part, though, they regarded their quest as subordinate to the larger goal of a closer unity with the divine. For instance, Abraham Abulafia in the thirteenth century wrote many manuals on how to attain the prophetic gift. He believed that it involves conscious learning, though a great deal of patience and discipline are also necessary. "Study the Sages of blessed memory with a clear and alert mind," he advised. "Gaze with divine intelligence into the works of the Kabbalists. . . . By means of these God will answer when you call upon Him."[9] As we have seen in Chapter 4, Abulafia specifically recommended permutations of the Hebrew alphabet as a technique to alter our daily consciousness and heighten the development of powers beyond the physical senses. Like those before him, Abulafia above all believed that such talents depend upon spiritual devotion. "It is well known that those who love prophecy love God and they are beloved of God,"[10] Abulafia commented. The connection, he felt, was clear.

In the sixteenth century, the Safed community in Palestine boasted several figures renowned for possessing extrasensory abilities. The most famous of these was Isaac Luria, who influenced the course of Judaism for centuries. His disciples credited him with clairvoyance, precognition, and the ability to "read" people's alleged past lives by interpreting auras he saw around them. Chaim Vital, his chief scribe and protégé, was not fascinated merely by the Jewish tradition concerning such phenomena, but he also regularly consulted mediums, psychics, and healers of every faith. In his intriguing book, *Joseph Karo, Lawyer and Mystic* (Jewish Publication Society: 1977), Professor R. J. Zwi Werblowsky of The Hebrew University comments that Vital's "autobiographical *Book of Visions* abounds with reports of visits to soothsayers, palmists, and oil-readers."[11]

In his writings, Chaim Vital gave careful attention to what we today would call parapsychology. He too was convinced that any person could attain higher powers, if manifesting the right spiritual integrity, preparation, and attitude. For him, the various stages of nonordinary modes of knowledge are to be approached methodically, in a step-by-step fashion of inner development. In this way, the potentially devastating mental and physical dangers involved—such as madness or actual death—can be held safely to a minimum. Like his teachers before him, he believed that to attempt to alter our normal ways of experiencing the world is not a task to be undertaken lightly. Chaim Vital also distinguished those psychic states in which the initiate is self-aware from those where lucidity falters. He cogently wrote:

> There are two different kinds of prophecy. a) The prophecy whose feat ... is like a trance. ... Light flows downward into the rational soul and is drawn into the animal soul where it becomes shaped into projections of the five inner senses. ... This kind of prophecy is called "dream," but we do not mean actual dream, but rather a "trance." b) The second prophecy is a perfect [one] in which the senses are not overwhelmed, where it all assumes its proper shape and this is the prophecy of the quality of Moses.[12]

Furthermore, Luria's influential disciple observed that our capacity to experience in full scale such higher states is molded by both our intellectual and bodily vitality. The healthier we are within, the greater the vistas that stretch before us. We must maintain our daily mental activities as well as physical strength, therefore, in order to climb the metaphorical Tree of Life in Vital's approach. "Thus you will understand why there are so many levels of prophecy," he explained. "The number of these levels is infinite."[13] This notion echoes the view set forth in the *Zohar* that every degree of elevated consciousness ultimately rests upon the quality of our daily frame of mind. For all depends on the type of speech, action, and intention to which we habituate ourselves, the *Book of Splendor* often declares.

Vital prescribed certain specific meditational exercises for awakening our psychic faculties, besides stressing the importance of everyday activity. His techniques involve the use of the imagination for visualizing each of the ten *Sefirot* in interplay with one another. As detailed in Chapter 4, the initiate learns to raise and exalt the divine light that flows through the *Sefirotic* system. Then, the adept draws the light back down, in a reverse process; in so doing, the energy centers within the human body are said to be activated. We must exert strong willpower in this practice, as "the desire to be raised to the higher levels ... opens the channel for the influence of thoughts to be attained as well as the intelligence being attained,"[14] Chaim Vital indicates. Intriguingly, other spiritual traditions like Yoga and Tibetan Buddhism similarly emphasize visualization in the mind's eye as a way to paranormal abilities.

Another important member of the Safed community who delved into the realm of extrasensory phenomena was Joseph Karo, a fascinating figure. The most influential Jewish legalist of his time—with an impact exerted through the present on Judaic law—Karo regularly experienced trance mediumistic states for nearly fifty years. In his secret diary, *Maggid Mesharim*, whose authenticity is beyond question today, he recorded the discourses of his *maggid*, or what he and his contemporaries regarded as an independent entity speaking through his lips. The historical evidence suggests that while alone (for occasionally the diary reports the abrupt cessation of the *maggid's* speech due to the sudden entry of strangers), Karo would spontaneously enter into this paranormal state.

Characteristically, Karo would retain awareness of what was happening as his voice would alter and its tone and rhythm drastically change. Without any conscious volition on his part, rational speech of an exotic nature would issue from his mouth. Claiming to be the spirit of the *Mishnah* (the Jewish holy book of biblical commentary), this secondary personality or *maggid* would speak on a wide range of esoteric topics—from analyzing the nature of higher consciousness and reincarnation to voicing actual prophecies.

Strikingly, as Professor Werblowsky notes in his book on Karo, some of these predictions actually came true. Moreover, this well-documented case of sixteenth-century trance mediumship bears intriguing parallels to similar phenomena studied by modern-day investigators. For instance, at the turn of the twentieth century, William James spent years researching the abilities of Mrs. Lenora Piper and concluded that orthodox science could not explain some of her talents. At present, Jane Roberts has published several books of wide appeal (*Seth Speaks, The Nature of Personal Reality*, etc.) in which she has recorded the dictations of what claims to be her spirit-guide or *maggid*. Several decades ago, the well-known psychic Edgar Cayce displayed a similar talent—and by now, the list of such persons in our own era is quite long indeed. Whatever the ultimate nature of this enigmatic phenomenon—and parapsychologists have no certain answers as yet—Joseph Karo's experience fits remarkably well with the pattern currently studied.

Not only did this brilliant Talmudic scholar accurately recall his *maggidic* revelations immediately after each experience, but he waited several hours before recording them. That is, most of the entries in his diary were communicated on Friday nights; to avoid profaning the Sabbath by writing, Karo wrote down the messages on the following night. Historically, few trance mediums have been able to assimilate their altered states of mind as easily as this. Indeed, Karo's unimpaired health and physical stamina, coupled with the intellectual rigor that he exhibited undimmed until his death at age eighty-seven, make his unusual psychological experiences quite compelling to us today. They also defy facile dismissal in view of this legalist's tremendous outpour of detailed, logical interpretations of Jewish law.

Interestingly, Karo's *maggid* offered its own explanation of how this baffling phenomenon worked: the more successful the individual in suspending the daily, conscious mind, the more easily a channel is thereby created through which extrasensory knowledge may enter. The accuracy of the information, in turn, depends on the completeness of this complex process.

"If you find occasionally that what I teach you is not quite correct," the *maggid* declared, "there may be wandering thoughts in your mind that interfere and these cause that not all my words [i.e., prophecies] come true . . . they also cause me to stammer and prevent me from revealing you everything."[15] It is compelling that Jane Roberts's "Seth" personality similarly states, "I project a portion of my reality as I dictate this book. . . . There are many manipulations necessary and psychological adjustments."[16]

Jewish historians are now finding more and more evidence of the pervasiveness of the *maggidic* phenomenon in Judaism's esoteric tradition. For example, not only was Karo's *maggid* not held in particular awe among fellow Kabbalists at Safed, but colleagues like Chaim Vital apparently viewed Karo as only a so-so medium. Vital believed that the quality of such paranormal communications related to the medium's own spirituality and indeed, Karo himself seemed to have hoped for a higher *maggid* to impart wholly accurate prophecies.

One martyred Kabbalist whom he admired very much in this respect was Solomon Molkho. Burned to death by the Inquisition in 1532, Molkho had precisely predicted such events as the overflow of the Tiber in 1530 and the great earthquake in Lisbon in 1531. Another of Karo's peers was Rabbi Joseph Taytazak who likewise was reputed to have psychic abilities, transmitted through automatic or spontaneous writing. The two men carried on an active correspondence on both Kabbalistic and mainstream aspects of Judaism.

In the eighteenth century, a major Kabbalist who regularly experienced trance mediumistic states was Rabbi Moses Chaim Luzzatto. Best known for his classical work on piety, *Mesillat Yesharim* ("Path of the Just"), in the 1730s and 1740s he wrote many treatises on esoteric psychology. While still a young man and unmarried, he succeeded in gathering round him a circle of followers in Italy. At the age of twenty his paranormal experiences apparently began. In a letter written about 1729 to a sympathetic friend, he reported:

> As I was performing a certain *yihud* [meditational exercise], I fell into a trance. When I awoke, I heard a voice saying: "I have descended in order to reveal the hidden secrets of the Holy King." For a while I stood there trembling . . . but the voice did not cease from speaking. . . . At the same time on the second day, I saw to it that I was alone in the room and the voice came again to impart a further secret to me. One day he revealed to me that he was a *maggid* sent from heaven.[17]

Like earlier Jewish mystics, Rabbi Luzzatto emphatically warned that such experiences are not to be pursued without the aid of a trained and knowledgeable guide. Perhaps he was speaking from his own experiments when he wrote in *The Way of God* that those who prepare themselves for prophecy must first learn various specific disciplines. Especially important, he stressed, is the guidance of an experienced prophet along each step of the way. This type of admonition seems central to many other spiritual traditions. The celebrated Italian visionary also provided a terse but evocative description of his particular *maggidic* phenomenon. In this same letter, he related that, "Souls whose identity I do not know are also revealed to me. I write down the new ideas each of them imparts to me. All these things happen while I am prostrate with my face to the ground and I see the holy souls in human form as in a dream."[18]

The Hasidim and the Paranormal

Several decades later, Jewish interest in the paranormal became closely intertwined with the new Hasidic movement that arose in Eastern Europe. While its early leaders did not emphasize the psychic world per se, they did stress the importance of the nonrational as a valid approach to the divine. In their belief that Talmudic study in itself was no sure path to higher consciousness, they adopted a tolerant attitude toward a wide range of extrasensory phenomena. Indeed, the Hasidic founder, Israel ben Eliezer, was regarded in his own lifetime as an awesome miracle worker with talents in virtually every aspect of paranormal ability. Even before he became acclaimed as the Baal Shem Tov—the charismatic spiritual guide for thousands of followers in villages and hamlets—he was known locally as a healer and clairvoyant. While it is nearly impossible today to separate fact from fiction in the countless tales that surround his exciting life, common themes do run through these stories. In this manner, they highlight Kabbalistic beliefs about certain specific psychic powers.

For instance, in several anecdotes the Baal Shem Tov meets with a supplicant who seeks the master's aid. Either simultaneously with or soon after speaking with the Besht, the individual finds that the desired event has occurred. In contemporary terms, this process is related to the phenomenon called *psychokinesis* and refers to mind over matter. In other incidents, the Hasidic founder is said to have correctly predicted specific happenings to befall people he meets—pointing to the power of precognition. Other stories recount how the Baal Shem Tov was able to accurately describe the history behind objects that he beheld for the first time—a phenomenon which parapsychologists term *psychometry.*

In one such anecdote, the Besht visits at a friend's house but is unable to sleep. When questioned by his puzzled friend the next morning, the Baal Shem Tov explains that he perceived that the man who had crafted the bed did so while in great sorrow. Consequently, his feelings or "vibrations" remained as a psychic residue around the wood and kept the Besht awake. What is fascinating about this sort of story is that it parallels closely the descriptions offered today by equally psychic persons. This type of intuition has been studied in recent years by scientific investigators; in his book, *The Medium, the Mystic, and the Physicist* (Viking: 1974) Dr. Lawrence LeShan devotes detailed attention to this precise phenomenon.

As the Hasidic movement spread, many of its leading figures were likewise credited with paranormal abilities. These illustrious teachers included Rabbi Dov Baer of Mezritch (the *Maggid*), Rabbi Schneur Zalman of Liady—founder of the Lubavitcher sect flourishing today—and Rabbi Nachman of Bratslav. As true with the tales that encircle their mentor, it is not easy for us now to accurately distinguish truth from embellishment. Nevertheless, some of these stories do help parallel current documentation in this interesting field.

For example, in one anecdote Rabbi Jacob Samson of Spitovka one day in 1791 suddenly saw a vision: the *Shekinah* (the female component of the deity) appeared to him in the form of a bitterly weeping woman. Rabbi Jacob Samson thereupon cried with grief that his friend Rabbi Pinchas of Koretz had just died. Weeks later, the news came that his colleague had indeed passed on at the exact date. The mourning Hasid explained that he had interpreted the symbol of the lamenting woman to represent the celestial reaction to his friend's demise.

Here again, contemporary speculation on extrasensory perception is strikingly predated by centuries of Kabbalistic thought. The prevailing theory today is that in such psychic phenomena—just as in our more ordinary mental affairs—our unconscious mind works by use of symbols. It is little known as yet, for instance, that Freud himself advanced this hypothesis to explain seemingly paranormal events he encountered with his patients, commenting that "Psychoanalysis may do something to advance the study of telepathy."[19]

The type of example often cited by investigators is of a man who, say, has a vivid daydream of a bird being hurled out of the sky by a falling object. The individual dismisses the apparently nonsensical vision, only to learn hours later that his wife, known affectionately as "Birdie," was hit by a truck as she crossed a street—at the exact moment of her husband's daydream. Freud's disciple Carl Jung was also convinced of the importance of symbols in our integration of Self in our lives. He helped his patients pinpoint and understand the symbols contained in their thoughts and dreams, paranormal or otherwise.

One prominent Hasidic master who was particularly renowned for his clairvoyant abilities was Rabbi Jacob Isaac of Lublin, popularly referred to as the "Seer." In his own lifetime, he was celebrated for his paranormal talents by followers who journeyed from far-off towns for spiritual "readings" and healings. Intriguingly, the half-legendary biographical information about him indicates that he was hardly ecstatic about his unusual talents as a young man. In fact, he sought to eliminate them and viewed them as something of a curse, declaring that they detracted from his love for humanity. Only later, under the careful guidance of older Hasidic teachers, did he come to accept his psychic gift and make use of it in his rabbinical work.

Indeed, as the Hasidic movement took root in the late eighteenth century, large numbers of its adherents began to place more and more importance on the manifestation of such powers. Many Jews were simply not able to meet the spiritual rigors demanded by the Hasidic founders, however gentle their message. Consequently, the role of the *zaddik* changed. No longer venerated merely for his piety, this intermediary between the earthly and the divine came to be increasingly associated with almost superhuman abilities. Nearly every small cluster of Hasidim boasted of the miraculous capabilities of its local *zaddik*, and eventually, neighboring communities would vie for the fame and honor of having a wonder-working rabbi as their leader. Some *zaddikim* no doubt encouraged their followers to spread such tales, but others viewed this element in the Hasidic swelling of ranks with alarm. They felt that psychic powers were of only secondary significance next to the spiritual development of each human being.

It is fascinating that the esteemed Elijah Gaon of Vilna— the titular chief of opposition to the Hasidim in Lithuania— was said to be quite gifted in the realm of parapsychology. The most acclaimed Talmudic scholar and teacher of his day, he was fiercely opposed to the Hasidic view. Yet, he was certainly no rationalist hostile to the Kabbalah's allure. Historians have often made this error in interpreting his battle with his foes. Actually, the Gaon of Vilna readily acknowledged the existence of extrasensory powers. Moreover, he appears to have regularly experienced paranormal states, including *maggidic* phenomena, for many years. What he objected to, it seems, was what he regarded as the Hasidic over-reliance on nonsensory forms of knowledge—such as gleaned through intense meditation—to the exclusion of traditional Torah study.

Thus, one of his closest disciples and a fellow Talmudist of fame reported in an account first published in 1820, "I heard from his holy mouth that many times *maggidim* from Heaven appeared to him, requesting to deliver unto him the mysteries of Torah without any effort, but he would not harken unto them. . . . When one of the maggidim insisted very much, . . . he answered, 'I do not want my understanding of the Torah to be mediated [by others].' "[20]

Either consciously or unconsciously paralleling Joseph Karo's stance more than two hundred years earlier, the Gaon of Vilna refused to be swayed in his interpretations of Jewish law by his own unusual, mediumistic experiences. Although he conceded their potential value, he advised his disciples not to depend on such phenomena or seek shortcuts to the divine. Furthermore, he stressed, such experiences were almost by their very nature often misleading. Therefore, "the important achievement," the Gaon of Vilna declared, "is what a man acquires in this world through his labor and efforts."[21] Consequently, he explained to his followers that they should heed only those psychic phenomena that complemented the information gained from their daily spiritual activity.

Interestingly, the Gaon of Vilna emphasized the higher nature of dreams as one permissible gateway and commented that "God created sleep to this end only, that man should attain the insights that he cannot attain . . . when the soul is joined to the body; [for] . . . during sleep . . . the soul is out of the body and clothed in a supernal garment."[22]

It was not long before the Hasidic masters themselves began to accent similar cautions about not attaching too much importance to extrasensory experiences per se. No doubt, they too were uneasy with the tremendous emphasis their supporters had come to place on the superhuman aspects of the *zaddik*'s role in community life. The Hasidic leaders therefore insisted ever more explicitly that psychic powers should not be pursued for their own sake; they were ends not means. For even the *Zohar* had stated, "It is a dictum of our teachers that a man should not rely on miracles."[23] Moreover, such phenomena were to be viewed dispassionately and taken in stride when they occurred. If an individual underwent a genuine paranormal experience, then he or she should thank the Maker and then go about life as usual, the Hasidic teachers preached.

Thus, in one parable that has come down to us, several Hasidim were recounting the many miracles that the *zaddikim* were reported to be performing. Their rabbi, listening patiently, suddenly declared, "The more miracles are attributed to the *zaddikim*, the more the ground is prepared for deception by ... charlatans."[24] Another Hasidic master, Rabbi Baruch of Medziboz, commented in a similar situation, "How utterly useless they [miracles] are! When Elijah performed miracles, we are told that the people exclaimed, 'The Lord is God.' But nowadays, the people grow enthusiastic over the reputed miracle-worker and forget entirely to say: 'The Lord is God.' "[25]

Strikingly, this same attitude toward paranormal abilities is common to several other spiritual disciplines, such as Hinduism and Tibetan Buddhism. These Oriental paths to knowledge have for centuries downplayed the significance of special talents in our day-to-day inward evolution. For instance, John Blofeld in *The Tantric Mysticism of Tibet* (Causeway: 1974) observes, "Marked progress in spiritual communion brings with it what are generally termed psychic powers, of which telepathy is the most common. Adepts are warned against cultivating such powers for their own sake or deliberately using them except in cases of dire emergency."[26] Similarly, Lama Govinda in *The Way of the White Clouds* (Shambhala: 1970) comments that, "In the original system of Buddhist meditation the attainment of [psychic] power is a mere by-product and is looked upon rather as a danger than as a stimulus on the higher path, which aims at liberation and abhors the exhibition of occult forces."[27]

The parallels between the Kabbalistic and Eastern approach to this whole subject are compelling indeed. In the archetypal tale, Buddha was accosted beside a river by a monk. The man exclaimed that he had spent the past decade, day after day, intensely practicing how to cross the river by levitation. Today he had finally accomplished the task! To this, the Buddha calmly replied, "What a pity! You could have taken the ferry ten years ago."

The corresponding Hasidic parable likewise takes place against a backdrop of water and boat. Rabbi Schneur Zalman of Liady was crossing a river on ferry at night. He suddenly spied the crescent of the new moon in the sky and asked the captain to stop the boat briefly so that the prayer for the new moon might be said. The captain politely refused. Within seconds, the ship stopped as if rooted on an iceberg. Then, after a few more seconds, it began to move again. When Rabbi Schneur Zalman repeated his request, this time the captain, obviously shaken, agreed. Why hadn't the Hasidic founder simply kept the ferry stationary the first time? Rabbi Joseph Isaac, his descendant, explained that to do so would have been to needlessly display a paranormal capability. Hence, the great Hasid "asked the man to have the boat stopped by human, natural means."[28]

CHAPTER EIGHT

LIFE AND DEATH: THE IMMORTAL SOUL

"Each spark descended into this world—indeed a profound descent and a state of true exile—to be clothed in a body and vital soul . . . so as to join and unite them with the Light."

—Rabbi Schneur Zalman of Liady

"This world is like the shore and the World to Come like the sea."

—Rabbi Moses Chaim Luzzatto

FOR JEWISH MYSTICS, with their fundamental belief in the divine mission of each person on earth, we are confronted continually with glimpses of our transcendence. Whatever our station in life, every one of us is inextricably related to the furthest reaches of the ultimate Essence, the *Ein Sof* ("Infinite"). For us even to exist as separate points of being, some of the awesome quality of the Light must be withdrawn, the Kabbalah teaches. But the seeming absence of this illumination is merely an illusion; through inner growth, we are told, we become increasingly aware of the intensity and splen-

185

dor of the Source that animates us. "The *neshamah* [spiritual aspect] of man," writes Rabbi Schneur Zalman of Liady, "naturally desire[s] and yearn[s] to separate from the body in order to unite with its origin ... the fountainhead of all life."[1] In meditation and prayer, in response to people around us, and in the simplest tasks of daily living, we may feel the reality of a world beyond the senses. In such moments—which psychologist Abraham Maslow aptly referred to as "peak experiences"—we are suddenly reminded of our true nature.

Yet, the Kabbalists have hardly subscribed to a blindly optimistic view of human nature.They have certainly been realists enough to be quite familiar with the almost ceaseless stream of day-to-day diversions and petty annoyances that can make us lose sight of our higher aspects. Indeed, they have emphasized that the sensation of being "trapped" in the mundaneness of ordinary things is a dangerous emotion, to be vigorously fought. For once this feeling starts to take over, it can lead to despair and the abandonment of all inner purpose. Hence, they have identified the recognition of *Divine Providence*, as they have called it, as a key guide for helping us to maintain direction in our lives.

The Jewish visionary tradition explains this phenomenon as encompassing events in our daily lives that are in some way uncanny, startling, or unbelievably coincidental so as to serve as clear signposts for us along the way. Such incidents can exert a tremendous force over the everyday world that lifts our routine frame of mind out of its doldrums. By remaining open and receptive to happenings around us, we become alert to such occurrences, the Kabbalists have stressed. Thus, for instance, Rabbi Luzzatto observed that there are many different reasons for everything that occurs to an individual in this world, for good or otherwise. "The Highest Wisdom," he noted, "perceives and knows what is best to rectify all creation."[2] Because everything that exists is in constant interplay, each element of the cosmos moves in correspondence to all others. As seen in Chapter 2, this notion of a universal harmony is central to the Jewish mystical way.

As we therefore gain in our own understanding of the cosmos, we can more easily read the pattern which lies behind outward events. We begin to see the common threads that bind seemingly unrelated occurrences. Whereas before we saw merely apparent chaos or misfortune—what Shakespeare's Hamlet bemoaned as the "slings and arrows of outrageous fortune"—now we perceive a unity. Rabbi Luzzatto gives such examples as that of a man whose cow broke its foot and fell, thereupon causing the irate owner to find a buried treasure. Also, he recounts the anecdote—familiar to many of us through our own lives—of a person who wants to embark on a trip and is suddenly detained, only to learn later that the fated journey would have ended in disaster. "Means such as these can be destined to affect the individual himself or to influence others," Rabbi Luzzatto writes. "Something can thus happen to a person in order to bring good or evil to someone else."[3]

Of course, we cannot always subject the most minute features of our days to great scrutiny. But the Kabbalists have always insisted that beneath the surface of what appear to be random events is actually a tightly woven pattern of meaning. With wisdom comes the gift of discernment, we are told, a power more prized than the simple flexing of extrasensory abilities.

This idea was similarly emphasized by the early Hasidim several generations later. They viewed odd or strange turns of events as very meaningful, to be interpreted on several levels. In one well-known Hasidic tale which illustrates this point, a disciple of the Koretzer *rebbe* was accidentally marooned on a deserted isle while en route to perform a *mitzvah* (good deed) for his mentor. He kept himself alive by eating wild fruit and berries. Eventually, he was taken off by a passing ship. Upon returning with remorse to the House of Study, he met the rabbi, who told him, "There were sparks of holiness on the island which it was necessary . . . to restore to their source. Regret not the opportunity granted you, for you served the Lord well."[4]

In another anecdote, the Baal Shem Tov and a disciple

were walking along the road. There was no water available for miles on the hot and dusty path; the disciple complained bitterly of his thirst. When asked by the Baal Shem Tov whether the disciple believed in Divine Providence, the man replied, "Yes." Suddenly a person appeared bearing a pail of water and offered a drink to the astonished Hasidic initiate. The Baal Shem Tov asked the man how he had come to be in such an out-of-the-way spot, ferrying water from a long distance. The man answered, "My master has just fainted not far from here, and I was compelled to bring water from a spring several miles distant." Thereupon, the Hasidic founder turned to his disciple and said, "You see, there are no coincidences in the universe."[5] This same belief permeates the stories of Isaac Bashevis Singer, the contemporary Yiddish writer and Nobel prize winner. Many of his evocative tales begin with an ostensibly happy and contented man suddenly thrust into a series of bewildering and initially devastating turn of events—only to meet a long-lost friend or lover, or find himself performing a crucial act of kindness to someone in danger.

This Kabbalistic notion is quite similar to Carl Jung's interesting concept of *synchronicity*. In his last two decades of life, the Swiss psychoanalyst developed a theory to explain the phenomenon of "meaningful coincidences." He believed that a divine harmony pervades the cosmos and that such events point to the fact that everything is ultimately interrelated. In his therapeutic work with patients, Jung stressed that these occurrences may provide deep significance and direction to those who feel trapped and lost. In her recent book, *The Tao of Psychology* (Harper & Row, 1979) Dr. Jean Shinoda Bolen, a practicing Jungian psychiatrist, devotes considerable attention to this subject. She writes:

> Paying attention to synchronicity, like paying attention to dreams, adds an extra dimension that enriches our inner lives, and adds another facet to our awareness.... We experience the point of intersection of the timeless with time ... and where what is inside of us and what is outside of us is unseparated.[6]

Interestingly, evidence from his personal correspondence indicates that Jung was familiar with the Kabbalah and the Hasidic tradition, though he could not read Hebrew. It is fascinating to speculate whether his concept of synchronicity was influenced by such sources, which he apparently studied at the same time he began to articulate this theory—now attracting increasing attention among physicists as well as psychologists.

However successful we are in heeding such exotic events as secret clues to our lives, the Kabbalah affirms, physical existence must come to an end. Its major thinkers have suggested that when the person's chief life-task is completed, his or her mission on earth is likewise over. It becomes time to move on. This notion was well accepted by the early Hasidim. In various anecdotes, they expounded upon the Lurianic doctrine.

In one incident, Rabbi Yekuthiel Teitelbaum became dangerously ill in old age. He declined to call in a doctor. When questioned by his amazed disciples, he explained that his work had ended, and therefore no physician could help him. As he predicted, he never recovered. In another tale, a Hasidic leader criticized a colleague for assuming massive responsibilities at too early an age for his congregation. When pressed for an explanation, the older *rebbe* said, "Every [person] is allotted by Heaven a term of service lasting for a certain number of years. Had [he] waited to commence his term at a more mature age, he would have enjoyed a longer life."[7] And, as the *rebbe* had surmised, his cohort passed away while still young.

It is intriguing to learn that Freud himself apparently ascribed to this classic Hasidic belief. In his authoritative biography, Dr. Ernest Jones relates that Freud feared his imminent demise after publishing *The Interpretation of Dreams* in 1899. Having completed his most significant work to date in his career, Freud felt that "his life's work was done, so that nothing more need to be expected of him."[8] Here again, we witness the hidden influence of the Kabbalah on one of the most important explorers of the human mind in modern civilization.

Beyond Death and Dying

In recent years, the subject of human death and dying has ceased to be the taboo that it was for many decades in Western society. In the universities, courses are now widely offered and research carried out in this provocative new field, known as *thanatology*. Under the pioneering efforts of innovators like Dr. Elisabeth Kubler-Ross, scientific investigators have begun to focus upon the psychological dimensions of physical mortality. Moreover, scholars have started to examine closely how death is regarded by different cultures and spiritual approaches. Here again, as editor of *Death: the Final Stage of Growth* (Prentice-Hall: 1975) Dr. Kubler-Ross has been a seminal figure in this work.

Thus far, however, the Kabbalah has yet to attract serious attention among persons interested in this area. This fact is surprising since the Jewish esoteric tradition has had a great deal to say on this precise matter. Not only have the Kabbalists dealt extensively with the psychology of death and dying, but they have also addressed more speculative questions, such as the continuity of consciousness after bodily death. Their compelling notions will no doubt draw increasing interest in coming years as thanatology continues to grow as a respected discipline.

In the Kabbalistic view, dying is indeed seen as an important stage of inner development. Rather than regarding this process as the finale to human existence, the Kabbalah depicts it as merely one stage in the evolution of the soul. That we are immortal beings is a fundamental principle for Jewish mystics; their entire system is based on it. However, what gives the act of dying its significance is that through it, we very much determine our next phase of being. For them, the moment of death and the interval immediately before it is a gateway to other realms of awareness. The quality of our frame of mind, in a sense, specifies which particular door will open for us.

Furthermore, the Kabbalah describes the ideal attitude with which to meet physical death. The goal is to be as lucid and self-composed as possible. The very worst kind of orientation encompasses fear, confusion, or outright denial. The more calm, trusting, and at peace is the individual, the better able he or she becomes in making a smooth and successful transition to the World to Come, we are told. For instance, one major Hasidic teacher commented, "Happy is he who ends his days in repentance and holy service, and dies with a clear conscience."[9] Another great Hasid likewise declared, "Death is merely moving from one home to another. If we are wise, we will make the latter the more beautiful home."[10]

It is to the credit of the Hasidic founders that they practiced what they preached in advocating this viewpoint. In reports of their last minutes on earth, they appear to have both emotionally as well as intellectually sustained this Kabbalistic precept. Thus, Rabbi Nachman of Bratslav on his deathbed was described by a disciple who was present as having died "bright and clear [and] passed away without any confusion whatsoever, without a single untoward gesture, in a state of awesome calmness."[11] A generation earlier, the Hasid Rabbi Schmelke spent his final moments "sitting erect in his chair, with face serene and vision undimmed,"[12] as he convoked his disciples around him. The renowned Rabbi Elimelech of Lizensk, as his death approached, was tranquil and cheerful. As he took the hand of a disciple, the Rabbi said, "Why should I not rejoice, seeing that I am about to leave this world below, and enter into the higher world of eternity?"[13]

In one of the most beautiful anecdotes that illustrates the Hasidic theory and practice, we are recounted how Rabbi Bunam lay on his deathbed whilst his wife wept bitterly beside him. Thereupon he said to her, "Why do you weep? All my life has been given merely that I might learn how to die."[14] This attitude might serve as a much-needed antidote to the more prevalent view of death among both Jews and non-Jews alike today. Indeed, in the rapidly growing "hospice" approach to care for the terminally ill, persons are similarly emphasizing the right of the dying to remain as lucid and aware as possible.

It is also striking to note the parallel between the Kabbalistic stress upon "conscious dying" and the views in several Eastern spiritual paths. In both Buddhist and Hindu writings, for instance, there is a comparable emphasis upon the moment of bodily death as a key event in the transition of our consciousness. Thus, in his incisive essay in *Death: the Final Stage of Growth*, Dr. J. Bruce Long observes that both the *Tibetan Book of the Dead* and the Hindu *Bhagavad Gita* espouse the identical concept in this regard. He comments:

> The *Gita* propounds the same belief that is central to the teachings of the *Tibetan Book of the Dead* at a much later time. Namely, the frame of mind in which one puts himself just prior to and at the moment of death, will determine the state of being into which he enters after death. . . . The dying person is instructed to close all the "doors of the senses," fix the consciousness with the heart-center and stabilize the breath . . . [then] "he will travel the highest path."[15]

Because Jewish visionaries have stressed the importance of daily consciousness as the chief indicator of our inner development, they have never attached much significance to deathbed confessions. Although they have certainly valued the individual who repents his or his misdoings or unexpressed longings, they have viewed such last-minute changes of heart with a healthy realism bordering on scepticism. As keen observers of the human scene, they have well understood the psychological tendency to "strike a bargain" with one's imagined deity for a few more years of life. Hence, this act has always been suspect in their eyes.

For example, Rabbi Zalman Hasid, while near death, declared to his friends that he seriously doubted whether a deathbed confession contained much merit; rather a person should "confess" when he or she is at his dining table and eating a tasty meal, he commented. For the Jewish esoteric tradition, what *is* crucial is how we lived, day in and day out; that is something that cannot be expunged or glossed over in any way.

Here again, the Kabbalistic way holds a fascinating parallel to several Eastern spiritual disciplines. Dr. Long further explains:

> The Buddhists, like the Hindus, believe that there are differences in the quality of deaths, just as there are differences in the quality of births and existences. [These] . . . depend upon the difference between disciplined and undisciplined living, between pure and impure mind or between "carefulness" and "carelessness."[16]

At the Gates of Death

The Kabbalah goes on to relate that at the exact moment of physical death, several specific changes occur— mental as well as physiological. The *Zohar* relates that the *nefesh* or bioenergy dissolves as the body deteriorates. The *ruach*, which is tied to the life energy flow, remains somewhat longer, but also ultimately dissipates. The transcendent part, the *neshamah*, leaves the corporal form entirely. This higher part of the Self is then greeted by the souls of persons familiar in earthly existence. The *Book of Splendor* vividly states:

> For we have learned that at the hour of a man's departure from the world, his father and his relatives gather round him, and he sees them and recognizes them, and likewise all with whom he associated in this world, and they accompany his soul to the place where it is to abide.[17]

Direct proof on this subject, of course, appears nearly impossible to obtain. And yet, investigators have been attempting precisely this goal in recent years. One method has been to clinically interview persons who were pronounced medically dead but revived. In both professional journals and popular accounts of their work, researchers like Dr. Karlis Osis (*At the Hour of Death*), Dr. Raymond Moody (*Life After Life*), and Dr. Kenneth Ring (*Life at Death*) have found compelling similarities among the private reports of such people. In what are now called "near-death experiences," researchers have consistently found that one common description is encountering the presence of other "souls"—explicitly mentioned by the *Zohar*. Dr. Moody intriguingly comments:

> Quite a few have told me that at some point while they were dying—sometimes early in the experience, sometimes only after other events had taken place—they became aware of the presence of other spiritual beings in their vicinity, beings who apparently were there to ease them through their transition into death.[18]

In the foreword to this same volume, Dr. Kubler-Ross briefly cites her own investigations on this issue and says that she has come to a similar conclusion. "With my own research," she writes, "most were aware of another person who helped them in their transition to another plane of existence. Most were greeted by loved ones who had died before them."[19]

Undoubtedly, the steadily growing scientific interest in the near-death experience—recently reviewed in the prestigious *American Journal of Psychiatry*—may help us shed further light on the accuracy of the Kabbalistic depiction of events after bodily death. At the very least, it is quite clear that this entire subject deserves the closest scrutiny. It is hardly irrelevant any longer to the study of our deepest potential.

In its discussion on this matter, the *Zohar* goes on to add:

> We have further learned that at the time of a man's death, he is allowed to see his relatives and companions from the other world. If he is virtuous, they all rejoice before him and give him greeting, but if not, then he is recognized only by [those] . . . who every day are thrust down to Gehinnom.[20]

For Jewish mystics, *Gehinnom* or Purgatory is hardly conceived of as a place of everlasting, torturous punishment, or even of rigorous retribution for our misdeeds. Rather, as Rabbi Zalman Schachter recently pointed out in his *Fragments of a Future Scroll* (Leaves of Grass Press: 1975), it is a state of consciousness in which the soul is purged of all defilement that has been amassed during its existence on earth. Indeed, the founder of Lubavitch Hasidism, Rabbi Schneur Zalman of

Liady commented in the *Tanya* that in this state the soul must be ridden of the uncleanness of mundane attractions and pleasures before it can evolve to a more exalted awareness of the divine. The Kabbalah affirms that *Gehinnom* is consequently the typical realm of existence immediately after physical mortality. Its purpose might be compared today to a person's necessity in taking a good, hard shower after a tiring physical workout, or even to a deep-sea diver who needs to enter a decompression chamber before returning fully to land.

Once this process is completed—and here our four-dimensional concepts like time lose all meaning, the Kabbalah warns—each soul then gravitates to its own level. The major Kabbalistic thinkers were emphatic that we cannot attribute any physical aspects to this World to Come. The *Tanya* declares that "in the supernal worlds . . . everything is timeless."[21] Another Hasidic leader commented that "There is neither fire nor water, nor any other material substance in the World of the Spirit."[22] And the Polnoer Hasidic master told his disciples that in this World Beyond, there is no eating or drinking or any other delights of the body. What happens is that, in a sense, each soul then creates its own "heaven" or "hell." Our consciousness during physical existence—what we think about and dream about in daily life within the privacy of our inner Self—determines totally what the subsequent state of awareness will be.

This concept, quite unlike mainstream Christian thought, is a central one in the Kabbalah. It pervades the *Zohar* and formed the foundation for much of the later Hasidic flowering centuries later in Eastern Europe. The *Book of Splendor* tells us again and again that depending entirely on our strivings in this world is our dwelling in the next. The Kabbalists thus do not posit the existence of one region of everlasting beneficence and one of eternal punishment. Rather, they consider there to be a virtually infinite number of realms—of consciousness—after bodily death, as varied in fact, as those during physical life. Just as people on earth range from the most kindly to the most murderous, so, too, this diversity is said to continue in the World to Come. This same view exists in Dante's *The Divine Comedy*, written about the time of the *Zohar*'s appearance. The "bible" of Jewish mysticism succinctly states, "For there are many abodes prepared by the Holy One, blessed be He, each one according to his grade. . . . As the works of the righteous differ in this world, so do their place and lights differ in the next world."[23]

Here, as before, the Kabbalah stresses the quality of our day-to-day frame of mind as the key. The type of inner discipline, piety, and spiritual devotion that surrounds our simplest and most commonplace acts, toward ourselves and toward one another, will create our experience in the next world. In a somewhat more elaborate explanation, the *Zohar* emphatically declares:

> It is the path taken by man in this world that determines the path of the soul on her departure. . . . the goal which a man sets himself in this world, so does he draw to himself [after bodily death]. If a man follows a certain direction in this world, he will be led further in the same direction when he departs . . . if holy, holy, and if defiled, defiled.[24]

This beautiful philosophy has often been depicted symbolically by Kabbalistic thinkers. Thus, the heaven of the sages has typically been portrayed as a spiritual region in which they continue to study and meditate upon the divine harmony and secrets of the universe. The characteristic metaphor is of the "Celestial Academy," where Prophets such as Elijah expound upon the great mysteries of the cosmos. As noted earlier, the Kabbalah hardly views the post-death realm as material in nature. So its image of the "Celestial Academy" is not to be taken literally but metaphorically. It is a state of awareness—and learning—without enmity, strife, or competion, where, as the Polnoer Hasidic *rebbe* explained, there are simply *zaddikim* deriving great joy from their nearness to the deity.

In keeping with this view, Jewish mystics have always insisted that the highest levels of the World to Come—poetically described as "the Garden of Eden"—is a spiritual region not *denied* to those without inner peace or knowledge, but one which such souls, by their very nature, deny themselves. The Polnoer *rebbe* continues, "What, then, can these [individuals] feel in Paradise but bitterness? Can they know the joy of the *Shekinah*'s [the female component of the deity] nearness, inasmuch as they never trained themselves for the enjoyments of the spirit?"[25]

Indeed, similar to other Kabbalistic teachings, the Hasidic masters made this doctrine more easily accessible to the large numbers of uneducated East European Jews. In a well-known parable attributed to the Baal Shem Tov as well as his disciples, an ignorant but devout coachman dies. He is unable to enjoy the highest regions of the World to Come, where other souls delve into abstruse matters to their utmost gratification. Thereupon, the "Heavenly Tribunal" sends him to a world where he is presented with a wondrous carriage harnessed to four magnificent horses, and where the roads stretch before him, always dry and even. Or, in more direct terms, the Maggid of Mezritch, the Baal Shem Tov's chief disciple, tersely explained, "Each man creates his own Paradise."[26]

Regardless of the ultimate truth of this outlook—and it may obviously be some time before investigators produce convincing evidence—its philosophical power is readily apparent. Contemporary humanistic psychologists have stressed precisely this point about our everyday lives. In a very real sense, we continually create our own happiness or dissatisfaction in each passing day. Gestalt Therapy founder Fritz Perls often emphasized this principle in his therapeutic work and writings. "Authenticity, maturity, responsibility for one's actions and life," he commented, ". . . is all one and the same thing."[27] His goal was to make his patients aware of how they made *themselves* tense, impatient, or miserable. Only in this way might they be able to change their attitudes and begin to enjoy life.

Not unlike the Hasidic leaders, Dr. Perls also admonished those who came to him for help to focus upon what made them feel most buoyant and alive. This approach has become explicitly stressed in many humanistic psychotherapies today. Patients begin to learn how they might be unconsciously contributing to their own lack of health through feelings of despair or hopelessness. In so doing, they discover that they shape their own emotional and physical reality. It seems clear that the Kabbalistic view of our inner world—and how we mold our experiences in life—has a great deal of present-day relevance.

Reincarnation: The Secret Jewish Doctrine

It may come as quite a surprise to those acquainted only with Judaism's legalistic side to learn of its embrace of the concept of the transmigration of souls. References to reincarnation can be found as early as the *Sefer Bahir* ("Book of Brilliance"), which first appeared around the year 1175 in Provence. About a century later, the *Zohar* dealt more extensively with this theme. But with the tremendous Kabbalistic germination in sixteenth-century Safed, this provocative doctrine became a key element in the Jewish esoteric tradition. In fact, during this period, as Professor R. J. Zwi Werblowsky of Hebrew University notes, "Trying to identify the souls inhabiting their colleagues became a passionate and serious [activity]. . . . Luria was considered by his followers as the supreme authority."[28] The Hasidic masters likewise ascribed to this notion and incorporated it as a significant feature in their message for the discouraged and impoverished masses of East European Jewry.

In the modern Jewish era, belief in an immortal soul rapidly declined, not to mention belief in its physical return. Outside of the various Hasidic sects, few Jewish theologians or philosophers have paid the scantest attention to the doctrine of reincarnation. Today, however, with the burgeoning interest in Eastern spiritual disciplines, there has been a marked fascination in the West—among both Jews and non-Jews alike—in this ancient belief. What the Kabbalah has to say about the subject is not only interesting in its own right, but also provides some startling parallels to ideas set forth in other paths, such as Hinduism and Tibetan Buddhism.

Though the Kabbalists, as we have seen, emphasize the existence of a spiritual realm beyond the physical world, they also stress that each soul must return to earth until all its tasks are completed. In heaven, the Self only gains a deeper understanding of its corporal life. It is essential, the Kabbalah affirms, that the soul reincarnate, in order to fulfill all of its unmet commandments. These might vary radically from person to person—hence, the basic Kabbalistic view that we each have a unique mission to accomplish. Indeed, works such as the *Zohar* assert that the very fact of our physical existence indicates our incomplete inner development. Except for one rather notable exception—to be discussed shortly—we would not even be here in material form unless it were necessary.

> The Holy One ... permits [the human being] ... to start anew, and labor for himself in order to make good his deficiency. In addition, it must be remembered that the man has to undergo transmigration because he is not, in any case, of great merit; since if he were so he would not have had to pass into another form and live again upon the earth, but would at once have "a place better than sons and daughters."[29]

The *Book of Splendor* specifically mentions several causes that necessitate additional lifetimes in the physical realm—what the Kabbalah calls *gilgulim* (transformations). One of these is the failure to raise a child, another is not having married. Thus, we are told, if an individual marries but dies without children, husband and wife undergo reincarnation and unite again as they were before. For the Kabbalists, the union between man and woman—encompassing physical, emotional, and spiritual dimensions—is a key pathway to the divine. Not surprisingly, therefore, initiates have viewed marriage—as well as other close relationships—as almost inevitably involving reincarnational dramas.

In fact, in the Jewish mystical tradition, spouses are regarded as having typically known each other in past lives. Joseph Karo's *maggid* thus declared that one of Karo's wives had actually been a well-known male scholar in an earlier existence. The *maggid* intriguingly stated:

> Since she is a male soul she is not really your mate; you
> received her as "ownerless property" [i.e., not as your true
> partner]. . . . Because her soul is essentially a male soul, she
> could not produce offspring for you.[30]

In another discourse on reincarnation, the *maggid* related:

> You already know that she has lived twice before and that in
> her second existence she was a miser . . . transmigrated this
> time in order . . . to be perfected through you. . . . She too
> will acquire merits, for through the money that she has brought
> you and through her serving you, you will be privileged to
> teach *Torah*.[31]

Throughout its exotic messages, Karo's *maggid* expounded
upon a favored theme among the Safed Kabbalists: that the
arena of sexuality and marriage is an inportant testing ground
for our spiritual development. Spouses are here together to
work out unresolved conflicts impeding inner growth. In this
context, the *Zohar* tersely observes that each spouse gets the
one he or she deserves. Similarly, the childrearing experience
is seen as an important aspect of earthly existence and no one
is considered able to pass beyond this realm without having
raised—in at least one lifetime—a child to adulthood.

Isaac Luria and his followers devoted a great deal of attention to the subject of the transmigration of souls. They elevated this earlier concept to a key element in their entire
teaching about the nature of human destiny and the divine
order. In his book, *Sefer Ha Gilgulim* ("The Book of Transformations"), Chaim Vital discussed this issue in detail. To
summarize his rather elaborate system, he argued that each
person must normally carry out all of the various commandments. If a single commandment is not fully observed, then
transmigration has to occur. But Vital drew a distinction
between those commandments which the person is capable of
fulfilling and those which he or she is not. For instance, a
woman is obviously unable to complete tasks that Judaism
specifies for men only. In such cases, Luria's protégé explained,
if we do not have the opportunity to fulfill them, we need not
transmigrate because of their incompletion. Moreover, every

commandment must ultimately be carried out not just physically, but with the proper intentionality and concentration. "If some spark of a soul has not fulfilled even one aspect of those three—deed, speech, and thought—it must transmigrate until it fulfills all of them,"[32] he wrote.

Chaim Vital also helped to promulgate the evocative Lurianic doctrine that various people on earth are secretly or inwardly related to one another because of their joint origin in the same "family of souls." Many historical developments among apparently disparate groups or nations, therefore, are seen to stem from longstanding reincarnational ties. The early Hasidic leaders, more than two hundred years later, stressed this same concept to their minions; in fact, some Hasidic founders explicitly identified their colleagues—and even themselves—as prominent biblical figures in prior lifetimes. Inevitably, the Kabbalah tells us, our purpose on earth relates to our own previous lifetimes and those of others around us, especially intimates. "As a result of this," Rabbi Moses Chaim Luzzatto comments, "all men [are] bound to each other."[33]

In the Jewish esoteric discipline, the goal of the *gilgulim* is for each soul to end its repetitive cycles of death and rebirth in the physical world. This viewpoint is strikingly similar to Buddhist and Hindu teachings, which likewise preach that when we attain sufficient spiritual awareness, the cycle is finally over. Thus, in *The Tantric Mysticism of Tibet*, John Blofeld observes:

> Clinging to the false notion of its permanency, the wretched ego suffers successive rounds of death and rebirth, aeon upon aeon.... None of the infinite number of states ... is altogether satisfactory.... The remedy lies in freeing oneself from [the cycle] forever by destroying the last shreds of egohood.[34]

In an identical belief, Jewish mystics have seen the necessity to return to earthly existence as a distinct burden. Thus, Chaim Vital relates that Moses died in bitterness because he knew that he had not yet fulfilled all of the commandments and would therefore need to reincarnate. Indeed, the *Zohar* stresses that in the World to Come souls must oftentimes be forced to transmigrate as they are quite uneager and even unwilling to voluntarily return to the obvious travails of this domain.

It should be recognized too that the early Kabbalah additionally makes reference to a Resurrection for humanity at some future date. At that time, we are told, the perfected soul of each person will reenter the body, which itself will be infinitely more perfect and radiant than what we are intimately familiar with. As to how this heavenly event relates to reincarnation, the *Book of Splendor* not only deals with this question but raises it as well. "What will happen to a number of bodies which shared in succession the same soul?" it asks. "Only the last that had been firmly planted and took root will come to life."[35] The Safed Kabbalists, however, decidedly downplayed the notion of a Resurrection. Similarly, the early Hasidim de-emphasized this concept, interpreting it metaphorically as referring to a spiritual rebirth of the soul.

In a final and striking parallel to Eastern paths like Tibetan Buddhism, the Kabbalah has asserted that the most spiritually evolved persons voluntarily return to this existence, though they have freed themselves of the cosmic wheel or *gilgulim*. The Kabbalists have regarded such figures as making the ultimate sacrifice to raise up their fellow human beings—to come back to our corporal world, with all its despair and disorder, after having tasted the inexpressible delights of the World of the Spirit. The sixteenth-century mystic Solomon Alkabez describes such souls as ". . . those who return not on account of their having omitted a religious duty, let alone for having committed a trespass, but solely out of compassion with their contemporaries."[36]

Similarly, Buddhism has for centuries offered its utmost admiration for the *bodhisattva*, the perfected individual who chooses to continue his or her cycle out of love for others still chained to the karmic wheel of earthly life. As Lama Govinda comments in *Foundations of Tibetan Mysticism* such an enlightened being "is willing to descend into the suffering world of mortals, in order to spread the happy tidings of liberation."[37] In this perspective, bodhisattvas walk quietly amidst us, attracting no attention, yet exerting a tremendous influence.

In the Jewish esoteric tradition, too, a handful of concealed sages in each generation are said to sustain all of humankind. Unbeknownst, their efforts keep the world going. For the Hasidim especially, this idea became important. Released from the conceit which is often associated with fame, these secret holy persons (known as the *Lamed-vov* or "thirty-six") are portrayed in some legends as possessing the highest psychic powers and divine knowledge of death and life. The very doors of heaven are said to be open before them. Yet, they present themselves as the simplest of folk. All the while, though, wherever they stand, they raise the fallen sparks of light back to their primal Source. This notion underlies the entire Kabbalistic approach to the mysteries of human existence.

As the Gerer *rebbe* declared, "Exile contains redemption within itself, as seed contains the fruit. Right work and real diligence will bring out the hidden reward."[38]

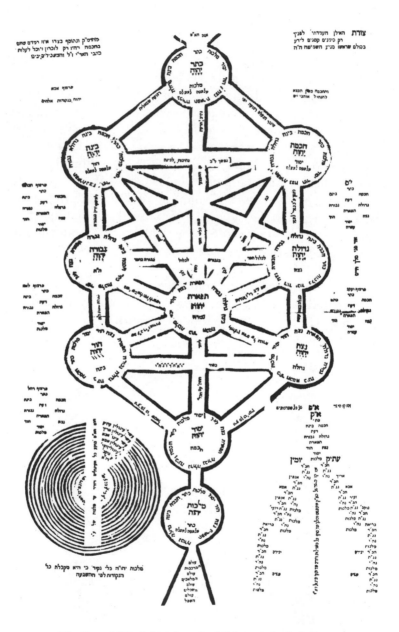

The Tree of Life derived from the Safed mystical school (Amsterdam, 1708).

CHAPTER NINE

THE NEW LAND
OF THE MIND

"The old way of choosing one path and following it patiently can no longer prevail. We have developed far beyond this. To embrace all paths and to integrate them into a full and secure harmony—this is the beginning of . . . [our] sacred responsibility."

"From the illumination of our souls . . . flashes of light will shine on the world. . . . The mystical meanings will be disclosed, the intimations will be clarified, the homiletical pronouncements will be made explicit, and the obvious will be raised to a higher significance. They will all together fill the world with abundance."

—Rabbi Abraham Isaac Kook

WE ARE IN THE MIDST of a momentous transformation in the scientific approach to the human mind. Though for many decades, a mechanistic perspective has held sway, new directions for investigation have rapidly begun to emerge. Some of these—such as the relation between our emotional and physical health, as well as the nature of altered states of awareness—have already attracted serious attention. Others, like the meaning of near-death experiences, are just beginning to attain widespread interest.

These intriguing concerns have started to push the boundaries of orthodox science into areas traditionally regarded as the realm of religion. More conservative figures, to be sure, eye this trend with unease. Yet, it seems clear, the view that we are nothing more than the sum of our most primitive instincts has become less and less convincing. The fragmented picture of our personality is no longer sufficient to many. That portrayal may have been adequate for an earlier period of science, but a growing number of persons are actively looking for alternatives. As the awesome complexity of our inner makeup has steadily unfolded, the search for a unified vision of the human potential has intensified.

However, this quest has itself been no overnight development. As far back as the turn of the twentieth century, William James railed against what he termed the "medical materialism" then first assuming dominance in the budding field of psychology. The illustrious Harvard professor flatly rejected as unjustified its eagerness to dismiss all unusual mental phenomena—such as the reports of great mystics—as signs of physical abnormalities like epilepsy or indicators of outright madness. To try to shrink the vistas of human experience to the confines of the clinic or laboratory would be a foolhardy and ultimately self-limiting venture, he warned. What is needed instead, James urged, is an open-minded respect and indeed a reverence for all of the elusive, often baffling aspects of the world within us.

Thus, in his seminal work, *The Varieties of Religious Experience*, presented as lectures in 1901–1902 in Edinburgh, this brilliant thinker advocated that the spiritual and scientific paths to knowledge of the cosmos be harmonized. "Science and religion are both of them genuine keys for unlocking the world's treasure-house," he poetically wrote. "Neither is exhaustive or exclusive of the other's simultaneous use."[1] The universe looms as an incredible "complex of many interpenetrating spheres of reality," James observed. "On this view, religion and science, each verified in its own way from hour to hour and from life to life, would be co-eternal."[2]

Unfortunately, James's farsighted vision was well beyond the grasp of most of his colleagues. They attacked him as a romantic and a dreamer, much too impractical for the rigors of the times. After all, they countered, wasn't this now the twentieth century, the age of objectivity? There was no room in science for the spiritual musings that so entranced the eminent Harvard academician, his critics insisted.

For well over the next sixty years, psychology and its allied disciplines firmly maintained this position. Under the twin turrets of Freudian theory and behaviorism, investigators were mainly concerned with studying the most mentally deranged individuals or drawing analogies between the behavior of animals like rats or pigeons and that of humans. Outside of a handful of iconoclasts like Carl Jung, whose restless intellect roamed in fields ranging from mythology and symbolism to schizophrenia and parapsychology, the kind of unified perspective anticipated by William James remained an unrealized image.

Beginning in the late 1960s, though, this orientation proved increasingly alluring. Such leading figures as Abraham Maslow and Gestalt Therapy cofounder Fritz Perls, argued persuasively that a more thorough, all-embracing model of human personality had to be developed. In Maslow's apt metaphor, Freud and his followers may have well probed the basement or subterranean depths of the mind, with its dark, twisted currents. What is now imperative, Maslow insisted, is a corresponding beacon to light up the way into the attic or highest chambers of our consciousness.

Thus, in his major volume, *Toward a Psychology of Being* (Van Nostrand: 1968), Maslow explored in detail the characteristics of the peak or transcendent experience. As we have seen, he believed that such episodes are associated with the pinnacles of mental health. "Clearly any psychology of religion, either supernatural or natural," he observed, "must take account of these happenings."[3] William James would certainly have agreed with this assessment.

Since then, a great deal has happened in the field. A variety of professional publications have flowered and taken root, such as the *Journal of Humanistic Psychology* and the *Journal of Transpersonal Psychology*. Around the globe, conferences have focused on the importance of the shamanistic or sacred dimensions of human life. There has been a steady stream of books on how the world's great spiritual traditions can offer us a better understanding of our psychological makeup. Perhaps even more significantly, our society as a whole has come to accept and adopt many of the exciting ideas within this movement.

And yet, still lacking has been the beacon to make sense of the largely unknown terrain inside us. Bits and pieces of ideas and techniques—even from the great spiritual traditions of the East—have simply not been adequate. There is one longstanding and cogent body of knowledge that may still provide the much needed vision—and that, as I have sought to illustrate throughout this book, is the Kabbalah. In this final chapter, it may therefore be helpful to briefly summarize its key features as they relate to the search for a new conception of the mind.

Toward a Kabbalistic Psychology

Certainly one of the fundamental Kabbalistic premises to assist in guiding the emergent psychology is that everything in the cosmos is a unity—that we cannot study persons as separate entities, apart from the rest of the universe. It is ironic though not really surprising that the modern behavioral sciences have clung to an outworn, mechanistic perspective long since discredited and abandoned in physics and most other branches of study. Borrowing its tools of inquiry from the nineteenth-century disciplines, the young field of psychology seized upon statistical and laboratory methods. For instance, its researchers firmly believed they could isolate an animal from its natural habitat as well as other members of its species, observe it under quite artificial laboratory conditions, and yet somehow draw meaningful conclusions about human nature.

For many years, this approach went virtually unchallenged. With the advent of ecology, though, biologists—especially those who study animal behavior—have convincingly argued against its validity. Such an orientation, they have insisted, has hindered our understanding of simpler organisms, let alone of humans. Furthermore, this issue is not merely of academic interest. That is, the idea that we can analyze living creatures in a manner unrelated to their surroundings has also frustrated the attempts of environmental psychologists to assess the very real effect of sound, light, and other energies upon us. For instance, at this very moment—if you inhabit a large city—you are being bombarded by low-level microwaves. What is their impact upon your emotional and physical well-being? No one knows.

To take another example, recent research has clearly demonstrated that apes and other mammals seem to "sense," hours or days in advance, when a major earthquake is on its way. They become markedly more agitated in their movements. Other reports have scientifically documented how lower animals as well as people are intimately affected by fluctuations in humidity, ion concentration, and even the phases of the moon.

It is thus proving apparent across many areas of knowledge that the lines that demark one academic discipline from another are in reality an illusion. We exist in one vast network of force. The departmental system may be an administrative asset to universities, but it does not make for very good science. In fact, it has been far from unusual for an academic psychologist in, say, Texas, to be literally in closer communication with his or her counterpart in England than with colleagues in biology or physics downstairs in the same building. Fortunately, this situation has begun to change for the better.

As noted earlier, the notion that the cosmos is an indivisible whole is hardly foreign to the Jewish esoteric tradition. For centuries, its chief thinkers have insisted that an irreducible order permeates the universe. From the flights of birds to the movement of galaxies, everything is seen as interconnected. Therefore, any accurate model of the human personality must, for the Kabbalists, start with this central assumption—

succinctly stated by Rabbi Nachman of Bratslav, "All things have one root."[4] Undoubtedly, this orientation will lead to a greater understanding of ourselves as well as of the outer world—just as works like the *Zohar* have declared for more than a half-millenium.

Another key Kabbalistic feature relevant to the new psychology is the age-old viewpoint that each person comprises several distinct but interrelated dimensions of consciousness. As keen observers of the human condition, the Kabbalah's teachers have always acknowledged the power of our lower impulses. We have strong drives for selfish and immediate gratification, whether for food, drink, sex, or material possessions, they have emphasized. Indeed, in its readiness to face our dark, animalistic side, the Kabbalistic way shows greater wisdom than often espoused by some glib figures on the contemporary humanistic or "pop" psychology scene. Having experienced firsthand bloodthirsty and sadistic oppression, its leaders—long before the Holocaust—have been very open-eyed about the incredible brutality that lurks within us. Their willingness to confront our tendencies for violence offers a much needed antidote to the more extreme, superficially "optimistic" models of human personality currently being touted.

And yet, the Kabbalah portrays our essence as inherently neither all-destructive nor wholly all-loving. Rather, we are composed of a multitiered array of attributes. Jewish mystics have stressed that we each have inner needs and capabilities far beyond those involved in ordinary, day-to-day living. Though we rarely make full or even partial use of these latent potentialities, adepts have long asserted, they are nevertheless of crucial importance. From this uncompromising standpoint, no conception of our makeup can be complete without a thorough comprehension of our most exalted capacities for transcendence.

In this respect, the Kabbalistic approach incorporates both Freudian and behavioral perspectives, yet implies that at superior levels of our being, both viewpoints are erroneous and inoperable. Just as Newton's laws of physics were not overturned but merely made a subset of Einstein's more in-

clusive theory of relativity—so too may these twin psychological orientations be found valid for certain lower states of
consciousness. For people functioning at greatly enhanced
levels—those whom the Kabbalah calls *zaddikim*—a wholly
new set of principles would have to apply. Thus, prominent
Kabbalists like Rabbi Schneur Zalman of Liady would definitely agree with psychoanalytic notions that most persons
are unaware of their animal-like drives. However, this Hasidic leader went on to argue that each of us can learn to
control and guide such impulses, even raising them upward
for noble purposes. Similarly, he and his colleagues nearly
two hundred years ago would probably have found little fault
with behavioral insights that we move through daily life in an
almost ceaseless routine of habit, blindly shaped by events
around us. But the early Hasidic masters preached that we
have the capacity to wholly overcome our negative habits and
unthinking actions.

Interestingly, Abraham Maslow's theory of the "hierarchy
of human needs" probably comes closest to the Kabbalistic
perspective. Raised in an ethnic, Brooklyn Jewish home,
Maslow seems to have intuitively arrived at this same notion
that we possess a spectrum of capabilities, ranging from the
most survival-oriented to the most immaterial. Only in truly
"self-actualizing" people, Maslow incisively observed, do these
higher faculties become fully awakened and active. For such
individuals, their desire for greater states of creativity, aes-
thetics, and morality in some way "absorbs" or overrides the
petty concerns with which we are all too familiar.

Another major and germane Kabbalistic view is its emphasis on our intentionality. Modern psychodynamic theory has
contributed much to our understanding of the extent to which
people may be ruled by unconscious feelings such as those
stemming from biological forces. It has become clear to us in
the twentieth century that persons often act from motives
that are rarely wholly pure. Yet, the Kabbalah indicates that
humans also comprise a higher motivating power, without
which little personal growth can be accomplished at all.

From the days of the great visionary Isaac Luria, Kabbalists have emphasized that a primary need for each of us is to lift up the "fallen sparks" that we encounter in daily life. They have taught that no matter what our chronological age, degree of education, or profession, we each long to create meaning and wholeness out of the fragmented occurrences of the mundane. Rather than simply alluding to conscious willpower, the term *kavvanah* thus refers to an intentionality that emerges from our entire being. At a certain stage of mental development, every person—with both conscious and unconscious impulses—above all strives to help redeem the world.

Jewish mystics have indicated that we must deliberately cultivate this quality within, for it will not develop automatically. Certainly for large numbers of people, it may lie almost totally dormant. Nevertheless, from the Kabbalah's perspective, modern psychology has severely slighted this innate human attribute. Anyone can start to initiate dramtic changes at any moment in his or her life, the Kabbalistic way declares. In fact, a common theme in the tales surrounding the Hasidic founders is precisely that we are each capable of the most profound self-transformation. The psychological orthodoxy, however, has typically depicted us as near automatons, programmed like computers, and lacking the power to make immediate and far-reaching decisions. Perhaps, under the sway of this ideology, many of us feel we can do little to alter our way of life or inner state of being. And so, a most destructive, self-fulfilling prophecy has dominated much of our thinking.

In my own therapeutic work with both hosptialized and community patients, I have often encountered this attitude, sometimes directly expressed. "What can you expect of me?" the person bemoans. "After all, I had such a miserable childhood." Or, "I'm mentally ill," some articulate schizophrenics will readily comment. "I can't get any better because my condition is permanent. You know that, Doc." Indeed, a psychotherapist with a strict Freudian or behavioral set of values will be hard pressed to respond with an appropriate reply— for neither of these psychological systems has ever stressed our will to grow and change.

It is encouraging, though, that in recent years an increasing number of humanistic psychologists have sought to reassert the primacy of our intentionality in self-development. Contemporary thinkers like Rollo May and Robert Assagioli have forcefully argued that the concept of our conscious willpower—and its awesome power—be brought back into the forefront of the science of the mind. Long decades of ignoring this vital human characteristic, they claim, have badly crippled the discipline. As the Kabbalists have for centuries been aware, the key to any successful course of therapy is the activation of this quality—and once this happens, we may begin to marshall new inner resources rapidly and confidently.

Another central lesson the Jewish visionary tradition holds for us today lies in its sophisticated model of both ordinary and altered states of awareness. Since the first intensive investigations in the 1960s on the effects of certain chemicals on humans, researchers have increasingly grappled with the fundamental nature of consciousness. How is it that seemingly normal, well-adjusted and even fairly unimaginative persons can within an hour or two of psychedelic ingestion experience the pinnacles of religious ecstasy or the depths of terror? Is our mental structure really that fragile? Furthermore, sensory deprivation studies—such as popularized in John Lilly's intriguing books—have shown that even without taking hallucinogens into their bodies, many people quickly undergo powerful personality changes—within a few scant hours—if simply denied all external, sensory stimulation, including light, sound, and motion.

Such findings pose no surprises for the Kabbalah. For centuries, its sages have stressed that our typical waking state is severely limited by "blinders" inside us, said to screen out the dazzling realms that exist at every step we take. We walk through our days as though surrounded by veils, the Kabbalists observe, which hide these other dimensions from our habitual awareness. Often, we behave as though half asleep, never fully experiencing what is around us. As the thirteenth-century *Zohar* declares, "How blind are the children of men, who neither see nor perceive what the foundation is of their world!"[5] Yet, as related in Chapter 6, the Kabbalah affirms that our inner shutters are absolutely necessary. Without them, we would soon be overwhelmed by the awesome celestial brilliance.

For this reason, adepts have never advocated instant "trips" into other states of consciousness, but rather, a slow, steady progress, grounded in physical activity and community involvement. From their perspective, it is quite expected that any sudden means to batter down our blinders within—whether through drugs or highly intensive isolation—would cause us to lose our mental stability. For our ordinary mind is indeed regarded as a very delicate instrument, not to be idly tampered with. Thus, Jewish visionaries argue, it is no great feat to "enter the garden of heavenly visions." The trick is getting out again with our life and sanity intact.

Here, the Kabbalistic viewpoint has already been incorporated into much of the contemporary behavioral sciences. The notion that we contain a "sensory filter," built into our nervous system since birth or earlier, is now well accepted in the mainstream. In fact, this principle has been gaining more and more credence. First articulated by William Broadbent in the late 1950s, it has guided a growing body of research in the study of severe mental illness, particularly schizophrenia and autism. Rather than blaming the patient's family for "causing" these baffling conditions, investigators are approaching the syndromes as essentially disorders of attention—the way in which we process sensory information from the world. Hence, innovative therapists try to teach such patients how to cope with situations that may "overload" them with too much stimulation. They must learn to avoid intense excitement lest they become overwhelmed and suffer a "breakdown."

An additional, relevant feature of the Jewish mystical tradition is its premise that our mind and body are closely intertwined. Its chief texts have insisted that our emotional and physical well-being are inextricably tied to one another. We do not *have* a mind and body; we *are* mind and body in the same organism. Centuries before the current boom in holistic health, the early Hasidic masters accurately pinpointed such mental states as unexpressed anger and depression as two primary causes of bodily illness. The Hasidic founders cogently urged their followers to ventilate their feelings on a regular basis and to take time to self-reflect and review each day's events dispassionately.

Furthermore, adepts have consistently taught that we must not reject our physical makeup, nor abuse it through overwork. They have explicitly condemned overexertion as detrimental to our emotional and bodily health. The Baal Shem Tov himself is said to have commented, "Do not consider the time you spend for eating and sleeping wasted. The soul within you is rested during these intervals, and is enabled to renew its holy work with fresh enthusiasm."[6]

In keeping with their belief in the sanctity of the human body, the Kabbalists have long emphasized the importance of an active sex life. To be sure, works like the *Zohar* clearly indicate that sexuality is sacred only within the context of the marital relationship. Yet, concerning this domain, they have prized the delights of sexual intercourse with love and even deemed it a gateway to higher reaches of ecstasy. For them, the bliss of true lovemaking is an earthly counterpart to the most exalted union occurring in the divine realm. Indeed, the *Book of Splendor* is replete with descriptions of the conjugal state that are so explicit that they would probably have been banned in any other format less than a generation ago.

Of course, in the last few years, the field of behavioral medicine has grown more and more aware of the vital link between our mind and body. There is now at least the rudiments of a research literature documenting this connection for virtually every major noninfectious illness, from asthma and migraine to heart disease and cancer. Some of these studies even point to sexual repression as a contributor to the onset of physical ailments like prostate and vaginal disorders. Undoubtedly, the new science of the mind will be solidly based on the longstanding Kabbalistic principle that our mental and bodily states constitute a unity.

Strikingly, what have always appeared as strictly mythological parts of the Kabbalah are now beginning to find acceptance among many scientific investigators. For instance, the notion that each of us includes a *neshamah*, or transcendent self, has always been basic to the Jewish esoteric way. Its practitioners have therefore acknowledged the existence within us of extrasensory abilities—which in biblical times were usually associated with divinely-inspired acts of prophecy. Though they have never urged that psychic powers be sought for their own sake, the Kabbalists have unquestionably believed that every human has potentialities for perceptions not bound by ordinary rules of time and space. The more advanced we become within, the further such capacities are awakened. Thus, dreams are said to not only convey valuable insights about our everyday life, but also harbor clairvoyance and telepathy. Jewish visionaries have accorded the highest respect to dreams and other manifestations of our unconscious. By getting in better touch with these normally hidden dimensions of our being, the Kabbalah stresses, we may gain a more exalted state of consciousness. "A dream is more precise than a vision," the *Zohar* recounts, "and may explain what is obscure in a vision."[7]

Though the study of our extrasensory talents has often been ridiculed by more conservative figures, it has also attracted some of the most gifted minds in modern psychology. William James, battling his critics, devoted more than twenty years of active research to the germinating discipline of parapsychology. He personally investigated countless phenomena in England and the United States, finally concluding near the end of his life that orthodox science could not explain some of what he had witnessed. In 1909, he issued his last report, entitled, "The Final Impression of a Psychical Researcher." The incisive thinker flatly declared, "I wish to go on record for . . . the presence, in the midst of all the humbug, of really supernormal knowledge. By this I mean knowledge that cannot be traced to the ordinary sources of information—the senses, namely."[8]

Though for many decades, mainstream researchers would not even entertain the possibility of our possessing extrasensory abilities, this situation has begun to change significantly.

It would currently be misleading to suggest that most professionals in this field are firmly convinced of the reality of psychic states; nevertheless, a steadily growing number are eager for a more flexible, open-minded perspective. In fact, the *American Journal of Psychiatry*—the most prestigious publication of the discipline—recently reported the encouraging results of a national survey on this subject. Dr. Stanley Dean, a pioneer in the understanding of schizophrenia, found that over one-half of psychiatrists polled believe that medical schools should provide curricular instruction on parapsychology. It may therefore be not too long before future physicians receive training in clairvoyance, telepathy, spiritual healing, and other latent human capacities delineated in the Kabbalistic path.

Perhaps even more interesting than its views on the psychic is the Kabbalah's provocative descriptions of events at the "hour of death"—and beyond. Dating back to its first written sources, the Jewish esoteric system has painted a vivid picture of the importance of a person's final moments on earth. The Hasidic literature is especially filled with accounts of how its founders died "serene and undimmed," in full control of their faculties until the end. Such figures well-illustrated their own message that the ideal way to die is with total awareness. Today, this same concept has been wholeheartedly endorsed by the burgeoning hospice movement. Emphasizing the right of every individual to die with dignity, this orientation likewise extols the intrinsic worth of a "good death," as the fitting conclusion of a decent life. As Parker Rossman describes this trend in *Hospice* (Fawcett: 1977), its key assumption is that, "Dying people have the right to die when their body and spirit are ready."[9] For many decades, this topic was a taboo subject in orthodox psychology—perhaps due to the unconscious reluctance of middle-aged researchers to confront this approaching stage in their own lives. Now, however, *thanatology* has become a respected branch of scientific inquiry, complete with its own journals, professional associations, and research symposia.

But physical death is hardly the end, the Kabbalah has always asserted. Its major thinkers have regarded bodily mortality as simply the doorway to other dimensions of experience. Chief texts like the *Zohar* clearly portray the act of dying as a transition—with definite aspects—to further levels of being. Moreover, Kabbalists have emphasized, there is full continuity of consciousness from one state to the next. "If a man follows a certain direction in this world, he will be led further in the same direction when he departs,"[10] observes the *Book of Splendor*. It informs us too that at the moment of death, we typically feel the presence of loved ones who have already died, as well as the sensation of being enveloped in a brilliant, celestial light, the *Ein Sof*. Other Kabbalistic reports describe dramatic out-of-the-body episodes in which sages have found themselves catapulted beyond their physical form while close to death or even in ecstatic meditation. Of course, such exotic commentaries have almost unanimously been rejected as pure superstition since the inception of modern psychology. For fear of being labeled as dabblers in the occult, only a handful of iconoclasts have dared to so much as glance at this literature.

Thus, it is fascinating that contemporary explorers of the mind are now beginning to focus on this extremely provocative topic, well analyzed in the Kabbalah. What was only a few years ago dismissed by nearly every respectable modern thinker has become the target of exciting speculation and scientific research. A variety of recent books and articles have all highlighted the same basic phenomenon—known as the "near-death experience"—and offered incredible parallels to what ancient spiritual paths like the Kabbalistic way have long demarked.

Again and again, persons who have been pronounced medically dead but who were later revived, have reported sensing the presence of departed loved ones and also encountering a "being of light," wondrous above all description. For many, this event utterly changed their attitude toward death—as well as toward day-to-day existence. They have become far more sure of the intrinsic meaning of their own lives and of the entire cosmos. As Dr. Raymond Moody wrote in his influential book, *Life After Life* (Bantam: 1978), "Their vision left them with new goals, new moral principles, and a renewed determination to try to live in accordance with them."[11]

Although it is still impossible to identify with certainty the ultimate substance of this phenomenon, a host of innovators in the behavioral sciences are taking it quite seriously indeed. In the October 1980 issue of the *American Journal of Psychiatry*, Dr. Bruce Greyson and Dr. Ian Stevenson reported in their own survey results on the "near death experience." Both for what it may reveal about the very nature of life and its uncanny power to transform our innermost values, they argued that the phenomenon deserves our closest attention. For more than a half-millenium, Jewish visionaries have been saying precisely the same thing. Furthermore, they have not hesitated to incorporate these findings into their overall conception of human personality and our highest reaches.

To summarize, then, once the Kabbalah's abstruse symbolism is penetrated, this ancient tradition hardly appears as a hodgepodge of garbled mumbo jumbo or nonsense. To be sure, its terminology is difficult and initially unfamiliar to Western ears. Symbolic references to thrones of glory, celestial kings and queens, and date palms, have little import for us today. Yet, it seems evident that the Jewish esoteric system offers a remarkably comprehensive, lucid, and consistent picture of the human mind. It is striking that in nearly all respects, the new psychology has converged on the exact portrayal of our inner makeup that the Kabbalists have for centuries espoused.

To Every Thing a Season

Given the extraordinary sophistication of this pathway to the divine, why did it languish so long in obscurity? It is a sad fact that in the current era the Jewish visionary tradition has probably been more neglected by farsighted scientists than any of the world's other major spiritual systems. From the material presented in this book, this observation is extremely ironic. For instance, in his brilliant lectures on "The Varieties of Religious Experience," William James identified

Christian, Hindu, Buddhist, and Islamic teachings as treasure houses of psychological wisdom. Conspicuously absent
in his discussions was any serious mention of Judaism and its
mystical offshoot. Until the last few years, this trend has
continued. There have been several interesting reasons for
this historical situation.

For one thing, the major Kabbalistic texts have almost never
been readily accessible to mainstream Western audiences.
Much of the *Zohar* was only first translated into English in
the 1930s; most of the other chief works have waited to the
last twenty years for their modern translation. For example,
the first English edition of the enigmatic, twelfth-century
Bahir did not appear until 1980. Prior to Gershom Scholem's
thorough analyses and excerpts of the Kabbalah's critical states
of development, there was little available for American or
West European investigators curious about this longstanding
discipline.

Who then could James and his colleagues have turned to for
guidance in the Kabbalistic way? The authoritative writings
of Heinrich Graetz and his fellow German-Jewish rationalists
depicted the Kabbalah as the den of ignoramuses, fools, and
madmen. To this day, this description still influences many
people involved with Jewish culture. What about knowledgeable, living Kabbalists in the West? Virtually all have been of
Orthodox religious practice and extremely guarded about freely
dispensing the esoteric teachings to outsiders. It has only
been in the last few years that groups like the Lubavitcher
Hasidim have begun to publicize the mystical tradition. The
image of Professor James and his Harvard brahmins converging en masse for information upon the elders of some poor,
Orthodox Boston synagogue is quite implausible. For those
interested in Jewish mysticism, virtually the only "outside"
source until well into the mid-twentieth century was Martin
Buber's stylistic interpretation of the beginnings of Hasidism.

Today, there is an unparalleled fascination in the Western
world for the Kabbalah. Nevertheless, several key volumes—
such as Moses Cordovero's *Orchard of Pomegranates* and Chaim
Vital's *Tree of Life*—remain unavailable to all but an elite

coterie of professional scholars. Some works now exist in modern Hebrew editions in Israel. But others still lie in their original manuscripts, hidden away in university and national archives. Each year, more of these volumes are translated and made accessible to the interested public. However, the sheer lack of ready information on Kabbalistic thought has unquestionably impeded its promulgation in the contemporary era .

Another reason for the general ignorance that has enshrouded this ancient tradition must be attributed to the inclinations of the early scientific explorers of the mind. Seminal thinkers of modern psychology and psychotherapy, like Freud, Erich Fromm, Wilhelm Reich, and Fritz Perls, were all of Jewish ancestry, yet eager to shed their ethnic and religious identity. Freud was far more sympathetic to mysticism than is ordinarily known and was intrigued by the evidence for psychical phenomena. However, throughout his life, he kept this interest carefully hidden. Perhaps he had correctly appraised his own historical situation when he bitterly commented that psychoanalysis would have met with far quicker acceptance had its progenitor not been a Jew. In fact, as late as 1927, Freud's ground-breaking *The Interpretation of Dreams*, published in 1899, was attacked by a prominent colleague as a work of mystical rubbish like "the well-known dream books, printed on bad paper, which may be found in cooks' drawers."[12]

In his interesting autobiography, *From Berlin to Jerusalem* (Schocken: 1980), Gershom Scholem relates that in the early 1920s, Erich Fromm briefly studied the *Zohar* with him in Berlin. But four years later, as Scholem reminisces, Fromm "was an enthusiastic Trostkyite and pitied me for my petit-bourgeois parochialism."[13] Wilhelm Reich, the influential sexual revolutionary, had little respect for Jewish culture, especially its traditional roots. Though like Freud he seems to have had a famous rabbi among his ancestors, Reich outdid his mentor by disaffiliating with anything deemed even remotely "Jewish" in content. Late in his career, Reich devoted considerable attention to the psychology of religion, gradually drawing more sympathetic to its aims. Yet he never sought to examine either mainstream or esoteric Judaism. Fritz Perls, at the end of his life, issued a semi-autobiographical account. In it, this inventive psychotherapist mirrored Reich's open disdain for Jewish teachings. Interestingly, all of these figures came from rather assimilated German-Austrian families. Whether they had read Graetz's vicious diatribes against the Kabbalah is a moot question. But with the possible exception of Freud, they shared Graetz's contempt for it. It held absolutely no interest for them.

It is again ironic that of the many gifted innovators of modern psychology, only one—Carl Jung, the son of a Protestant minister—recognized the Kabbalistic system as a true wellspring of psychological knowledge. Moreover, Jung arrived at the Jewish esoteric path not through any of its own gateways, but rather by the seventeenth-century Latin treatise on it by Knorr von Rosenroth.

In his posthumously published private correspondence, the Swiss psychoanalyst made several references to the Kabbalah. He even alluded to some of its more technical terms, such as the Lurianic concept of the "shattering of the vessels" of creation. Most interestingly, in a letter he penned in 1957, Jung explicitly pinpointed the connection between Jewish mysticism and Freudian theory. A true understanding of this powerful innovator's work, he wrote, "would carry us beyond Jewish orthodoxy into the subterranean workings of Hasidism . . . and then into the intricacies of the Kabbalah, which still remains unexplored psychologically."[14]

Though Freud may have denied the existence of this link, there are readily discernible similarities between psychoanalysis and Kabbalistic notions. In innumerable ways, in fact, this longstanding discipline has effectively foreshadowed nearly every important insight in the behavioral sciences. Acknowledging his lack of familiarity with the primary Jewish sources, Jung was unable to complete his quest for a demonstrable psychology of the divine. But he saw Jewish mysticism as a beacon to light the way. In a time when a new vision of the human potential is now sought by many, the Kabbalah speaks to us with a relevance perhaps unprecedented since its inception.

NOTES

INTRODUCTION

1. Abraham Isaac Kook, *The Lights of Penitence, Lights of Holiness, The Moral Principles, Essays, Letters, and Poems,* translated by Ben Zion Bokser (New York: Paulist Press, 1978), p. 67.

CHAPTER 1

opening quotes:

C.G. Jung, *Letters,* volume 2, edited by Gerhard Adler (Princeton: Princeton University Press, 1975), p.155.

Herbert Weiner, *9½ Jewish Mystics* (New York: Collier, 1969), p.17.

1. Louis Jacobs, *Jewish Mystical Testimonies* (New York: Schocken, 1978), p. 31.
2. Detlef Ingo Lauf, *Secret Doctrines of the Tibetan Books of the Dead* (Boulder: Shambhala, 1977), p. ix.
3. *Bahir,* translated by Aryeh Kaplan (New York: Weiser, 1980), 1, p.1.
4. Ibid., 4, p.2.
5. Ibid., p. vii.
6. Jacobs, p.62.
7. *Zohar,* volume 1, translated by Harry Sperling and Maurice Simon, (London: Soncino Press, 1933), pp. 323–324.
8. Lao Tzu, *Tao Te Ching,* translated by D.C. Lau (Baltimore: Penguin, 1974), p.125.
9. *Zohar,* volume 1, p.160.
10. *Zohar,* volume 1, p. xiii–xiv.
11. Solomon Schechter, "Safed in the Sixteenth Century," *Studies in Judaism,* second series (Philadelphia: Jewish Publication Society, 1908), p.223.
12. Moses Cordovero, *The Palm Tree of Deborah,* translated by Louis Jacobs (New York: Sepher-Hermon, 1974), p. 117.
13. R.J. Zwi Werblowsky, *Joseph Karo, Lawyer and Mystic* (Philadelphia: Jewish Publication Society of America, 1977), p. 15.
14. Gershom Scholem, *Major Trends in Jewish Mysticism* (New York: Schocken, 1974), p. 254.

15. Louis I. Newman, *Hasidic Anthology* (New York: Schocken, 1975), p. 203.
16. Ibid., p. 137.
17. Ibid., p. 158.
18. J.G. Weiss, "Via Passiva in Early Hasidism," *Journal of Jewish Studies,* 1960, *11*, p. 149.
19. Louis Jacobs, *Hasidic Thought* (New York: Schocken, 1976), p. 72–73.
20. Newman, p. 476.
21. Jacobs, *Hasidic Thought*, p. 132.
22. Schneur Zalman of Liady, *Tanya*, translated by N. Mindel (New York: Kehot Publication Society, 1973), p. 79.
23. Jacobs, *Hasidic Thought*, p. 131.
24. *Rabbi Nachman's Wisdom,* translated by Aryeh Kaplan (Brooklyn: Aryeh Kaplan, 4804-16th Avenue, 1976), p. 151.
25. Weiner, p. 198.
26. Michael Meyer, *Ideas of Jewish History* (New York: Behrman House, 1974), p. 217.
27. Ibid., p. 217.
28. Heinrich Graetz, *History of the Jews,* volume 4 (Philadelphia: Jewish Publication Society of America, 1894), p. 14.
29. Ibid., volume 5, pp. 375–376.

CHAPTER 2

opening quotes:
   Zohar, volume 2, p. 36
   Rabbi Nachman's Wisdom, p. 142.
1. Fritjof Capra, *The Tao of Physics* (Boulder: Shambhala, 1975), p.25.
2. Abraham Maslow, *The Psychology of Science* (New York: Harper and Row, 1966), p. 1.
3. Ibid., pp. 4–5.
4. *Zohar,* volume 1, p. 84.
5. Moses Chaim Luzzatto, *The Way of God,* translated by Aryeh Kaplan (Jerusalem: Feldheim, 1978), p. 195.
6. *Zohar,* volume 1, p. 146.
7. Ibid., p. 121.
8. *Zohar,* volume 2, p. 121.
9. *Zohar,* volume 1, p. 177.
10. *Rabbi Nachman's Wisdom,* p. 143.
11. Capra, pp. 154–155.
12. *Zohar,* volume 1, p. 63.
13. *Book of Creation,* translated by Irving Friedman (New York: Weiser, 1977), 1, p. 1.
14. Schneur Zalman of Liady, pp. 89–91.
15. *Bahir,* 172, p. 65.
16. Albert Einstein, *Cosmic Religion* (New York: Covici, Friede, 1931), p. 102.
17. Albert Einstein, *The World as I See it* (New York: Covici, Friede, 1934), p. 264.

CHAPTER 3

opening quotes:

  Zohar, volume 1, p. 286.

  Newman, p. 384.

1. *Zohar*, volume 2, p. 280.
2. *Rabbi Nachman's Wisdom*, p. 156.
3. *Zohar*, volume 3, p. 227.
4. Ibid., p. 231.
5. *Rabbi Nachman's Wisdom*, p. 141.
6. Kook, p. 67.
7. Newman, p. 267.
8. Ibid., p. 53.
9. Ibid., p. 506.
10. Ibid., p. 244.
11. Ibid., p. 244.
12. Zalman M. Schachter, "The Dynamics of the *Yehudit* Transaction." *Journal of Psychology and Judaism*, Fall 1978, 3(1), pp. 11, 14.
13. *Zohar*, volume 1, p. 44.
14. *Zohar*, volume 2, p. 205.
15. *Zohar*, volume 1, p. 293.
16. Luzzatto, *The Way of God*, p. 63.
17. *Rabbi Nachman's Wisdom*, p. 132.
18a. Moses Chaim Luzzatto, *The Path of the Just*, translated by Shraga Silverstein (Jerusalem: Feldheim, 1966), p. 189.
18b. Ibid., p. 215.
19. Newman, p. 18.
20. Irving Block, "Chabad Psychology and the *Benoni* of *Tanya*," *Tradition*, Fall 1963, 6(1), p. 35.
21. Newman, p. 257.
22. *Zohar*, volume 4, p. 334.
23. Raphael Patai, *The Hebrew Goddess* (New York: Avon, 1978), p. 104.
24. Ibid., p. 111.
25. *Bahir*, 131, p. 48.
26. Ibid., 198, p. 80.
27. Ibid., 155, p. 56.
28. *Zohar*, volume 2, pp. 174–175.
29. *Zohar*, volume 5, p. 93.
30. *Zohar*, volume 1, pp. 113–114.
31. Ibid., p. 159.
32. *Zohar*, volume 2, p. 212.
33. Newman, pp. 254–255.

CHAPTER 4

opening quotes:

Rabbi Nachman's Wisdom, pp. 150–151.

Martin Buber, *The Tales of Rabbi Nachman*, translated by Maurice Friedman (New York: Avon, 1970), p.37.

1. *Rabbi Nachman's Wisdom*, p. 189.
2. Luzzatto, *The Way of God*, p. 45.
3. *Rabbi Nachman's Wisdom*, p. 416.
4. Schneur Zalman of Liady, p. 47.
5. Abraham ben Samuel Abulafia, *The Path of the Names,* translated and adapted by Bruria Finkel, Jack Hirschman, David Meltzer, and Gershom Scholem (Berkeley: Trigram, 1976), p. 24.
6. Luzzatto, *The Path of the Just*, p. 329.
7. *Rabbi Nachman's Wisdom*, p. 324.
8. Luzzatto, *The Way of God*, p. 199.
9. *Zohar*, volume 1, p. 243.
10. Itzhak Bentov, *Stalking the Wild Pendulum* (New York: Dutton, 1977), p. 225.
11. Abulafia, p. 25.
12. Ibid., p. 25.
13. *Rabbi Nachman's Wisdom*, p. 401.
14. Ibid., p. 179.
15. Ibid., p. 151.
16. *Oxford Annotated Bible*, edited by Herbert C. May and Bruce M. Metzger (New York: Oxford University Press, 1962), 1 Ezekial 15–29, p. 1001.
17. Gershom G. Scholem, *Jewish Gnosticism, Merkabah Mysticism, and Talmudic Tradition* (New York: Jewish Theological Seminary of America, 1965), p. 15.
18. *Book of Creation*, 5, p. 15.
19. Abulafia, p. 39.
20. Ibid., p. 39.
21. Ibid., p. 24.
22. Jack Hirschman, "On the Hebrew Letters," *Tree*, Summer 1971, 2, pp. 37–38.
23. *Zohar*, volume 2, p. 159.
24. Carl G. Jung, *Man and his Symbols* (New York: Doubleday, 1964), p. 90.
25. Metzger, p. 189.
26. J.G. Weiss, "The Kavvanoth of Prayer in Early Hasidism," *Journal of Jewish Studies*, 1958 (9), p. 179.
27. Schneur Zalman of Liady, p. 225.
28. Ibid., p. 225.
29. *Rabbi Nachman's Wisdom*, p. 266.
30. Louis I. Jacobs, *Hasidic Prayer* (New York: Schocken, 1978), p. 105.
31. Ibid., p. 107.
32. Ibid., p. 108.

33. *Rabbi Nachman's Wisdom*, p. 177.
34. Frederic J. Heide and Thomas D. Borkovec. "Relaxation-Induced Anxiety: Psychophysiological Evidence of Anxiety Enhancement in Tense Subjects Practicing Relaxation." Paper presented at the 1980 Annual Convention of the Association for Advancement of Behavior Therapy, New York, p.1.
35. *Rabbi Nachman's Wisdom*, p. 191.
36. Ibid., p. 303.

CHAPTER 5

opening quotes:
Buber, p. 35.
Zohar, volume 1, p. 16.
1. Frank Goble, *The Third Force* (New York: Pocket Books, 1974), p.54.
2. Ibid., p. 54.
3. *Zohar*, volume 1, p. 323.
4. Luzzatto, *The Way of God*, p. 61.
5. Ibid., p. 63.
6. *Zohar*, volume 1, p. 332.
7. *Zohar*, volume 3, p. 77.
8. Gershom Scholem, *The Messianic Idea in Judaism*, translated by Michael Meyer and Hillel Hankin (New York: Schocken, 1978), p. 224.
9. Newman, p. 474.
10. Schneur Zalman of Liady, p. 237.
11. *Rabbi Nachman's Wisdom*, p. 148.
12. Ibid., p. 179.
13. Luzzatto, *The Way of God*, p. 103.
14. *Bahir*, 190, p. 75.
15. *Zohar*, volume 3, p. 217.
16. *Zohar*, volume 2, p. 152.
17. Schneur Zalman of Liady, pp. 77–79.
18. *Rabbi Nachman's Wisdom*, p. 222.
19. Norman Garmezy, "The Psychology and Psychopathology of Attention," *Schizophrenia Bulletin*, 1977, 3(3), p. 365.
20. Keith H. Nuechterlein, "Reaction Time and Attention in Schizophrenia: a Critical Evaluation of the Data and Theories," *Schizophrenia Bulletin*, 1977, 3(3), p.403.
21. Ibid., p. 403.
22. Aldous Huxley, *The Doors of Perception and Heaven and Hell* (New York: Harper and Row, 1963), pp. 22–23.
23. Ibid., p. 57.
24. *Rabbi Nachman's Wisdom*, p. 129.
25. Scholem, *Major Trends in Jewish Mysticism*, p. 254.
26. *Rabbi Nachman's Wisdom*, p. 105.
27. Luzzatto, *The Path of the Just*, p. 41.
28. *Zohar*, volume 4, p. 14.

29. Abulafia, p. 26.

30. Ibid., p. 26.

31. *Zohar*, volume 1, p. 84.

32. *Zohar*, volume 3, p. 74.

33. Huxley, p. 22.

34. Govinda, *The Way of the White Clouds*, p. 103.

35. *Zohar*, volume 3, pp. 47–48.

36. Huxley, title page.

CHAPTER 6

opening quotes:

   Zohar, volume 2, p. 200

   A. Z. Idelsohn, *Jewish Music and its Historical Development* (New York: Schocken, 1967), p. 414.

1. Newman, p. 447.

2. *Zohar*, volume 1, p. 303.

3. Newman, p. 447.

4. Moshe Halevi Spero, "Anticipations of Dream Psychology in the Talmud," *Journal of the History of the Behavioral Sciences*, October 1975, *11*(4), p. 376.

5. *Zohar*, volume 2, p. 259.

6. Ibid., p. 200.

7. Ibid., p. 258.

8. Ibid., p. 228.

9. Ibid., p. 236.

10. *Zohar*, volume 1, p. 116.

11. Ibid., p. 164.

12. *Zohar*, volume 2, p. 259.

13. Werblowsky, p. 182.

14. *Zohar*, volume 5, p. 140.

15. Werblowsky, pp. 47–48.

16. *Zohar*, volume 2, p. 199.

17. Ibid., p. 79.

18. Stanley Krippner, "Dreams and other Altered Conscious States," *Journal of Communication*, Winter 1975, p. 174.

19. Ibid., p. 177.

20. Montague Ullman, "The Role of Imagery," *Journal of Communication*, Winter 1975, p. 163.

21. Ibid., p. 163.

22. *Zohar*, volume 4, p. 225.

23. *Oxford Annotated Bible*, 2 Kings 3:15, p. 457.

24. Ibid., 1 Samuel 16:16, p.353.

25. Scholem, *Jewish Gnosticism, Merkabah Mysticism, and Talmudic Tradition*, p. 11.

26. Ibid., p. 21.

27. *Bahir*, 47, p. 17.

28. Amnon Shiloah, "The Symbolism of Music in the Kabbalistic Tradition," *World of Music*, 1978, 20(3), p. 58.

29. Jacobs, *Jewish Mystical Testimonies* (New York: Schocken, 1978), p. 60.

30. *Oxford Annotated Bible*, Joshua 6:20, p. 269

31. *Zohar*, volume 3, p. 59.

32. Ibid., p. 60.

33. Dov Baer of Lubavitch, *Tract on Ecstasy*, translated by Louis Jacobs (London: Vallentine Mitchell, 1963), p.78.

34. Ibid., p. 77.

35. Ibid., p. 77.

36. Ruth Rubin, *Voices of a People* (New York: McGraw-Hill, 1973), p. 247.

37. Ibid., p. 247.

38. Yaacov Mazor and André Hadju, "The Hasidic Dance *Nigun*," *Yuval*, 1974, 3, p. 139.

39. Gordon Epperson, *The Musical Symbol* (Ames, Iowa: Iowa State University, 1967), p. 25.

40. Newman, p. 203.

41. Joseph Haleri, "My Hasidic Adventure," *East West Journal*, October 1974, 4, p. 31.

42. Robert Bruce Williams, "Music Therapy: How It Helps the Child," *Psychology of Music*, 1978, 6(1), p. 57.

43. Helen I. Bonny and Walter N. Pahnke, "The Use of Music in Psychedelic (LSD) Psychotherapy." *Journal of Music Therapy*, summer 1972, 9, p. 70.

44. W. Otto Meissner, *Your Need of Music* (Milwaukee: Meissner Institute of Music, 1926), p. 23.

CHAPTER 7

opening quotes:

  Luzzatto, *The Way of God*, p. 121.

  Zohar, volume 2, p. 199.

1. *Zohar*, volume 1, p. 139.

2. *Zohar*, volume 2, p. 20.

3. Luzzatto, *The Way of God*, p. 389.

4. Ibid., p. 391.

5. Ibid., p. 217.

6. Ibid., p. 233.

7. *Zohar*, volume 5, p. 363.

8. Luzzatto, *The Way of God*, p. 233.

9. Abulafia, pp. 60–61.

10. Ibid., pp. 56–57.

11. Werblowsky, p. 56.

12. Meltzer, p. 190.

13. Ibid., p. 190.

14. Ibid., p. 190.

15. Werblowsky, p. 263.

16. Jane Roberts, *Seth Speaks* (Englewood Cliffs, New Jersey: Prentice-Hall), pp. 30 & 6.

17. Jacobs, *Jewish Mystical Testimonies*, p. 143.

18. Ibid., p. 144.

19. Sigmund Freud, *Studies in Parapsychology,* translations by Alix Stratchey, C.J.M. Hubback, and Edward Glover (New York: Collier, 1966), p. 87.

20. Werblowsky, p. 314.

21. Ibid., p. 314.

22. Ibid., p. 315.

23. *Zohar*, volume 1, p. 352.

24. Newman, p. 262.

25. Newman, p. 262.

26. Blofeld, p. 92.

27. Govinda, *The Way of the White Clouds*, p. 82.

28. Naftali Hertz Ehrmann, *The Rav*, translated by Karen Paritzky, (Jerusalem: Feldheim, 1977), p. 117.

CHAPTER 8

opening quotes:

   Schneur Zalman of Liady, pp. 174–175.

   Luzzatto, *The Path of the Just*, p. 23.

1. Schneur Zalman of Liady, p. 79.

2. Luzzatto, *The Way of God*, p. 127.

3. Ibid., p. 129.

4. Newman, pp. 174–175.

5. Ibid., p. 128.

6. Jean Shinoda Bolen, *The Tao of Psychology* (New York: Harper and Row, 1979), pp. 47–48.

7. Newman, p. 373.

8. Edwin Wallace, "Freud's Mysticism and its Psychodynamic Determinants." *Bulletin of the Menninger Clinic*, May 1978, 42 (3), p. 207.

9. Newman, p. 67.

10. Ibid., p. 71.

11. *Rabbi Nachman's Wisdom*, p. 445.

12. Newman, p. 71.

13. Ibid., p. 70.

14. Ibid., p. 70.

15. J. Bruce Long, "The Death that Ends in Hinduism and Buddhism." Edited by Elisabeth Kübler-Ross, *Death, the Final Stage of Growth* (Englewood Cliffs, New Jersey: Prentice Hall, 1975), p. 62.

16. Ibid., p. 66.

17. *Zohar*, volume 2, p. 307.

18. Raymond Moody, *Life after Life* (New York: Bantam, 1976), p. 55.

19. Ibid., Foreword by Elisabeth Kubler-Ross.

20. *Zohar*, volume 2, p. 309.

21. Schneur Zalman of Liady, p. 127.

22. Newman, p. 2.
23. *Zohar*, volume 2, pp. 17–18.
24. *Zohar*, volume 1, p. 324.
25. Newman, p. 3.
26. Ibid., p. 1.
27. Fritz Perls, *Gestalt Therapy Verbatim* (New York: Bantam, 1972), p. 56.
28. Werblowsky, p. 245.
29. *Zohar*, volume 3, p. 333.
30. Werblowsky, p. 113.
31. Werblowsky, pp. 114–115.
32. David Meltzer, *The Secret Garden: an Anthology in the Kabbalah* (New York: Seabury, 1976), p. 193.
33. Luzzatto, *The Way of God*, p. 121.
34. John Blofeld, *The Tantric Mysticism of Tibet* (New York: Causeway, 1974), pp. 47–48.
35. *Zohar*, volume 2, p. 22.
36. Werblowsky, p. 241.
37. Lama Anagarika Govinda, *Foundations of Tibetan Mysticism* (New York: Weiser, 1975), p. 247.
38. Newman, p. 97.

CHAPTER 9

opening quotes:
Kook, p. 340.
Kook, p. 351.
1. William James, *The Varieties of Religious Experience* (Garden City, New York: Doubleday, 1978), p. 133.
2. Ibid., p. 133.
3. Abraham Maslow, *Toward a Psychology of Being* (New York: Van Nostrand, 1968), p. 113.
4. *Rabbi Nachman's Wisdom*, p. 142.
5. *Zohar*, volume 3, p. 79.
6. Newman, p. 451.
7. *Zohar*, volume 2, p. 79.
8. *William James on Psychical Research*, edited by Gardner Murphy and Robert O. Ballou (Clifton, New Jersey: Augustus M. Kelley, 1973), p. 322.
9. Parker Rossman, *Hospice* (New York: Fawcett, 1977), p. 39.
10. *Zohar*, volume 1, p. 324.
11. Moody, p. 93.
12. Ernest Jones, *The Life and Work of Sigmund Freud*, edited by Lionel Trilling and Steven Marcus (New York: Basic Books, 1961), p. 235.
13. Gershom Scholem, *From Berlin to Jerusalem*, translated by Harry Zohn (New York: Schocken, 1980), p. 156.
14. Carl Jung, *Letters*, volume 2, edited by Gerhard Adler (Princeton: Princeton University Press, 1975), p. 359.

GLOSSARY

Adam Kadmon. The primordial human in the creation of the universe. Each of us is said to mirror the makeup of this archetypal figure.

Baal Shem Tov. "Bearer of the Good Name," the popular appellation of Israel ben Eliezer (c. 1698–1760), the charismatic Hasidic founder.

Bahir. The "Book of Brilliance," anonymously written, which first appeared in Provence, southern France, about the year 1175.

Besht. An abbreviation of the Hebrew name, "Baal Shem Tov."

Bittul Ha-Yesh. Hasidic term for self-annihilation of the ego, in order to experience higher states of consciousness.

Chabad. The metaphysical system developed by Rabbi Schneur Zalman of Liady (1747–1812). The basis for Lubavitcher Hasidic thought, this term derives from the abbreviation of the first letters of the highest three *sefirot*—*chochmah* (wisdom), *binah* (understanding), and *daath* (knowledge).

Devekuth. The inward state of cleaving to the divine.

Ein Sof. The "Infinite," from which all forms in the universe are created. This concept is similar to the Eastern notion of the "luminosity-emptiness."

Gematriyah. Meditational technique in which Hebrew words with dissimilar meanings but equivalent numerical values are probed for their secret correspondences.

Gilgulim. The "cyles" or "transformations" of each soul's journey to complete enlightenment. This concept assumes the existence of reincarnation and many lifetimes on earth for each person.

Halacha. The legal system of orthodox Judaism. Its subtleties have been viewed by Kabbalists as reflecting many levels of hidden meaning.

Hasidism. The popular, charismatic movement which arose among East European Jewry in the late eighteenth century. *Hasid* means

232

"devout" in Hebrew; in twelfth-century Germany, an unrelated group was likewise known as the *Hasidim*.

Hekhalot. The "heavenly halls" glimpsed during meditation, as practiced by Jewish visionaries in the first century B.C.E. through the tenth century C.E.

Hitlahavut. The mental state of "burning enthusiasm" for the divine in all aspects of life.

Kabbalah. From the Hebrew root-word "to receive." Often used as a generic term for Jewish mysticism per se, it more precisely refers to its esoteric thought from the late twelfth century onward.

Kavvanah. The classic rabbinical term for mental concentration. Among the Hasidim, *kavvanah* came to be associated with the type of "one-pointedness" of intent necessary for higher realms of awareness.

Kavvanoth. The technical name for the meditative exercises developed by Kabbalists in sixteenth-century Safed. These methods involve a complex visualization format related to the ten *Sefirot*.

Kelipot. The "shells" or forces of impurity that arose during the creation of the universe. Each person is said to have the responsibility to heal the *kelipot* he or she encounters in daily life.

Keter. The "crown" or highest of the ten *Sefirot*; it is also regarded as the active, penetrating force in the cosmos.

Maggid. A supposed spiritual entity that communicates through the adept when in a trance state; *maggid* also refers to a spiritually advanced human.

Malkuth. The "kingdom" or lowest of the ten *Sefirot*; it is also regarded as the passive, receptive force in the cosmos. *See also keter.*

Maskilim. "Enlightened Ones," referring to the first assimilationists among Western Jews in the late eighteenth and early nineteenth centuries. The *Maskilim* were highly contemptuous of Kabbalistic and Hasidic elements of Judaism.

Mittnagedim. Orthodox Jews who were "Opponents" of the Hasidic movement. The *Mittnagedim* went to great lengths to attempt to supress the spread of Hasidism among East European Jewry.

Nefesh. The lowest, most physical portion of the human Self. The *nefesh* is said to dissolve upon physical mortality.

Neshamah. The nonphysical, transcendent part of the Self. The *neshamah* continues after bodily death; some Kabbalists suggest that two other, still more immaterial components exist within each of us.

Niggun. Hasidic melody without words.

Notarikon. Meditational technique which breaks Hebrew words into sentences composed of initial letters, to attain esoteric knowledge.

Rebbe. Hasidic term for spiritual teacher.

Ruach. That portion of the human Self that is intermediate in nature between the *nefesh* and *neshamah*. The *ruach* dissipates shortly after bodily death.

Sefer Yetzirah. "Book of Creation," anonymously written between the third and sixth centuries C.E. It represents the earliest metaphysical text in the Hebrew language.

Sefirot. The ten energy-essences that are said to be in constant interplay and underlie all of the universe. The *sefirot* have historically been portrayed in various arrangements, the most significant being the Tree of Life.

Shekinah. The female aspect to the deity. The *Shekinah* is described as dwelling amongst holy persons but as being in exile from its own Source.

Talmud. The summary of the Judaic oral law, compiled in writing by sages in Palestine and Babylonia. Completed about 500 C.E., it exists in two editions, one for each center of world Judaism of the time. While many major Kabbalists were quite knowledgeable in Talmudic study, some Hasidic figures downplayed its significance; they thereby incurred the wrath of the *Mittnagedim.*

Tanya. "It Has Been Taught," the title of the major theoretical work by Rabbi Schneur Zalman of Liady. Its chief section was first published in 1796 and has been intensively studied by Lubavitcher Hasidim and others ever since.

Tikkun. The divine restoration of the cosmos. Each human act is described as either aiding or impeding this process.

Torah. In a narrow sense, the Pentateuch. More widely, Torah is understood to comprise the twenty-four books of the Bible and the Talmud.

Tree of Life. The central metaphor for the universe and every aspect of it. The ten *Sefirot* are most typically arranged in a pattern known as the Tree of Life; all animate and inanimate forms are said to mirror this structure.

Yichud. A meditational exercise involving mental visualization and the ten *Sefirot*; this technique was developed by the sixteenth-century Kabbalists of Safed.

Zaddik. "Pious One." In Hasidism, the *zaddik* is the spiritual leader of the community and is regarded as an intermediary between it and the divine world.

Zohar. The "Book of Splendor," which first appeared in late thirteenth-century Spain. It is the "bible" of the Kabbalah and its most influential work. Ascribed to Simeon bar Yochai of the second century by traditionalists, scholars today attribute it to Moses de Leon, who is said to have composed most of it in the 1280s or 1290s.

BIBLIOGRAPHY

Aberbach, David. "Freud's Jewish Problem." *Commentary*, June 1980, 69(6), 36–39.

Abulafia, Abraham ben Samuel. *The Path of the Names*. Translated and adapted by Bruria Finkel, Jack Hirschman, David Meltzer, and Gershom Scholem. Berkeley: Trigram, 1976.

Alvin, Juliette. *Music Therapy*. New York: Basic Books, 1975.

Ausubel, Nathan. *The Book of Jewish Knowledge*. New York: Crown, 1964.

Bachya, ben Joseph ibn Paquada. *Duties of the Heart*, volumes 1 and 2. Translated by Moses Hyamson. Jerusalem: Feldheim, 1978.

Bahir. Translated by Aryeh Kaplan. New York: Weiser, 1980.

Bakan, David. *Sigmund Freud and the Jewish Mystical Tradition*. New York: Schocken, 1958.

Bentov, Itzhak. *Stalking the Wild Pendulum*. New York: Dutton, 1977.

Bergman, Paul. "Music in the thinking of great philosophers." *Music Therapy*, 1952, 2, 40–44.

Bindler, Paul. "Meditative Prayer and Rabbinic Perspectives on the Psychology of Consciousness: Environmental, Physiological, and Attentional Variables." *Journal of Psychology and Judaism*, Summer 1980, 4(4), 228–248.

Black Elk Speaks. Lincoln: University of Nebraska Press, 1961.

Block, Irving. "Chabad Psychology and the Benoni of Tanya." *Tradition*, Fall 1963, 6(1), 30–39.

Blofeld, John. *The Tantric Mysticism of Tibet*. New York: Causeway, 1974.

Blumenthal, David R. *Understanding Jewish Mysticism*. New York: Ktav, 1978.

Bokser, Ben Zion. "The Religious Philosophy of Rabbi Kook." *Judaism*, Fall 1970, 19(4), 396–405.

Bolen, Jean Shinoda. *The Tao of Psychology.* New York: Harper and Row, 1979.

Bonny, Helen I. "Music and Consciousness." *Journal of Music Therapy,* Fall 1975, *12*(3), 121–135.

Bonny, Helen I. and Pahnke, Walter N. "The Use of Music in Psychedelic (LSD) Psychotherapy." *Journal of Music Therapy,* summer 1972, 9, 64–67.

Book of Creation. Translated by Irving Friedman. New York: Weiser, 1977.

Boxberger, Ruth. "Historical Bases for the Use of Music in Therapy." *Music Therapy,* 1951, *11*(2), 125–165.

Broadbent, William. *Perception and Communication.* Oxford: Pergamon, 1958.

Buber, Martin. *Hasidism and Modern Man.* Translated by Maurice Friedman. New York: Horizon, 1958.

Buber, Martin. *I and Thou.* Translated by Ronald Gregor Smith. New York: Charles Scribner's Sons, 1958.

Buber, Martin. *Tales of the Hasidim: the Early Masters.* New York: Schocken, 1961.

Buber, Martin. *The Tales of Rabbi Nachman.* Translated by Maurice Friedman. New York: Avon, 1970.

Bulka, Reuven P. *Mystics and Medics.* New York: Human Sciences Press, 1979.

Capra, Fritjof. *The Tao of Physics.* Boulder: Shambhala, 1976.

Chapman, J. and McGhie, A. "A Comparative Study of Disordered Attention in Schizophrenia." *Journal of Mental Science,* 1962, *108*, 487–500.

Chapman, Loren J. "Recent Advances in the Study of Schizophrenic Cognition." *Schizophrenia Bulletin,* 1979, *5*(4), 568–580.

Chazan, Robert and Raphael, Marc Lee. *Modern Jewish History, A Source Reader.* New York: Schocken, 1974.

Comay, Joan. *The Temple of Jerusalem.* New York: Crown, 1964.

Cordovero, Moses. *The Palm Tree of Deborah.* Translated by Louis Jacobs. New York: Sepher-Hermon Press, 1981.

Daly, Mary. *Beyond God the Father.* Boston: Beacon, 1973.

Dean, Stanley R., Plyer, C.O. and Dean, Michael L. "Should Psychic Studies be Included in Psychiatric Education?" *American Journal of Psychiatry,* October 1980, *137*(10), 1247–1249.

Dimont, Max I. *The Jews in America.* New York: Simon and Schuster, 1980.

Dov Baer of Lubavitch. *Tract on Ecstasy.* Translated by Louis Jacobs. London: Vallentine Mitchell, 1963.

Ehrmann, Naftali Hertz. *The Rav.* Translated by Karen Paritzky. Jerusalem: Feldheim, 1977.

Einstein, Albert. *Cosmic Religion.* New York: Covici, Friede, 1931.

Einstein, Albert. *The World as I See it.* New York: Covici, Friede, 1934.

Epperson, Gordon. *The Musical Symbol.* Ames, Iowa: Iowa State University, 1967.

Epstein, Perle. *Kabbalah, the Way of the Jewish Mystic.* New York: Doubleday, 1978.

Epstein, Perle. *Pilgrimage.* Boston: Houghton Mifflin, 1979.

Fleer, Gedaliah. *Rabbi Nachman's Foundation.* New York: Ohr MiBreslov, 1976.

Frey-Wehrlin, C.T. "Reflections on C.G. Jung's Concept of Synchronicity." *Journal of Analytic Psychology,* January 1976, *21* (1), 37–49.

Freud, Sigmund. *The Interpretation of Dreams.* Translated by James Stratchey. New York: Basic Books, 1965.

Freud, Sigmund. *Studies in Parapsychology.* Translations by Alix Stratchey, C.J.M. Hubback, and Edward Glover. New York: Collier, 1966.

Garfield, Patricia. *Pathway to Ecstasy.* New York: Holt, Rinehart, and Winston, 1979.

Garmezy, Norman. "The Psychology and Psychopathology of Attention." *Schizophrenia Bulletin,* 1977, 3(3), 360–369.

Goble, Frank. *The Third Force.* New York: Pocket Books, 1974.

Govinda, Lama Anagarika. *Foundations of Tibetan Mysticism.* New York: Weiser, 1975.

Govinda, Lama Anagarika. *The Way of the White Clouds.* Boulder: Shambhala, 1970.

Graetz, Heinrich. *History of the Jews.* Philadelphia: Jewish Publication Society of America, 1894.

Greeley, Andrew M. *The Sociology of the Paranormal.* New York: Sage, 1976.

Greyson, Bruce and Stevenson, Ian. "The Phenomonology of Near-Death Experiences." *American Journal of Psychiatry,* October 1980, *137* (10) 1193–1196.

Grof, Stanislav and Halifax, Joan. *The Human Encounter with Death.* New York: Dutton, 1977.

Haleri, Joseph. "My Hasidic Adventure." *East West Journal,* October 1974, *4*, 30–31.

Halevi, Z'ev ben Shimon. *Adam and the Kabbalistic Tree.* New York: Weiser, 1974.

Halevi, Z'ev ben Shimon. *Kabbalah.* New York: Thames and Hudson, 1980.

Halpern, Steven. *Tuning the Human Instrument*. Belmont, California: Spectrum Research Institute, 1978.

Head, Joseph and Cranston, S.L. *Reincarnation: the Phoenix Fire Mystery*. New York: Crown, 1977.

Heide, Frederic J. and Borkovec, Thomas D. "Relaxation-Induced Anxiety: Psychophysiological Evidence of Anxiety Enhancement in Tense Subjects Practicing Relaxation." Paper presented at the 1980 Annual Convention of the Association for Advancement of Behavior Therapy, New York.

Heifetz, Harold. *Zen and Hasidism*. Wheaton, Illinois: Theosophical Publishing House, 1978.

Hirschman, Jack. "On the Hebrew Letters." *Tree*, Summer 1971, 2, 34–45.

Hoffman, Edward. "The Kabbalah: its Implications for Humanistic Psychology." *Journal of Humanistic Psychology*, Winter 1980, 20 (1), 33–47.

Huxley, Aldous. *The Doors of Perception and Heaven and Hell*. New York: Harper and Row, 1963.

I Ching. Translated by Richard Wilhelm, rendered into English by Cary F. Baynes. Princeton: Princeton University Press, 1967.

Idelsohn, A.Z. *Jewish Music and its Historical Development*. New York: Schocken, 1967.

Illich, Ivan. *Medical Nemesis*. New York: Pantheon, 1976.

Jacobs, Louis. *Hasidic Prayer*. New York: Schocken, 1978.

Jacobs, Louis. *Hasidic Thought*. New York: Schocken, 1976.

Jacobs, Louis. *Jewish Mystical Testimonies*. New York: Schocken, 1978.

James, William. *The Varieties of Religious Experience*. Garden City, New York: Doubleday, 1978.

William James on Psychical Research. Gardner Murphy and Robert O. Ballou, editors. Clifton, New Jersey: Augustus M. Kelley, 1973.

Jones, Ernest. *The Life and Work of Sigmund Freud*, edited by Lionel Trilling and Steven Marcus. New York: Basic Books, 1961.

Jung, Carl. *Man and his Symbols*. New York: Doubleday, 1964.

Jung, Carl. *Letters*, volume 2. Edited by Gerhard Adler. Princeton: Princeton University Press, 1975.

Kook, Abraham Isaac. *The Lights of Penitence, the Moral Principles, Lights of Holiness, Essays, Letters, and Poems*. Translated by Ben Zion Bokser. New York: Paulist Press, 1978.

Krippner, Stanley. "Dreams and other Altered Conscious States." *Journal of Communication*, Winter 1975, 173–182.

Kübler-Ross, Elisabeth. *Death, the Final Stage of Growth*. Englewood Cliffs, New Jersey: Prentice-Hall, 1975.

Kübler-Ross, Elisabeth. *On Death and Dying.* New York: Macmillan, 1969.

Lamm, Norman. "The Letter of the Besht to R. Gershon of Kutov." *Tradition,* Fall 1974, *14*(4), 110–125.

Lao Tzu. *Tao Te Ching.* Translated by D.C. Lau. Baltimore: Penguin, 1974.

Lauf, Detlef Ingo. *Secret Doctrines of the Tibetan Books of the Dead.* Translated by Graham Parkes. Boulder: Shambhala, 1977.

LeShan, Lawrence. *The Medium, the Mystic, and the Physicist.* New York: Viking, 1975.

Lieber, Arnold L. and Sherin, Carolyn R. "Homicides and the Lunar Cycle: Toward a Theory of Lunar Influence on Human Emotional Disturbance." *The American Journal of Psychiatry,* July 1972, 129 (*1*), 101–106.

Lieber, Arnold L. "Human Aggression and the Lunar Synodic Cycle." *Journal of Clinical Psychiatry,* May 1978, 39 (5), 385–387.

Lieber, Arnold L. *The Lunar Effect.* New York: Doubleday, 1979.

Love, Jeff. *The Quantum Gods.* London: Comptom Russell, 1976.

Luce, Gay Gaer. *Body Time.* New York: Pantheon, 1971.

Luzzatto, Moses Chaim. *The Path of the Just.* Translated by Shraga Silverstein, Jerusalem: Feldheim, 1966.

Luzzatto, Moses Chaim. *The Way of God.* Translated by Aryeh Kaplan. Jerusalem: Feldheim, 1978.

Mann, W. Edward and Hoffman, Edward. *The Man Who Dreamed of Tomorrow: a Conceptual Biography of Wilhelm Reich.* Los Angeles: Tarcher, 1980.

Maslow, Abraham. *The Psychology of Science.* New York: Harper and Row, 1966.

Maslow, Abraham. *Toward a Psychology of Being.* New York: Van Nostrand, 1968.

Mazor, Yaacov and Hadju, André. "The Hasidic Dance *Niggun.*" *Yuval,* 1974, 3, 136–265.

Meissner, W. Otto. *Your Need of Music.* Milwaukee: Meissner Institute of Music, 1926.

Meltzer, David. *The Secret Garden: an Anthology in the Kabbalah.* New York: Seabury, 1976.

Meyer, Michael. *Ideas of Jewish History.* New York: Behrman House, 1974.

Minkin, Jacob S. *The Romance of Hassidism.* North Hollywood, California: Wilshire, 1971.

Mishra, Rammurti. *Fundamentals of Yoga.* New York: Lancer, 1959.

Moody, Raymond. *Life after Life.* New York: Bantam, 1976.

Najaro, Claudio and Ornstein, Róbert. *On the Psychology of Meditation*. New York: Viking, 1971.

Newman, Louis I. *The Hasidic Anthology*. New York: Schocken, 1975.

Nuechterlein, Keith H. "Reaction Time and Attention in Schizophrenia: a Critical Evaluation of the Data and Theories." *Schizophrenia Bulletin*, 1977, 3(3), 373–428.

Olan, Levi A. *Judaism and Immortality*. New York: Union of American Hebrew Congregations, 1971.

Osis, Karlis and Haraldsson, E. *At the Hour of Death*. New York: Avon, 1977.

Oxford Annotated Bible. Edited by Herbert G. May and Bruce M. Metzger. New York: Oxford University Press, 1962.

Pagels, Elaine. *The Gnostic Gospels*. New York: Random House, 1979.

Patai, Raphael. *The Hebrew Goddess*. New York: Avon, 1978.

Perls, Fritz. *Gestalt Therapy Verbatim*. New York: Bantam, 1972.

Petuchowski, Jacob J. *Prayerbook Reform in Europe*. New York: World Union for Progressive Judaism, 1968.

Playfair, Guy L. and Hill, Scott. *The Cycles of Heaven*. New York: St. Martin's Press, 1978.

Poncé, Charles. *Kabbalah*. Wheaton, Illinois: Theosophical Publishing House, 1978.

Rabbi Nachman's Wisdom. Translated by Aryeh Kaplan. Brooklyn: Aryeh Kaplan, 4804-16th Avenue, 1976.

Reed, Henry. "Dream Incubation: a Reconstruction of a Ritual in Contemporary Form." *Journal of Humanistic Psychology*, Fall 1976, *16* (4), 53–70.

Ring, Kenneth. *Life at Death*. New York: Coward, McCann, and Geoghegan, 1980.

Roberts, Jane. *Seth Speaks*. Englewood Cliffs, New Jersey: Prentice-Hall, 1972.

Rosner, Fred. "Mental Disorders: A Chapter from the Work of Preuss." *Journal of Psychology and Judaism,* Winter 1978, 3(2), 126–142.

Rossman, Parker. *Hospice*. New York: Fawcett, 1977.

Rubin, Ruth. *Voices of a People*. New York: McGraw-Hill, 1973.

Safran, Alexandre. *The Kabbalah*. Translated by Margaret A. Pater. Jerusalem: Feldheim, 1975.

Saminsky, Lazare. *Music of the Ghetto and the Bible*. New York: Bloch, 1934.

Schachter, Zalman M. "The Dynamics of the *Yehudit* Transaction." *Journal of Psychology and Judaism*, Fall 1978, 3(1), 7–21.

Schachter, Zalman M. *Fragments of a Future Scroll.* Germantown, Pennsylvania: Leaves of Grass Press, 1975.

Schaya, Leo. *The Universal Meaning of the Kabbalah.* Translated by Nancy Pearson. Baltimore: Penguin, 1974.

Schechter, Solomon. *Studies in Judaism,* 2nd series. Philadelphia: Jewish Publication Society, 1908.

Schneur Zalman of Liady. *Tanya.* Translated by N. Mindel. Brooklyn: Kehot Publication Society, 1973.

Scholem, Gershom G. *From Berlin to Jerusalem.* Translated by Harry Zohn. New York: Schocken, 1980.

Scholem, Gershom G. *Jewish Gnosticism, Merkabah Mysticism, and Talmudic Tradition.* New York: Jewish Theological Seminary of America, 1965.

Scholem, Gershom G. *Major Trends in Jewish Mysticism.* New York: Schocken, 1974.

Scholem, Gershom G. *The Messianic Idea in Judaism.* Translated by Michael Meyer and Hillel Halkin. New York: Schocken, 1978.

Scholem, Gershom G. *On the Kabbalah and its Symbolism.* Translated by Ralph Manheim. New York: Schocken, 1965.

Schullian, Dorothy M. and Schoen, Max. *Music and Medicine.* New York: Henry Schuman, 1948.

Shah, Idries. *The Sufis.* New York: Doubleday, 1964.

Shamir, Yehuda. "Mystic Jerusalem." *Studia Mystica,* Summer 1980, 3(2), 50–60.

Shiloah, Amnon. "The Symbolism of Music in the Kabbalistic Tradition." *World of Music,* 1978, 20(3), 56–64.

Singer, Isaac B. *Reaches of Heaven.* New York: Farrar, Straus and Giroux, 1980.

Soyka, Fred. *The Ion Effect.* New York: Bantam, 1978.

Spero, Moshe Halevi. "Anticipations of Dream Psychology in the Talmud." *Journal of the History of the Behavioral Sciences,* October 1975, 11(4), 374–380.

Steinsaltz, Adin. *The Essential Talmud.* Translated by Chaya Galai. New York: Basic Books, 1976.

Steinsaltz, Adin. *The Thirteen Petalled Rose.* Translated by Yehuda Hanegbi. New York: Basic Books, 1980.

Stoddard, Sandol. *The Hospice Movement.* New York: Vintage, 1978.

Stone, Merlin. *When God was a Woman.* New York: Dial, 1976.

Suares, Carlo. *The Cipher of Genesis.* Boulder: Shambhala, 1978.

Suares, Carlo. *The Resurrection of the Word.* Translated by Vincent and Micheline Stuart. Boulder: Shambhala, 1975.

Tart, Charles C. *Altered States of Consciousness.* Garden City, New York: Anchor, 1972.

Tart, Charles C. *States of Consciousness.* New York: Dutton, 1974.

Tart, Charles C. *Transpersonal Psychologies.* New York: Harper and Row, 1975.

Toben, Bob. *Space-Time and Beyond.* New York: Dutton, 1975.

Trachtenberg, Joshua. *Jewish Magic and Supersitition.* New York: Atheneum, 1975.

Tree, Summer 1971, 2.

Tree, Winter 1972, 3.

Tree, Winter 1974, 4.

Tree, Summer 1975, 5.

Ullman, Montague and Krippner, Stanley, with Alan Vaughan. *Dream Telepathy.* New York: Macmillan, 1973.

Ullman, Montague. "The Role of Imagery." *Journal of Communication,* Winter 1975, 162–175.

Unterman, Alan. *The Wisdom of the Jewish Mystics.* New York: New Directions, 1976.

Van Dusen, Wilson. *The Presence of Other Worlds.* New York: Harper and Row, 1974.

Waite, Arthur E. *The Holy Kabbalah.* Secaucus, New Jersey: University Books, 1975.

Wallace, Edwin R. "Freud's Mysticism and its Psychodynamic Determinants." *Bulletin of the Menninger Clinic,* May 1978, 42 (3), 203–222.

Watts, Alan. *Psychotherapy East and West.* New York: Pantheon, 1961.

Weiner, Herbert. *9½ Mystics.* New York: Collier, 1969.

Weiss, J.G. "The Kavvanoth of Prayer in Early Hasidism." *Journal of Jewish Studies,* 1958 (9), 163–192.

Weiss, J.G. "Via Passive in Early Hasidism." *Journal of Jewish Studies,* 1960, *11,* 137–155.

Werblowsky, R.J. Zwi. *Joseph Karo, Lawyer and Mystic.* Philadelphia: Jewish Publication Society of America, 1977.

Werner, Eric. *A Voice Still Heard.* University Park, Pennsylvania: Pennsylvania State University Press, 1976.

White, John. *A Practical Guide to Death and Dying.* Wheaton, Illinois: Theosophical Publishing House, 1980.

Wiesel, Elie. *Souls on Fire: Portraits and Legends of Hasidic Masters.* New York: Random House, 1972.

Wijnhoven, Jochanan H.A. "Gershom G. Scholem: the Study of Jewish Mysticism." *Judaism,* Fall 1970, *19*(4), 468–481.

Williams, Robert Bruce, "Music Therapy: How it Helps the Child." *Psychology of Music, 1978, 6* (1), 55–59.

Wilson, Colin. *New Pathways in Psychology*. New York: Mentor, 1974.

Zohar, volumes 1–5. Translated by Harry Sperling and Maurice Simon. London: Soncino Press, 1931–1934.

INDEX

Credits

Quotations from *Joseph Karo, Lawyer and Mystic* by R.J. Zwi Werblowsky
are used with the courtesy of the copyright holder, The Jewish Publication Society.

Quotations from *The Way of God* by Moses Chaim Luzzatto and *Rabbi
Nachman's Wisdom* are used with the permission of the copyright
holder and translator, Rabbi Aryeh Kaplan.

Quotations from the *Zohar*, volumes 1–5, translated by Harry Sperling
and Maurice Simon are used with the courtesy of the publisher, Soncino
Press, London.

Figure 1 (The Tree of Life) and figure 2 (Adam Kadmon) from *Adam
and the Kabbalistic Tree* by Z'ev ben Shimon Halevi are used with the
permission of the publisher, Samuel Weiser, Inc., York Beach, Maine.

Figure 3 (The Distribution of the Ten Sefirot Through the Four Worlds)
from *Kabbalah* by Charles Ponce is used with the permission of the
publisher, The Theosophical Publishing House, Wheaton, Illinois.

Edward Hoffman received his doctorate in psychology from the University of Michigan. He is currently Director of Psychology and Acting Clinical Director at Hollywood Pavilion in Hollywood, Florida. Dr. Hoffman serves as an adjunct professor at Nova University and maintains a private practice as a clinical psychologist. He recently co-authored *The Man Who Dreamed of Tomorrow: A Conceptual Biography of Wilhelm Reich.*